Ross Deuchar

Gangs and Spirituality

Global Perspectives

Ross Deuchar
Interdisciplinary Research Unit on Crime,
  Policing and Social Justice, School of
  Education
University of the West of Scotland
Ayr, UK

ISBN 978-3-030-07675-7   ISBN 978-3-319-78899-9   (eBook)
https://doi.org/10.1007/978-3-319-78899-9

© The Editor(s) (if applicable) and The Author(s) 2018
Softcover re-print of the Hardcover 1st edition 2018
This work is subject to copyright. All rights are solely and exclusively licensed by the Publisher, whether the whole or part of the material is concerned, specifically the rights of translation, reprinting, reuse of illustrations, recitation, broadcasting, reproduction on microfilms or in any other physical way, and transmission or information storage and retrieval, electronic adaptation, computer software, or by similar or dissimilar methodology now known or hereafter developed.
The use of general descriptive names, registered names, trademarks, service marks, etc. in this publication does not imply, even in the absence of a specific statement, that such names are exempt from the relevant protective laws and regulations and therefore free for general use.
The publisher, the authors and the editors are safe to assume that the advice and information in this book are believed to be true and accurate at the date of publication. Neither the publisher nor the authors or the editors give a warranty, express or implied, with respect to the material contained herein or for any errors or omissions that may have been made. The publisher remains neutral with regard to jurisdictional claims in published maps and institutional affiliations.

Cover image: © Photologue/Getty

Printed on acid-free paper

This Palgrave Macmillan imprint is published by the registered company Springer International Publishing AG part of Springer Nature
The registered company address is: Gewerbestrasse 11, 6330 Cham, Switzerland

Gangs and Spirituality

"In *Gangs and Spirituality*, Ross Deuchar traverses three continents and great disciplinary divides to arrive at conclusions about masculinities and crime or religion and criminal justice that provoke thought, emotion, and, hopefully, action. Academic writing with this much humanity and practical significance is rare. Featuring the voices of gang members in their own words and powerful stories of redemption, *Gangs and Spirituality* is a first-rate book; a must-read for anyone involved in gang research or interested in desistance from crime."
—James Densley, *Associate Professor of Criminal Justice, Metropolitan State University, USA*

"Ross Deuchar brings us inside the lives of marginalized men across the globe who turn to gang violence to achieve masculine identity. In a heartening way, he teaches us that hopeful endings are possible. He chronicles how support and spirituality provide these otherwise lost souls with a pathway to desistance and a meaningful future. This is an important book, with valuable insights for scholars interested in, among other areas, theory, life-course criminology, gender, violence, and corrections."
—Francis T. Cullen, *Distinguished Research Professor Emeritus, University of Cincinnati, USA*

"The publication of Ross Deuchar's *Gangs and Spirituality: Global Perspectives* marks an important milestone in gang research. It unites a focus on spirituality, religiosity and religion in the study of gang members ... This work should re-focus attention on spiritual beliefs and their power to change lives."
—Scott H. Decker, *Foundation Professor of Criminology and Criminal Justice and Faculty Affiliate in the Center on the Future of War, Arizona State University, USA*

Foreword

The publication of Ross Deuchar's *Gangs and Spirituality: Global Perspectives* marks an important milestone in gang research. It unites a focus on spirituality, religiosity, and religion in the study of gang members. There are dribs and drabs of such work scattered about the field, yet no unifying force has assumed the monumental task of making sense of the disparate work in this area. Spirituality must clearly play a role in transitions in and out of crime, gangs and from antisocial to pro-social roles. But that role is complicated, rarely linear and nuanced at every step of the way.

Life is a series of transitions. Transitions imply that individuals move across different states and stages in the course of their lives. The transition from gang member to ex-gang member is not the last transition to be made in the life of a gang member. Indeed, until the transition to death is complete, the next transition is just head in life. And even in death, transitions persist as family, friends, enemies and the public change and reimagine their appraisal of an individual. After all, biographic reconstruction is a major function of funeral activity. Recall the classic scene from *Waking Ned Devine*, when Jackie O'Shea offers a tribute to his 'departed friend' Michael O'Sullivan and chooses to reinterpret his life and their friendship:

> What a wonderful thing it would be to visit your own funeral. To sit at the front and hear what was said, maybe say a few things yourself. Michael and I grew old together. But at times, when we laughed, we grew young. If he was here now, if he could hear what I say, I'd congratulate him on being a great man, and thank him for being a friend.

It is important to understand life's transitions, and yet social science struggles to do so. Most of social science provides a slice of life, a cross-sectional view of what life looks like at a moment in time. The past is presumed, the future unknown. At best, social science provides a view of multiple time points, some fixed moment in the past, the present and an additional measurement at some future point.

This is a major challenge for our understanding of 'social facts.' This challenge is especially important (and difficult) for criminologists, because crime is fleeting; involvement in crime peaks dramatically in the late teens and early twenties and then declines rather precipitously. Depicting individuals as 'criminals' sheds light only on brief glimpses of individuals' transitions through the life course and a bad sample at that. This is a bigger challenge for those who work with youth and adults who are involved in gang life, victimized by its high levels of violence and who bear the effects of both being a victim and a perpetrator.

This is a book about the search for meaning in a series of life transitions. Such a search is common to us all, but is particularly challenging for those who are involved in crime, gangs, and incarceration. The constant in such transitions is their dynamic nature, as Deirdre Healy (2010) makes abundantly clear in her brilliant work on desistance. Transitions are often accompanied by ambiguity, dissonance, and uncertainty. Such is the case in transitions from 'drug user' to 'drug-desister,' a transition characterized by self-doubt and anticipation of failure. The lives of adolescents are often characterized as being tumultuous, difficult times for the youth who experience them and their parents as well. No wonder transitions are difficult. Helen Ebaugh (1988) discussed the transitions in becoming an 'ex,' ex-drug addict, ex-alcoholic, ex-physician, and ex-nun. She describes a pattern of intermittency where individuals involved in a transition from one state to another are uncertain about whether they are one thing or the other. Mixing and maintaining dual identities is not easy, and surely must be the cause of regression to old, familiar habits and friends. One solution to the challenges posed by such 'betwixt and between' living is to resume old lifestyles. But change cannot be escaped. As Father Greg Boyle observed (2010):

> There is nothing 'once and for all' in any decision to change. Each day brings a new embarking. It's always a recalibration and a reassessing of attitude and the old tired ways of proceeding, which are hard to shake for any of us.

Ross Deuchar has jumped into the middle of the existential transitions experienced by gang members. His focus is on spirituality, the beliefs of an individual, typically independent of formal religion and religious practices, but not always. He examines these in three specific contexts: Los Angeles, Scotland and Denmark, and Hong Kong. In each of these settings, he pays close attention to how gang life is conditioned by context, history, and culture. It is this latter consideration—culture—that offers the most insight for his examination of spirituality. Membership in a group includes a number of important characteristics: activity, group process, group structure, and beliefs. Beliefs include perceptions of self and group, as well as the intersection of the two. Beliefs are contextualized by social position, a key element of which is the pressures and perceptions of the group and the individual by external groups such as community and society. In this context, Deuchar considers the role of masculinities in gang membership across the three geographic settings in which he studies gangs. Masculinities play key roles in attracting individuals to gangs and binding them to the group. As masculinities interact with the larger culture, they are changed and change the individual.

There has been a good deal of attention to codes, values, and culture among street gang members (Mitchell et al. 2017). These values play an important role in the lives of gang members. In this respect, gang members are not much different from other individuals of their age; they possess certain values and beliefs that help them form opinions, make decisions, and cope with the world. This is analogous to the role that spirituality plays for individuals with such beliefs, though certainly the content differs. In addition to congregate activities, shared beliefs help to motivate individual gang members, give them a set of values to follow and be judged by and judge others. It is possible to conceive of masculinities performing a similar function to that of spirituality—a set of values to shape behavior and evaluate circumstances so as to know how to act.

What Deuchar does is to find a place in transition narratives for spirituality. Groups and individuals need narratives to situate their behavior as well as to transition between states and stages of life. While in the gang, such narratives abound:

The rival gang is out to get you.
Members of your gang have your back.
The cops will do anything to bust you.
Your gang is your family.
Blood in, blood out.

But once the foundation of gang membership begins to show cracks, a new narrative is needed, particularly for individuals who find that gang narratives have begun to conflict with reality, or no longer work for their stage of life. Since many gangs lack established roles for middle-aged gang members,[1] there are few if any transitional narratives for long-term gang members, ironically especially for those who remain out of prison. For those who have been to prison, there are roles in the community and the gang for an 'ex-con' or 'old head.' After all, thirty-year-olds cannot maintain the intense masculinities so common among late adolescence. As the masculinities associated with young gang membership no longer square with the life experiences of those in their late twenties, a new narrative of spirituality is needed.

---

[1] This generalization is not true of all gangs.

One aspect of such spirituality provides a way to cope with the violence that older gang members have experienced. Unlike their younger gang counterparts, older gang members gain a sense of their own mortality through aging as well as inflicting violence and death and witnessing violence and death among members of their own gang. Life course events such as becoming a parent (Pyrooz et al. 2017) are also influential in loosening the bonds to old beliefs, relationships, and activities. Spirituality, in this case religious beliefs in an afterlife,[2] requires a mechanism to cope with the recognition that many gang members did evil things, and there might be consequences for such evil. Prayer, a religious routine activity, is one way to cope with such circumstances:

Interviewer: Do you miss those guys?

Interviewee: Yeah… they were my friends, (voice cracks), and they're not here anymore to share the things that I wish I could share with them now. I just pray to God they're not burning in hell.[3]

While Deuchar's methodology and emphasis on spirituality is unique, his work on exiting the gang builds on work done in Great Britain. The work of Crewe (2009), Healy (2010), Liebling (2004), and Maruna et al. (2006) in Great Britain is especially noteworthy in this process. Much of this work emphasizes a 'spiritual' element to the disengagement process, as identity and narrative both are heavily aligned with spiritual processes.

Disengaging from groups involved in crime can be a difficult process owing to the group process and ties among individuals in such groups. While individuals engaged in traditional forms of street crime (robbery, burglary, drug selling, etc.) offend in groups, these groups lack persistence, structure and generate limited loyalty among their participants. Exiting from such groups is generally less problematic. However, disengaging from groups with more persistence and structure, such as gangs,

---

[2] It is important to keep in mind that there are at least three different types of afterlife: heaven, purgatory, and hell.
[3] Research subject from the GOOGLE Ideas Project (Decker and Pyrooz 2011).

terror groups, drug smugglers, and the like, can pose greater challenges. Such groups generate relationships and dependence among their members that make disentangling oneself from them considerably more complicated. What many researchers have missed in this context is the role that spiritual beliefs play in decisions about staying in a group or leaving that group.

Despite a surge of interest in disengagement, the exit process is not well understood (Carson and Vecchio 2015). This is particularly true for our understanding of how gang members come to leave their gang and forge new identities. The creation and maintenance of new identities as an 'ex' (Ebaugh 1988) is important for understanding disengagement from gangs as well as terror groups, organized crime and religious cults. Creating a new identity can be accomplished through the creation of 'scripts' or narratives. Such narratives often include a new conception of self or new worldview. In some cases, this is accomplished through adopting a religious transformation or more spiritual view of oneself or one's role in the world, which is something the extant literature on gangs and disengagement has alluded to but not formally tested (Pyrooz and Decker 2011; Carson et al. 2013; Flores 2013; Decker et al. 2014; Flores 2016).

There is not a solid body of research findings to document the effect, if any, of religion on desistance from crime and departures from crime groups. Among the few direct studies of this process, Giordano et al. (2008) used a life course perspective to examine 'hooks for change.' While the quantitative results did not find an effect for religion on desistance from crime, in qualitative interviews subjects identified that spirituality did play a role in such decisions. Drawing on this work, Veysey et al. (2013, p. 246) identified four 'mechanisms' that spirituality worked through as a hook for change, including: (1) a form of social capital, (2) religious teachings that encourage pro-social behavior, (3) as resources for emotional coping, and (4) by providing opportunities to build pro-social relationships. This is a useful framework to use in conceptualizing how spirituality can assist with the desistance process, one consistent with Deuchar's approach.

While in other disciplines there has been attention to religious practice and spirituality, there has been little attention to these topics among criminologists who study gangs in the USA. A 2013 publication by the National Gang Center and the Office of Juvenile Justice and Delinquency Prevention (OJJDP) titled 'Getting out of Gangs, Staying out of Gangs' makes no mention of these topics. In a recent comprehensive review of the literature on gang disengagement (Carson and Vecchio 2015), religion and spirituality received scant attention, owing to the paucity of research on the topic. Other studies, however, have examined the link between religion, spirituality, and gangs.

Owing to the strong presence of Catholicism and the Catholic Church in Central America, it is perhaps not surprising that there has been significant work in that region involving the role of religion in exiting gangs. El Salvador in particular has been the site of multiple examinations of the role of religion and spirituality in youth violence and gang involved youth. Salas-Wright et al. (2013) have led the work in this area. In a community sample of 290 high-risk and gang involved youth in San Salvador, they found inverse relationships between *religious coping* and *spirituality* and reduced levels of antisocial bonds. Antisocial bonds are the indirect measure between religious coping and spirituality and the outcome measure of youth violence. Antisocial bonds are reduced by religious coping and spirituality. Given the high levels of violence, especially gang violence in El Salvador (Katz and Amaya 2015), this represents an important test of the role of religious coping and spirituality. In another analysis (Salas-Wright et al. 2012), they found that the effect of spirituality was mediated by social development factors, though spirituality remained an important protective factor against delinquency involvement.

The most direct study of the role of spirituality and desistance from gangs is found in Flores' work (2009, 2014, 2016) with gangs in Los Angeles. His work is based on a series of interviews and fieldwork in two Los Angeles neighborhoods among 'recovering' gang members and is framed in the contexts of masculinities, immigration, religions, and marginalization. He pays particular attention to the role of two long-standing efforts to encourage reintegration of gangs in Hispanic neighborhoods in Los Angeles, *Homeboy Industries* and *Victory Outreach*. Both programs have a strong redemptionist character to their approach to moving gang members away from their gangs and integrating them in less destructive (individually and socially) life styles. Much like Decker et al. (2014; Pyrooz and Decker 2011), the disengagement processes Flores describes emphasize the role of the process of leaving rather than describing gang leaving as a discrete event. Spirituality, rather than religious practices, plays a role in this process from Flores' perspective, yet is not defined as the sole component of such a process.

Deuchar's work is not traditional social science hypothesis testing and therein lies its strength. *Gangs and Spirituality* is a journey, a personal journey across time and space, with intimate visits into the lives of his subjects. He passionately recounts their struggles to make sense of their own lives, struggles that often end in a search for an external locus or power to believe in. This work should refocus attention on spiritual beliefs and their power to change lives.

Arizona, U.S.
Scott H. Decker
Arizona State University

References

Boyle, G. (2010). *Tattoos on the heart*. New York, NY: Free Press.

Carson, D. C., & J. M. Vecchio. (2015). Leaving the gang: A review and thoughts on future research. In S. H. Decker & D. C. Pyrooz (Eds.). *The Handbook of Gangs* (pp. 257–275). New York: Wiley.

Carson, D. C., Peterson, D., & Esbensen, F.-A. (2013). Youth gang desistance: An examination of different operational definitions of desistance associated with leaving the gang on the motivations, methods and consequences of youth gang desistance. *Criminal Justice Review, 38*(4), 510–534.

Crewe, B. (2009). *The prisoner society: Power, adaptation, and social life in an English prison*. Oxford: Oxford University Press.

Decker, S. H., & Pyrooz, D. C. (2011). Gangs and the internet: Logging Off and Moving On. Google Ideas. Washington, DC: Council on Foreign Relations.

Decker, S. H., Pyrooz, D. C., & Moule, R. K., Jr. (2014). Disengagement from gangs as role transitions. *Journal of Research on Adolescence, 24*(2), 268–283.

Ebaugh, H. (1988). *Becoming an ex: The process of role exit*. Chicago: University of Chicago Press.

Flores, E. O. (2009). 'I am somebody': Barrio Pentecostalism and gendered acculturation among Chicano ex-gang members. *Ethnic and Racial Studies, 35*(6), 996–1016.

Flores, E. O. (2014). *God's gangs: Barrio ministry, masculinity, and gang recovery*. New York: New York University Press.

Flores, E. O. (2016). Grow your hair out: Chicano gang masculinity and embodiment in recovery. *Social Problems, 63*(4), 590–604.

Giordano, P. C., Longmore, M. A., Schroeder, R. D., & Seffrin. P. M. (2008). A life course perspective on spirituality and desistance from crime. *Criminology 46*(1), 99–131.

Healy, D. (2010). *The dynamics of desistance*. London: Willan.

Katz, C. M., & Amaya, L. E. (2015). *The gang truce as a form of violence intervention*. San Salvador: FUNDE.

Liebling, A. (2004). *Prisons and their moral performance: A study of values, quality and prison life*. Oxford: Clarendon Press.

Maruna, S. L., Wilson, K., & Curran, K. (2006). Why god is often found behind bars: Prison conversions and the crisis of self-narrative. *Research in Human Development, 3*(2–3), 161–184.

Mitchell, M. M., Fahmy, C., Pyrooz, D. C., & Decker, S. H. (2017). Criminal crews, codes, and contexts: Differences and similarities across the code of the street, convict code, street gangs, and prison gangs. *Deviant Behavior, 38*(10),1197–1222.

Pyrooz, D. C., & Decker, S. H. (2011). Motives and methods for leaving the gang: Understanding the process of gang desistance. *Journal of Criminal Justice, 39*, 417–425.

Pyrooz, D. C., McGloin, J. M., & Decker. S. H. (2017). Parenthood as a turning point in the life course for male and female gang members: A study of within-individual changes in gang membership and criminal behavior, *Criminology, 55*(4), 869–899.

Salas-Wright, C. P., Olate, R., & Vaughn, M. G. (2012). The protective effects of religious coping and spirituality on delinquency. *Criminal Justice and Behavior, 40*(9), 988–1008.

Salas-Wright, C. P., Olate, R., Vaughn, M. G.,& Than, T. V. (2013). Direct and mediated associations between religious coping, spirituality, and youth violence in El Salvador. *Rev Panam Salud Publica, 34*(3), 183–189.

Veysey, B., Martinez, D., & Christian, J. (2013). 'Getting out': A summary of qualitative research on desistance across the life course. In C. Gibson & M. Krohn (Eds.), *Handbook of life course criminology: Emerging trends for future research* (pp. 233–260). New York: Springer.

Acknowledgements

I would like to thank the men of all age groups who participated in the research featured within this book and who gave up their time to talk so openly and candidly to me, even when times were tough for them. Also to all of the personal mentors, pastors, chaplains, and coaches I met around the world who opened so many doors for me and allowed me access to their hugely inspiring organisations and interventions. I feel privileged to have shared so many journeys with so many people during the fieldwork, and to also have experienced a little bit of the peace and love that the interventions generated.

I am deeply thankful to Professor Scott Decker for writing the eloquent Foreword, and to Professor Frank Cullen, Dr. James Densley, Professor Wing Lo and Dr. Simon Harding for kindly reviewing earlier drafts of the book and providing me with invaluable feedback.

Thanks also to the Carnegie Trust for the Universities of Scotland and the University of the West of Scotland for providing the funding that supported the research.

My special thanks, as always, go to Karen and Alan for all their love and support.

Finally, to all of those who inspired—and continue to inspire—my own spiritual journey … this book is a reminder to you of the impact you have had on me.

Contents

Part I   Introduction

1   Gangs in Global Perspective   3

Part II   Gangs, Masculinity and Spirituality: Existing
          Theories and Insights

2   Gang Members 'Doing Masculinity'   19

3   Religious and Spiritual Desistance From Gangs   39

Part III Los Angeles, USA: From Gangs and Guns
          to Love and Compassion

4   Amplified Masculinity Among Los Angeles Homeboys   63

5   Love, Compassion and Therapeutic Communities
     in *Homeboy Industries*   89

xvii

Part IV Scotland and Denmark: From Violence, Offending and Prison Life to Religiosity, Yoga and Breathing

6   Masculinity, Morality and Offending in Scotland and Denmark — 117

7   Support in Times of Trouble: Chaplaincy in Scottish and Danish Prisons — 143

8   'Warriors' to 'Peacemakers': Yoga, Breathing and Meditation in Denmark — 169

Part V Hong Kong: From Triad-Affiliated Gangsters to Christian Brothers

9   Foot Soldiers, Gangsters and Drug Addicts in Hong Kong — 195

10   From Criminal Gangsters to Men of God — 219

Part VI Conclusion

11   From Masculine Criminal Distinction to Masculine Spiritual Distinction — 245

Index — 261

List of Figures

Fig. 11.1 Subfields in the *field of masculinity* and the transition to gang membership and '*masculine criminal distinction*' (Adapted from Coles 2009, p. 40) — 248

Fig. 11.2 Subfields in the *field of masculinity* and the transition from '*masculine criminal distinction*' to '*masculine spiritual distinction*' (Adapted from Coles 2009, p. 40) — 255

List of Tables

Table 4.1	The research participants in Los Angeles	67
Table 6.1	The research participants in Scotland and Denmark	124
Table 7.1	The sub-group of research participants engaged with Prison Chaplaincy	146
Table 8.1	The sub-group of research participants engaged with 'Prison Smart'/'Breathe Smart'	173
Table 9.1	The research participants in Hong Kong	200

Part I
Introduction

1

Gangs in Global Perspective

In this opening chapter, I provide an account of the professional journey that led me to write this book. I make it clear that the focus of the book is on exploring and examining the relationship between masculinity, gang disengagement, desistance and spirituality, and provide an overview of the research methods I used and the book's chapters and their content. Towards the end of the chapter, I briefly outline why I believe the book's content makes a special contribution to the field of Criminology, and to gangs research in particular.

Understanding Gang Desistance: Focusing on Masculinity and Spirituality

It is hard to believe that a decade has past since the first piece of qualitative research I conducted into gang culture and violence. From humble beginnings in Glasgow's housing schemes, over the years my continuing work as an ethnographic Criminologist has evolved and taken me to different corners of the world—from Scotland to Denmark, then to the United States and finally Asia. Travelling across three Continents,

© The Author(s) 2018
R. Deuchar, *Gangs and Spirituality*,
https://doi.org/10.1007/978-3-319-78899-9_1

my increasingly international insights have given me a deep understanding of the diverse nature of gang structures and the violence and wider criminality that emerges within them. Having studied the strongly territorial violence associated with street gangs in Glasgow, I moved on to learn about the motorcycle gang wars in Copenhagen, drive-by shootings emerging against the backdrop of racial oppression in Los Angeles and triad hierarchies and organised criminality in Hong Kong.

Although some (but not all) of the causes of gang formation and gang-related crime may be similar across the world, I have realised that no two gangs are exactly alike in 'form and function' (Densley 2013, p. 5). As Fraser (2013, p. 981) notes, one cannot subsume the distinctive cultural orientations, historical trajectories and meanings of gangs in different continents, countries and cities into a 'singular construction'. Accordingly, I have always avoided the tendency to search for a generic and precise definition of what a 'gang' actually is or to describe the nature of the criminal activity associated with gangs from the basis of *assumed similarity* (Fraser 2015). Rather, in the chapters of this book I make a concerted effort to focus on the wide-ranging global geographical, historical and cultural specificities that provided the backdrop to the gang-oriented criminality I have researched and the gang members I have interviewed and observed (Fraser 2015).

That said, against the diverse backdrop of geographical sites I have found myself located in and the multiplicity of insights I have gained I have become consistently conscious of three things. First, although the role of women in gangs has been well-documented (Campbell 1992; Miller 2001; Batchelor 2009), the vast majority of those responsible for gang-related crime within the cities where I have conducted research have been male. Second, among all of the male gang members I have met in different parts of the world I have continually identified strong links between their dominant views about masculinity and their tendency towards offending behaviour. In short, their somewhat narrow perceptions about what it means to be a man have often stimulated their violence and wider criminality. Third, and perhaps most surprisingly, I have become aware that gang members' decision-making and behaviour is often driven by moral codes, ethical precepts and (in some cases) subtle spiritual beliefs and awareness (White 2013).

My fascination with the above issues led me to explore the factors that tend to precipitate male gang members' eventual decision to change. I came to focus on the extent to—and ways in which—their perceptions of masculinity and proclivity towards spiritual beliefs, principles and practices might interact with this. Accordingly, this book is fundamentally about the relationship between masculinity, gang disengagement, desistance and spirituality. I have, of course, always recognised that it is important to some extent to distinguish between the processes of disengaging from gangs and discontinuing crime—one process does not necessarily predict or rely upon the other. However, since a considerable body of research reports that gang-involved males contribute disproportionately to crime in general and violence in particular (see, for instance, Decker 1996; Decker et al. 2008; Melde and Esbensen 2013; Melde et al. 2016), I have focused on the often-intertwined processes of gang detachment and criminal desistance—and the recognised links between them (Melde et al. 2016).

In doing so, I have been mindful of the fact that desistance does not simply come about as a result of transformations in offenders' life circumstances and personal situations. It is often stimulated by subjective processes, including offenders' narrative reconstructions of selves and identities (Maruna 2001; Giordano et al. 2002; Gadd and Farrell 2004; Giordano et al. 2008; Healy 2012). Moving beyond rational choice or life course perspectives on desistance (Cusson and Pinsonneault 1986; Laub and Sampson 2003), I have therefore drawn on cognitive transformation perspectives to explore the subjective nature of offenders' identity shifts (Giordano et al. 2002). However, I have also become increasingly interested in the routes that offenders may take to begin to engage in these reconstructions and the phases when and spaces where they might take place.

I have been inspired by the work of Deirdre Healy (2012) who has argued that, when researching the termination of criminal engagement, it is important not only to identify the 'factors that show a relationship with desistance' but also to uncover the 'processes underlying these relationships' (p. 38). Healy draws upon Turner's (1970) liminal theory to explore the 'rich landscape' inhabited by those who exist in the space 'betwixt and between' criminality and desistance and are on the threshold of change (ibid., p. 35, and see also Healy 2010). Having moved beyond a 'separation phase' where their thinking patterns, behaviour and values begin to change, she argues that liminal beings begin to distance themselves from their past selves and to construct new identities. As such, Healy proposes that the liminal phase is characterised as a time of 'fruitful darkness' when personal transformation, growth and identity reconstruction can occur.

Drawing on Healy's arguments, during my global ethnographic research I have focused on exploring the factors associated with masculinity and spirituality and their relationship with the intertwined process of gang disengagement and criminal desistance among male offenders who have found themselves in a liminal phase. In some cases, this liminal state emerged while the men were engaged in rehabilitation programmes in the community and in other cases while interacting with support structures in prison. Whatever the case, I have sought to gain a deeper understanding of what seemed to be occurring in the minds of those who could be described as 'early-stage desisters' or those who were on the 'threshold of change' when I met them (Healy 2012, pp. 35–36). Ultimately, I have found it useful to draw not only on theoretical perspectives on hegemonic masculinity and spirituality to understand these cognitive transitions but also on Bourdieusian social field analysis (Bourdieu 1969, 1984, 1991). Bourdieu's perspective accounts for the combination of structure and agency in the desistance process, which is necessary to advance a truly holistic account of the phenomenon.

Focus for and Content of the Book, Research Methods and Chapter Summaries

Across the pages of this book, I highlight the reasons that the men I worked with had first joined gangs and regularly engaged in violence and criminal offending. I also illustrate the way in which programmes and interventions saturated by spiritual perspectives and practices as well as faith-based religious principles and approaches were beginning to help them to redefine their views on masculinity and to take initial steps to leave gang and criminal lifestyles behind.

Overview of Part I and Chapter Summaries

In Part I, I begin by exploring some of the existing literary insights into gangs, masculinity and crime. I also examine the prevailing evidence on religion and spirituality as a potential resource for nurturing turning points, identity and behaviour change. I begin in Chapter 2 by providing an overview of existing international research that identifies links between social constructions of masculinity, gang culture, violence and offending. I explore the way in which, against the backdrop of social and cultural marginalisation, evidence suggests that hyper-aggressive forms of masculinity have become valorised in some contexts, with a tendency towards membership of male-dominated gangs, criminal activity and street violence. I begin to consider how reformatory interventions may be most effectively designed to enable male gang members to move towards criminal desistance while also creating contexts that will prevent them from feeling emasculated.

The spotlight is then placed on religion and spirituality as a potential resource for nurturing positive transitions in Chapter 3. Here, I explore the evidence that suggests that religious and/or spiritual practices can support masculinity identity reconstruction in such a way as to stimulate the desistance process. The process of faith conversion and the emergence of redemption scripts (Maruna 2001) is critically analysed, and I consider the potential salience of the way in which faith-based contexts may enhance some men's ability to publically project stories of change about their values, attitudes and priorities. I also examine the existing insights that suggest that engagement in wider, more holistic spiritual practices may also play a role in the type of identity and behaviour change that stimulates progression towards desistance.

Overview of Parts II–IV and Research Methods

In Parts II–IV of the book I take readers on a tour of the eclectic mix of global locations where I conducted my empirical work, describing in some detail the geographical, historical and cultural backdrops to the gang-oriented and wider criminality that my research participants had been involved in. I also share the insights from my empirical research, which drew upon ethnographic methods (Hammersley 2006). In so doing, I foreground the research participants' personal perspectives deriving from in-depth interviews as well as my own impressions and feelings that emerged from participant observation (Emerson et al. 1995).

Specifically, I draw on evidence gathered via life history and semi-structured interviews conducted with gang members and offenders in the USA, Scotland, Denmark and Hong Kong while they were engaged in rehabilitation programmes and interventions in local communities and prisons. I also share wider insights gained from interviews with personal mentors, pastors, chaplains and coaches. At the time that I collected the data, the men I interviewed were of various ages (from late teens to early sixties) but all of them could be described as existing in the liminal space 'betwixt and between' offending and desistance, striving as they were to change, progress and heal (Healy 2012, p. 35). Although the prominent focus of my research was on exploring the experiences of gang members, in a small minority of instances I was also able to examine the views and perceptions of wider groups of offenders. This included those who engaged in sexual violence or who engaged in drug dealing or armed robbery outwith gang contexts, and to an extent the emerging insights provided a nuanced contrast to those from the dominant sample. During interviews, I explored the social barriers that all of the men had come across during their early lives, and the perceived relationship between their socially constructed views on masculinity and involvement in gang violence and/or criminality. I also explored the motivations that they felt underpinned their initial desire to change and begin to transition away from offending lifestyles.

As well as conducting interviews, during the majority of my visits to intervention programmes within communities I employed the ethnographic research method of 'participant as observer' (Gold 1958). In employing this method, I maintained transparency with the research population by communicating my research intentions to the male participants, as well as the staff and mentors within the organisations responsible for the initiatives. In most cases, I participated actively alongside the men during intervention programmes. I observed them informally during their daily activities and explored their personal insights and views about the social, emotional and spiritual engagement that the programmes and interventions nurtured not only through initial and follow-up interviews but also through more informal discussions and interaction. Although somewhat more limited in my ability to participate in prison interventions due to access arrangements and security protocols, I was still able to engage informally with male inmates during their own participation in these initiatives.

In all cases, participants were accessed and recruited to the various sub-research studies voluntarily and consensually, mostly through specific gatekeepers (such as mentors, pastors, chaplains and coaches). For those who were in prison at the time of my research, formal access was arranged through specific prison authorities (namely the Scottish Prison Service and Danish Prison and Probation Service). Participants were assured of the confidentiality of information passed on during interviews. Once transcribed, fieldnotes and interviews were analysed thematically to detect salient patterns (Strauss and Corbin 1990), and pseudonyms used in order to ensure that anonymity was upheld in the reporting of the data.

Through drawing upon the emerging thematic insights, I rigorously explored the gradual shifts in 'cognitions and social circumstances' in the lives of the men I observed, interacted with and interviewed and ultimately considered the way in which they had entered a new social subfield (Coles 2009). These shifts and social changes were described and more loosely referred to in the data by the men themselves and those who worked intensively with them (Healy 2010, p. 419). I paid due attention to the perceived subtlety of these cognitive transitions, identity shifts and changes in social structures in the form of role transitions, and considered their consequence in terms of masculinity (re)construction and the men's attempts to change and transition towards gang disengagement and desistance (Decker et al. 2014). In the chapters in Parts II–IV, I examine the relationship between these emerging transitional changes and the men's religious and spiritual participation experiences within intervention programmes in prisons and local communities. I explore the extent to and ways in which these programmes and interventions appeared to support them in re-focusing their masculine orientations and enhance the natural social processes working to push and pull the men out of gangs and their criminal and violent lifestyles (Decker et al. 2014).

Further, more nuanced details about the approaches to data gathering used and the specificities associated with research participants in each particular international context are outlined in each chapter. In each one, salient extracts from interviews and fieldnotes are presented and are duly accommodated with insights from the existing literature.

Parts II–IV Chapter Summaries

Part II of the book places the spotlight on the USA, where gangs have been part of the cultural fabric for over 300 years. I focus specifically on Los Angeles, the city that gave America the modern street gang. In Chapter 4, I begin by considering the way in which issues of race, segregation and discrimination combined to create communities that spawned street gang formation in the city. I also discuss the way in which wider social marginalisation has sustained this. In the main body of the chapter, I share insights from life history interviews conducted with young Latino male gang members from the most socially disadvantaged areas of the city, all of whom were in the early stages of transition and change when I met them. I discuss the social barriers that they came across during their early lives, the profound lack of love and hope they experienced, their perceptions about masculinity and described involvement in gang-related offending. I also consider what motivated their initial desire to change and begin to move away from violent criminality.

Following on directly from this, in Chapter 5 I share insights from participant observation of the initiatives and strategies implemented within one of the biggest and most renowned gang intervention programmes in the world, *Homeboy Industries* in Los Angeles. I draw on ethnographic fieldnotes to provide illustrations of the holistic culture within the organisation, and the nature and potential impact of coaching and mentoring strategies and group therapy sessions. In addition, insights from follow-up interviews and informal interactions with the male reforming gang members I described in Chapter 4 illustrate the main factors that led to their motivation to engage with *Homeboy Industries*, and the perceived impact that it was having on them during the liminal phase (Healy 2012). Further, data gathered via semi-structured interviews with mentors, coaches and staff provide deeper insights into the ways—and extent to which—the structured programmes were providing an initial mechanism for changing perceptions about masculinity and nurturing greater commitment to criminal desistance.

In Part III, I move the focus of attention from the USA to northern Europe, and to Scotland and Denmark in particular. In Chapter 6, I firstly draw upon a comparative perspective to explore and examine the issues relating to gangs and masculinity in the two countries, highlighting the key similarities and differences. I draw upon insights gathered from life history interviews conducted not only with gang members but also several other types of offenders (such as drug dealers, armed robbers and sex offenders). These participants were mostly residing in Scottish and Danish prisons (or had recently been released) at the time of fieldwork. As in Part II, I explore the links between the interviewees' socially-constructed views of masculinity, their involvement in gangs and (in some cases) wider criminality. Towards the end of the chapter, I highlight the way in which the motivation for violence and crime among many of the Scottish and Danish men I interviewed often also seemed to be guided by strong moral and ethical codes, as were their initial attempts to desist.

In Chapter 7, I draw on insights from follow-up semi-structured interviews that I conducted with one smaller sub-sample of the men in Scottish and Danish prisons, as well as additional interviews with Christian and Muslim prison chaplains. I examine the way in which chaplains conducted religious and spiritual study groups and engaged in recreational pastimes and supportive one-to-one discussions with inmates. I consider the impact that the chaplains and the religious study groups and practices were having on the men's values, attitudes and self-identities while in the liminal phase (Healy 2012). I present case studies that illustrate the turning points and journeys that particular inmates experienced. I then draw conclusions about the way in which prison chaplaincy may provide added value in terms of nurturing a sense of peace, wellbeing, fulfillment and desistance-related attitudes amongst male gang members and offenders.

Moving on from religious engagement to wider ascetic-spiritual practices, in Chapter 8 I present insights from follow-up semi-structured interviews I conducted and wider informal discussions I had with a second sub-group of the Danish sample I referred to in Chapter 6. Some of these men were still incarcerated when I worked with them, but the majority had recently been released from prison. While most were former members of Danish street gangs and biker gangs, a minority had offending histories outwith gang structures. These men had regularly begun to participate in yoga exercises, dynamic breathing techniques and meditation practices, and in this chapter I combine their insights with some complementary ones from interviews I conducted with their coaches and instructors. I explore the way in which the men discussed and described the deeper cognitive and identity shifts they experienced through the practices, and the way in which they felt able to deal more effectively with negative and destructive emotions and the personal strains that had led them into gang violence and wider criminality. Additional, supplementary reflections on my own personal experiences of participating in the practices are also included in the form of fieldnotes from participant observation.

In Part IV, I focus attention on one final geographic location—Asia, with a specific spotlight placed on Hong Kong. The suggested connections between youth gangs and triad societies are examined, and I draw attention to the particular ways that male youth gang members can become 'triadized' and immersed in organised criminality. In Chapter 9, I share insights from life history interviews conducted with a small sample of men of various ages in Hong Kong who had become members of street gangs and slowly transitioned to become part of triad-affiliated crime groups. Through drawing on the most salient themes from interviews, I explore the underlying social and cultural influences that led the men to engage with and (in some cases) progress through triad hierarchies, and the links with masculinity. I also examine the range of factors that triggered a readiness for change among these men.

Following directly on from this, in Chapter 10 I move on to explore and examine the potential impact of a religious intervention that I refer to under the fictitious name of the *Hong Kong Christian Society (HKCS)*. I draw on additional insights from follow-up interviews and discussions with the same men I referred to in Chapter 9, as well as from fieldnotes constructed during participant observation and from interviews with staff and volunteers within *HKCS*. I explore and examine the nature of the Christian support sessions the men engaged in and their apparent impact in terms of supporting them with addiction issues, and enabling them to challenge their entrenched beliefs regarding criminal lifestyles. The insights are used to make inferences about the extent to and ways in which Christian-based interventions can potentially play a valuable role in supporting and enabling Hong Kong gang members to re-direct their entrenched beliefs about loyalty and obligation to brotherhood in non-criminal directions.

In Chapter 11, I draw upon Bourdieusian social field analysis combined with theoretical perspectives on hegemonic masculinity to provide a more granular analysis of the global insights outlined in the empirical chapters of the book. In doing so, I provide a deeper theoretical perspective on what provided the pathways into and out of gang membership, violence and criminality for the majority of the men I interviewed and the role of religion and spirituality in the latter. Towards the end of the chapter, final implications are made for future policy, practice and research.

Contribution to the Field

I believe that the global insights within the book will hold strong appeal for Criminologists and gang researchers as well as policy makers and practitioners around the world. For Criminologists, the book provides some unique empirical findings about the role that religion and spirituality can play in enabling some male gang members and offenders who have entered a liminal phase to transition into a new social sphere characterised by the presence of substitute forms of brotherhood and trust and alternative forms of masculine status. I am hopeful that these insights have the capacity to stimulate additional research that moves beyond the locations where I have worked and begins to capture the longer-term impact of religious and spiritual interventions on gender identity reconstruction and desistance.

For policy-makers and practitioners, the book includes some important perspectives on the extent to which religious and spiritual practices may enable male offenders to discover (or re-discover) *alternative* masculine identities and begin to view desistance as a realistic goal that they can achieve. Given the high rates of psychological problems, social pressures and reduced wellbeing experienced by offenders, the narrowly-constructed views on masculinity that gang members often embrace and the holistic nature of factors that have been found to contribute to the desistance process, the applied insights I present are timely. I believe that the described impact of the programmes I outline could be significant in terms of informing future policy-related decisions and practice orientations in different parts of the world and ultimately enabling more male gang members and offenders to desist.

References

Batchelor, S. (2009). Girls, gangs and violence: Assessing the evidence. *Probation Journal, 56*(4), 399–414.

Bourdieu, P. (1969). Intellectual field and creative project. *Social Science Information, 8*, 189–219.

Bourdieu, P. (1984). *Distinction: A social critique of the judgement of taste* (R. Nice, Trans.). Cambridge, MA: Harvard University Press.

Bourdieu, P. (1991). *Language and symbolic power*. Cambridge: Polity Press.

Campbell, A. (1992). *The girls in the gang*. Cambridge: Blackwell.

Coles, T. (2009). Negotiating the field of masculinity: The production and reproduction of multiple dominant masculinities. *Men and Masculinities, 12*(1), 30–44.

Cusson, M., & Pinsonneault, P. (1986). The decision to give up crime. In D. B. Cornish & R. V. Clarke (Eds.), *The reasoning criminal: Rational choice perspectives on offending* (pp. 72–82). New York: Springer.

Decker, S. H. (1996). Collective and normative features of gang violence. *Justice Quarterly, 13*(2), 245–264.

Decker, S. H., Katz, C. M., & Webb, V. J. (2008). Understanding the black box of gang organization: Implications for involvement in violent crime, drug sales, and violent victimization. *Crime and Delinquency, 54*(1), 153–172.
Decker, S. H., Pyrooz, D., & Moule, R. K., Jr. (2014). Disengagement from gangs as role transitions. *Journal of Research on Adolescence, 24*(2), 268–283.
Densley, J. (2013). *How gangs work: An ethnography of youth violence*. London: Palgrave Macmillan.
Emerson, R. M., Fretz, R., & Shaw, L. (1995). *Writing ethnographic fieldnotes*. Chicago: University of Chicago Press.
Fraser, A. (2013). Street habitus: Gangs, territorialism and social change in Glasgow. *Journal of Youth Studies, 16*(8), 970–985.
Fraser, A. (2015). *Urban legends: Gang identity in the post-industrial city*. Oxford: Oxford University Press.
Gadd, D., & Farrall, S. (2004). Criminal careers, desistance and subjectivity. *Theoretical Criminology, 8*(2), 1362–4806.
Giordano P. C., Cernkovich, S. A., & Rudolph, J. L. (2002). Gender, crime and desistance: Toward a theory of cognitive transformation. *American Journal of Sociology,* 107, 990–1064.
Giordano, P. C., Longmore, M., Schroeder, R., & Seffrin, P. (2008). A life-course perspective on spirituality and desistance from crime. *Criminology, 46*(1), 99–132.
Gold, R. (1958). Roles in sociological field observation. *Social Forces,* 36, 217–223.
Hammersley, M. (2006). Ethnography: Problems and prospects. *Ethnography and Education, 1*(1), 3–14.
Healy, D. (2010). Betwixt and between: The role of psychosocial factors in the early stages of desistance. *Journal of Research in Crime and Delinquency, 47*(4), 419–438.
Healy, D. (2012). *The dynamics of desistance: Charting pathways through change*. New York: Routledge.
Laub, J. H., & Sampson, R. J. (2003). *Shared beginnings, divergent lives: Delinquent boys to age 70*. Cambridge, MA: Harvard University Press.
Maruna, S. (2001). *Making good: How ex-convicts reform and rebuild their lives*. Washington, DC: American Psychological Association.
Melde, C., & Esbensen, F.-A. (2013). Gangs and violence: Disentangling the impact of gang membership on the level and nature of offending. *Journal of Quantitative Criminology, 29*(2), 143–166.

Melde, C., Esbensen, F.-A., & Carson, D. C. (2016). Gang membership and involvement in violence among US adolescents: A test of construct validity. In C. L. Maxson & F.-A. Esbensen (Eds.), *Gang transitions and transformations in an international context* (pp. 33–50). Switzerland: Springer.

Miller, J. (2001). *One of the guys: Girls, gangs and gender*. New York: Oxford University Press.

Strauss, A., & Corbin, J. M. (1990). *Basics of qualitative research: Grounded theory procedures and techniques*. London: Sage.

Turner, V. (1970). *The forest of symbols: Aspects of the Ndembus ritual*. London: Cornell University Press.

White, R. (2013). *Youth gangs, violence and social respect: Exploring the nature of provocations and punch-ups*. Basingstoke, UK: Palgrave Macmillan.

Part II

Gangs, Masculinity and Spirituality:
Existing Theories and Insights

2

Gang Members 'Doing Masculinity'

In this part of the book, I explore some of the existing literary insights into gangs, masculinity and crime. I also examine the prevailing evidence on religion and spirituality as a potential resource for nurturing turning points, identity and behaviour change. In this chapter I provide an overview of existing international research that identifies links between social constructions of masculinity, gang culture, violence and offending. I explore the way in which, against the backdrop of social and cultural marginalisation, evidence suggests that hyper-aggressive forms of masculinity have become valorised in some contexts, with a tendency towards membership of male-dominated gangs, criminal activity and street violence. I begin to consider how reformatory interventions may be most effectively designed to enable male gang members to move towards criminal desistance while also creating contexts that will prevent them from feeling emasculated.

Social Constructions of Masculinity, Marginalisation and Violence

It has long been recognised that crime (and particularly violent crime) is a phenomenon predominantly associated with masculinity (Honkatukia et al. 2007). As it has often been argued: to 'do crime' is to 'do masculinity' (Carlsson 2013, p. 662; see also Messerschmidt 1993). As opposed to prioritising biological accounts that stress genetic and physiological factors that may be responsible for instances of male criminality, I favour sociological and feministic-inspired perspectives. These tend to emphasize that the prevalence of male violence and criminality is very often dependent on the way in which masculinity is constructed and enacted in social contexts (Carrington et al. 2010). In this book, I concentrate mainly on examining gang-related violence and crime among disadvantaged males in urban communities. In order to contemplate how intervention programmes and initiatives may assist these men to re-focus their masculine orientations in such a way as to support desistance efforts, it is first important to consider the way in which masculinity is often socially constructed in their lives.

Classic American criminologists such as Edwin Sutherland and Albert Cohen focused attention on the gendered nature of street-oriented violence. However, they drew largely on biologically based sex-role theories that demonstrated no insight into the varieties of masculinities constructed throughout the life course (Messerschmidt 2005). Much evidence suggests that masculinities are multiple and are mediated by a complex array of social, cultural and historical factors (Connell 2005; Scott-Samuel et al. 2009). For instance, Messerschmidt (2005, p. 197) has argued that gender is a 'situated, social and interactional accomplishment that grows out of social practices in specific settings and serves to inform such practices in reciprocal relation'. In other words, we coordinate our activities to 'do' gender in situational ways. Messerschmidt highlights Connell's notion of 'hegemonic masculinity' as being crucial to understanding the power relations among men in certain social settings, due to its promotion of exaggerated forms of male identity (see also Baird 2012):

Hegemonic masculinity is the culturally idealised form of masculinity in a given historical and social setting. It is culturally honoured, glorified, and extolled situationally—such as at the broader societal level (e.g., through the mass media) and at the institutional level (e.g., in school)—and is constructed in relation to 'subordinated masculinities' (e.g., homosexuality) and in relation to women. (Messerschmidt 2005, p. 4)

In contemporary western working-class urban communities, cherished hegemonic masculine characteristics typically include physical strength, competitiveness, assertiveness and overt heterosexual behaviour combined with the rejection of femininity and weakness (Keddie 2003). Goodey (1997) refers to the notion of the 'masculine biography' and argues that men's gendered behaviour results from a 'lifetime of experiences and can only be understood in the context of these experiences' (Abrams et al. 2008, p. 25). Certainly, it is clear that socially-constructed masculinities alone do not generate violence and criminality in urban communities. However, evidence suggests that the interaction between young men's experiences of deprived socio-economic conditions and the messages they receive from those around them about what 'manhood' represents can provide an important indication as to why membership of armed gangs and participation in street violence and drug dealing may occur in some contexts more than others (Baird 2012).

Elaborating on this further, Messerschmidt (2005) argues that crime (and particularly violent crime) can become a resource for some men to enact hegemonic forms of masculinity at certain stages of their lives and for particular reasons. One common stimulus is continual exposure to social, structural and cultural disadvantage. In particular, Abrams et al. (2008) draw attention to issues related to black masculinity, arguing that the marginalisation that some ethnic minority men experience robs them of many of the resources needed to fulfil the hegemonic masculine ideal. If combined with economic disadvantage, the *multiple marginality* they experience (Vigil 1988) may sometimes lead on to public displays of 'exaggerated' masculinity characterised by violence and criminal behaviour (see also Abrams et al. 2008; Hagedorn 2008; Baird 2012).

Further, it has been argued that the construction of violence as a working class phenomenon stems partly from the 'importance of physicality – the body - in working class life and culture' (White 2013, p. 133). Accordingly, the centrality of physique can often translate into forms of aggressive masculinity that celebrate strength and physical prowess, while also being bound up with specific class codes of conduct. In a de-industrialised landscape, men who may have traditionally established their masculine credentials via physical work, but who have now become marginalised, may begin to define themselves through using their bodies to engage in anti-social forms of activity (White 2013).

Accordingly, working class males who become disadvantaged by a lack of meaningful opportunities for employment as well as experiencing the sense of powerlessness that arises from wider social and/or cultural oppression may over-compensate by engaging in 'masculine protest' (Connell 2005, p. 16). In such cases, anger and aggression come to the surface and violence becomes 'a marker of standing' (Carrington et al. 2010, p. 408; and see also Honkatukia et al. 2007). Wider sub-cultural values in these isolated, marginalised contexts may also reinforce this. In their interviews with 11–14 year-old boys in London, Phoenix et al. (2003) found that attributes such as 'hardness' were associated with being properly 'masculine', and that social class and race were identified as moderators of such masculinity (Palasinski and Riggs 2012, p. 465). Where monological expressions of masculinity are repeatedly given value by men in these social contexts, violence may become normalised and this may often include a tendency towards membership of gangs as vehicles for such violence (Carrington et al. 2010; Baird 2012).

Within the context of gang culture, White (2013, p. 138) argues that the 'valorisation of respect in the face of marginalisation' manifests itself through the privileging of in-group loyalty, toughness, fearlessness, mutual protection and fighting (see also Hallsworth 2011). As Baird (2012) argues, male gang members may occupy a significant ontological position in the field of masculinity, symbolised through the accumulation and display of power, respect and money. In turn, since young boys are often disposed to experiencing a process of masculine socialisation that reflects existing masculine identities around them, these gang members can become powerful role models for them. This is particularly the case in contexts where young men live their lives against the backdrop of poverty, class and/or race subordination and difficult family lives dominated by alcoholism or drug dependency (Deuchar 2009, 2013).

Drawing these insights together, in considering how social contexts may cultivate violent crime among men we need to recognise the multiplicity of ways that masculinity can become constructed. Since multiple marginality in the form of social and/or racial disadvantage may negatively influence men's masculine biographies and their ability to perform hegemonic masculinity in conventional ways, violent crime may become an alternative resource to fulfill hegemonic ideals. In socially disadvantaged settings, hanging around on the street clearly offers a 'field of possibilities' through which 'gender can be accomplished and the bounds of race and class can similarly be transcended' (Harding 2014, p. 223). Within this context, Harding (2014) argues that the gang acts as a particularly salient stimulus for 'doing masculinity' through physical violence and drug dealing, as other conventional opportunities are blocked off. As such, it provides a social arena where the very worst aspects of hegemonic masculinity often become reinforced. Indeed, evidence from around the world adds weight to this argument.

Gang Culture, Crime and Masculinity: International Perspectives

For over a Century, recurring evidence has suggested that disadvantaged males (and particularly younger men) often turn towards gang membership as a means of enacting 'hyper-masculinity' and sustaining a 'plausible male identity' (Pitts 2008, p. 108). As John Pitts (2008, p. 108) has highlighted, gang affiliation is often a 'product of socio-economically induced gender insecurity', while R. W. Connell (2005, p. 83) has argued that gang violence is a 'striking example of the assertion of marginalised masculinities against other men'. In this section, I explore a range of specific insights on this issue that have arisen from gang research conducted across the world.

In the early twentieth century, scholarly insights began to emerge through the work of the Chicago School of Sociology, where researchers such as Thrasher (1927) found 1313 gangs to be in existence in Chicago. For Thrasher, gang culture was a way to work out the masculine anxieties of immigrant young men (Hagedorn 2004). He highlighted that their disorder and violence could become so pronounced that they gave the impression of being 'beyond the pale of civil society' (Thrasher 1927, p. 6). Thrasher's pioneering research inspired later work on social disorganisation in the USA by authors such as Shaw and McKay (1942) in Chicago and Whyte (1943) in Boston. Subsequent ethnographic work by Cohen (1955, p. 164) highlighted that, by engaging in 'bad' and 'delinquent' behaviour', young male gang members actively denied their femininity and asserted their sense of working class masculinity (p. 164). Other mid-Century scholarly works by American criminologists such as Yablonski (1967), Cloward and Ohlin (1960) and Klein (1971) also focused on quintessentially male group processes inherent within urban street gangs. Walter Miller's (1958) classic work on lower-class urban gang delinquency in Boston also drew attention to key 'focal concerns' that underpinned gang members' outlooks. These included an admiration for and celebration of toughness, physical prowess, bravery and overt masculinity (Hayward and Ilan 2011).

Contemporary American gang research has expanded to include a focus on black and Chicano gangs and has identified the way in which they are often rooted in institutionalised racism, poverty and marginality (Vigil 1988; Anderson 1999; Alonso 2004; Flores 2014). In Elijah Anderson's (1999) pioneering ethnographic study into urban street life in Philadelphia, he highlights that the inclination to violence emerges from the circumstances of life among the ghetto poor. For young African American males in the ghettos, their lives are characterised by unemployment, the dominance of the drug trade and feelings of racial alienation and marginalisation. The most profound casualties adopt a 'code of the street', which amounts to a 'set of informal rules' that direct all of their interpersonal public behaviour, particularly violence' (Anderson 1999, p. 33). Anderson argues that the central issue of manhood is the 'widespread belief that one of the most effective ways of gaining respect is to manifest nerve'. Displaying 'nerve' is done in various ways, including taking another's possessions, messing with someone's woman, or pulling the trigger on rival drug dealers.

In research conducted in Los Angeles, California, Alonso (2004) has also drawn attention to the way in which, for Californian ethnic minority youths marginalised on several fronts, association with street gangs reinforces a masculine identity that in turn fuels the further growth of gang membership. In sum, many American criminologists have come to the conclusion that gang life is an expression of (multiply-) 'marginalised masculinity' (Flores 2014, p. 476).

It has been argued that, unlike in the USA, street gangs in some parts of Europe have fluid membership and flexible boundaries and are often involved in less criminally-oriented activity (Aldridge et al. 2008; Klein 2008). However, some authors have identified the way in which European street gangs are often also guided by a focus on marginalised masculinity. For instance, Lien's (2005) research in Oslo, Norway and Weitekamp et al.'s (2005) work with Russian immigrants in Germany both highlight the way in which young gang members talk constantly about their sense of honour and respect. They have to prove their sense of masculinity and courage in order to be given a place in street gangs against the backdrop of social and cultural disadvantage. Further, empirical work conducted in the Netherlands has identified that violence emerges on the streets between young white Dutch males and migrant young men, focused on the upholding of masculine honour and the need to claim the streets (Van Gemert and Stuifbergen 2008; Van Gemert et al. 2011, 2016). In addition, Kersten's (2001) research in Germany illustrates that the combined activity of neighbourhood gangs, skinheads and football hooligans represents attempts by underclass young men to claim hegemonic masculinity through violence.

In the UK, gang research first began in the 1960s in Glasgow through the work of James Patrick (1973). Patrick documented the strong subcultural emphasis on 'self-assertion', 'rebellious independence against authority' and the hallowing of violence as features of masculinity in Glasgow's housing schemes (see also Deuchar 2009, 2013). Wider British scholars initially resisted examining youth group dynamics in terms of 'gangs'. However, in more recent decades they have focused on attempting to dispel the proliferation of tabloid images while also working with communities to establish a wider knowledge base on youth groups with characteristics of street gangs (Joe-Laidler and Hunt 2012).

Harding's ethnographic research in south London (2014) applies Bourdieu's principles of social field analysis and habitus to gangs, and identifies the centrality of 'street capital'. Drawing on Sandberg and Pedersen (2011), he argues that street capital is more than 'simply street credibility' but is embodied in the 'knowledge, skills and objects that are given value in street culture' (Harding 2014, p. 60). Crucially, it is described as 'masculine in essence' (p. 61) and is allocated by others through informal networks. Within this context, Harding goes on to argue that the gang provides a social arena for disadvantaged (predominantly black) young males to construct a 'plausible gendered self' (p. 222). Crucially, he highlights that criminal activity becomes the primary resource for enacting street masculinity, and distinction in the 'street casino' is most commonly acquired through securing fast money from drug dealing and participating in violence (for further discussion on social field analysis, see Chapter 11).

In other research conducted in inner-city London, Densley (2015) has drawn attention to the way in which—against the backdrop of educational exclusion, unemployment and racism—disadvantaged young black men on occasions perform violence to gain acceptance as members of gangs. In addition, he describes an even darker side to the way in which violence can be used as a form of masculine power within street gangs. Elder members may use violence or the threat of violence to regulate the behaviour of their youngers. They may also use sexual violence as a means of addressing 'the supposed transgressions of women' or emasculating male gang youngers as punishment (Densley 2013, p. 96).

Although sceptical about the existence of gangs in the UK, Hallsworth (2011, p. 135) has identified the existence of various street-oriented 'outlaw groups' where the 'capacity to assert physical self is celebrated as a valid marker of being a man'. Indeed, Hallsworth identifies fighting as a recurrent feature of life on the streets for young men in Lambeth in inner London, and describes the type of lawlessness embraced by these young men as a type of 'purified masculinity' that disavows what society codes as feminine. This includes the need to avoid being 'overtly emotional, intimating care and evincing compassion for others' (Hallsworth 2011, p. 136).

In Scotland, my own previous research has also illustrated the way in which street gangs provide young men with opportunities to express narrowly-defined but widely accepted views of masculinity (Deuchar 2009, 2013). Violence is often seen as a way of helping them to cope with the social exclusion and multiple marginality that has emerged as a result of deindustrialisation. It is also a means of reacting to damaged mental health landscapes that are often a repercussion of early trauma in homes and communities (Holligan and Deuchar 2015). Specifically in Glasgow (Scotland's largest city), territorial violence is prevalent and young men's strong territorial identification is often a symptom of both the 'decline of industrialism' and erosion of traditional urban leisure space (Fraser 2015, p. 109).

Beyond the context of American and European gang research, wider global evidence also illustrates the close links between marginalisation, gang violence and masculine identity construction. In Australia, White (2013) has identified the way in which institutional racism and economic oppression experienced by ethnic minority young men leads to street gang formation. In some cases, the 'valorisation of respect in the face of marginalisation' manifests itself through 'being tough', engaging in territorial violence and behaving and dressing aggressively (p. 137). In particular, White argues that criminal acts such as armed robbery and assault as well as street fights are often viewed as being overtly masculine and a source of male adrenaline rush. However, many gang members create and maintain strong ethical and moral precepts including the recognised need for 'loyalty to the group and to each other', as well as displaying courage and a commitment to mutual protection (White 2013, p. 138). Many young men display compliance with the negative features or hegemonic masculinity as a last resort to status, which often manifests itself in the 'language of emasculation and effeminisation' used in their attempts to humiliate others (ibid.).

Although there has been a paucity of gang research emerging in Asian countries such as China, Pyrooz and Decker (2013, p. 267) have identified that the presence of household strains, low self-control, reduced levels of school and parental attachment and parental monitoring and association with delinquent peers can increase the tendency to engage in violence and wider criminality among 'Chinese youth and emerging adults'. Furthermore, they identify that 'groups matter' in the commission of delinquency among young men in China (ibid., p. 168). In addition, wider research by Lo (2010) suggests that street gang members in Hong Kong are often heavily influenced by triad subcultures. They draw upon hegemonic masculine values such as a commitment to sworn brotherhood to fuel their participation in organised forms of criminality including drug dealing and trafficking. They also believe they need to use violence as a means of protecting other fellow gang members whom they regard as 'blood brothers' (Chin 1990, and for extended discussion on this, see Chapter 9).

Accordingly, international evidence suggests that men (and particularly young men) become attracted to gang violence and criminality as a means of asserting the standard bearers of working class hegemonic masculinity (including toughness, physical prowess, respect and nerve), against the backdrop of marginalisation. Male gang members accrue street capital from other men and in the process construct respected and plausible gendered identities by hallowing violent physicality and engaging in high adrenaline pursuits, while at the same time overtly rejecting all forms of femininity. While firm compliance with these negative aspects of hegemonic masculinity is prioritised as a means of social status, in many cases strong ethical and moral precepts are also upheld. Again, these are strongly masculinized and include a focus on honour, loyalty and a commitment to sworn brotherhood.

However, while a great deal of empirical gang research has examined the nature and motivations of gang members and the ultimate impact of gang membership on criminological outcomes, fewer scholars have explored the 'motives and methods' for gang desistance (Pyrooz and Decker 2011, p. 422). It is to this under-examined issue that I now turn.

The Masculinization of Gang Desistance and Reformatory Interventions

Research on desistance from crime and violence has traditionally been dominated by life course perspectives. In particular, there has been a strong focus on how changes in life stages such as entry into marriage, employment or parenthood can function as drivers in desistance processes (Laub and Sampson 1993; Sampson and Laub 2005). In the field of gang research, much has also been written about the difficulties that members experience in trying to leave gangs. Some claims suggest that members often may have to 'get jumped out' to leave the gang as a result of the 'blood in, blood out' principle (Pyrooz and Decker 2011, p. 419; Decker et al. 2014, p. 270). While this may be common in some parts of the world, criminal desistance in general is more often a gradual and 'drifting' process that rarely follows a seamless transition and is usually conditional on a range of triggers, turning points and push/pull factors (Pyrooz and Decker 2011; Decker et al. 2014).

For gang members, pull factors tend to include taking on new responsibilities like getting a job or having children or perhaps being encouraged by significant influential others to leave the gang. Conversely, push factors include witnessing various types of violent incidents, on occasions becoming a victim of violence or simply becoming tired of the lifestyle (Deuchar 2009; Pyrooz and Decker 2011; Deuchar 2013; Decker et al. 2014; Carson and Esbensen 2016). Maruna and Farrall (2004) also differentiate between *primary* and *secondary* desistance: while the former is seen to be characterised by a 'hiatus in criminal activity', the latter is viewed as more of a long-term process which results in the 'reframing of personal identity into a new conventional self' (Healy 2012, p. 7).

It is clear, then, that desistance is not just about transformations in offenders' circumstances (Søgaard et al. 2016). It is often stimulated by (inter)subjective processes, including offenders' narrative reconstructions of selves and identities (Maruna 2001; Giordano et al. 2002; Gadd and Farrell 2004; Healy 2012). Thus, while life events can act as triggers for an individual's decision to change, social and structural changes will only be influential if a person considers these desirable (Søgaard et al. 2016). Consequently, desistance cannot occur without individual agency and the construction of events as meaningful (Healy 2012; Liebregts et al. 2015; Søgaard et al. 2016).

In previous sections, I explored the international evidence that suggests a strong relationship between marginalised masculinity and participation in gang violence and criminality as a means of expressing hegemonic ideals in exaggerated ways. Accordingly, my own interests have become centred on the vehicles that may exist for alternative masculine identity construction as a potential stimulus for initial behavioural change conducive to primary desistance and *prospective* secondary desistance. Carlsson (2013, p. 684) argues that, at certain points in the life course, desistance from crime can begin to be seen as a form of 'masculinity accomplishing' as part of the 'transition to male adulthood' (see also Gadd and Farrall 2004). Other recent criminological insights from the USA also suggest that initial gang disengagement and recovery is often stimulated by, or at the very least complemented with, changing personal definitions of masculinity (Flores 2014).

However, the process of masculinity identity reconstruction needs to be validated by securing legitimacy in the eyes of significant others in gang members' lives (Decker et al. 2014; Pyrooz 2014). Flores (2014, p. 176) discusses the need for reformatory interventions to support the reshaping of 'gang embodiment'. While 'hard' gang embodiment refers to permanent markers of street gang life, including subconscious aggressive verbal and nonverbal reactions, 'soft' embodiment refers to the malleable markers such as a shaved head, tattoos, and aggressive types of clothing. Densley (2013, p. 139) also highlights that the masculine status that gang membership initially brings ultimately leads on to 'stigmata' for many members, who often carry with them 'criminal records, violent reputations, tattoos, scars, ongoing vulnerability to reprisals and a residual territorial confinement' into their uncertain futures. At the heart of the male gang recovery and desistance process, there may be a need to encourage men to address the markers of gang embodiment that can ultimately become 'stigmata' while also preventing them from feeling emasculated in front of significant others (Densley 2013; Flores 2014; Pyrooz 2014).

Throughout the pages of this book, I continually draw upon the premise that disengagement from gangs and desistance from gang-related violence and crime among male offenders is potentially stimulated through nurturing role transitions and promoting alternative views of male identity and accomplishment. To date, there has been a paucity of research that has examined the extent to which interventions can support the re-writing of masculine biographies, encourage gang-affiliated men to disrupt their gendered selves, engage in role transition and experiment with alternatives to hegemonic masculinity in such a way as to potentially change their propensity towards (violent) criminality (Abrams et al. 2008; Decker et al. 2014). There is also a distinct lack of knowledge about the role that religion and spirituality can potentially play in this process. The chapters of this book help to address these existing knowledge gaps.

Concluding Discussion

Like others before me, in this chapter I have argued that violence and wider criminal offending among men often emerges as a result of the interaction between multiple marginality and the socially constructed forms of masculinity that surround them. I have drawn upon the evidence that suggests that gang membership provides a potent context for the re-assertion of marginalised masculinity through violent physicality.

In considering the subjective processes that may stimulate disengagement from gangs, violence and crime, in this book I focus on the potential that reformatory intervention programmes may have for supporting masculine identity reconstructions conducive to desistance. In doing so, I pay particular attention to the experiences of those male gang members and offenders who are on the threshold or early stages of change: those who could be described as 'early-stage desisters' or 'liminal beings' (Healy 2012, pp. 35–36). As Flores (2014, p. 487) has argued, not much is known about programmes that promote desistance from gang life, and even less is known about how gang recovery engages marginalised 'gang masculinity' among early-stage desisters. Undoubtedly, getting out and staying out of gangs requires resilience, particularly as many gang members carry 'stigmata' into their futures, may feel that they need to stay loyal to their gangs and live in constant fear of reprisals (Densley 2013).

A centrally recognised element in the process of desistance is the 'knifing off' of offenders from their immediate environment through introducing them to new institutional structures and routines (Laub and Sampson 2003, p. 145). Further, some have argued that desistance is best understood within the context of human relationships, and stimulated by supporting offenders to move away from old social networks and build new ones (McNeill 2004; McNeill and Maruna 2008; Healy 2012; Alós 2015; Birgden 2015). Maruna (2001) also highlights that the process of desisting from crime is often accompanied by an impulse towards generative care-giving, where offenders commit to 'making good' by drawing upon a 'damaged past' and using it to protect the future interests of others (McNeill 2004, p. 432). Drawing upon the identity theories of desistance associated with Criminologists such as Maruna (2001), Giordano et al. (2002) and Decker et al. (2014) suggests that creating opportunities for fostering social capital while facilitating the personal reflection and introspection needed to contest gang masculinity may best support the narrative reconstructions that stimulate disengagement from male gang culture and crime.

Ultimately, the complexities of masculinity construction and gang involvement suggest that intervention strategies designed to enable gang members to desist must incorporate a range of elements. These may need to include exit strategies and offer alternative sources of masculine expression and status accumulation. They may also need to focus on re-shaping gang embodiment indicators and nurturing the appropriate networks that will help to legitimise alternative constructs and roles (White 2013). In the next chapter, the spotlight is placed on religion and spirituality as a potential resource for nurturing positive transitions. I explore the existing literary evidence that suggests that religious and/or spiritual engagement can support masculinity identity reconstruction among offenders in such a way as to stimulate the desistance process.

References

Abrams, L. S., Anderson-Nathe, B., & Aguilar, J. (2008). Constructing masculinities in juvenile corrections. *Men and Masculinities, 11*(1), 22–41.

Aldridge, J., Medina, J., & Ralphs, R. (2008). Dangers and problems of doing gang research in the UK. In F. Van Gemert, D. Petersen, & I. L. Lien (Eds.), *Street gangs, migration and ethnicity* (pp. 31–46). Collumpton: Willan.

Alonso, A. (2004). Racialized identitites and the formation of black gangs in Los Angeles. *Urban Geography, 25*(7), 658–674.

Alós, R. (2015). Effects of prison work programmes on the employability of ex-prisoners. *European Journal of Criminology, 12*(1), 35–50.

Anderson, E. (1999). *Code of the street*. New York: W. W. Norton & Company.

Baird, A. (2012). The violent gang and the construction of masculinity amongst socially excluded young men. *Safer Communities, 11*(4), 179–190.

Birgden, A. (2015). Maximising desistance: Adding therapeutic jurisprudence and human rights to the mix. *Criminal Justice and Behaviour, 42*(1), 19–31.

Carlsson, C. (2013). Masculinities, persistence, and desistance. *Criminology, 51*(3), 661–693.

Carrington, K., McIntosh, A., & Scott, J. (2010). Globalization, frontier masculinities and violence: Booze, blokes and brawls. *British Journal of Criminology, 50*, 393–413.

Carson, D. C., & Esbensen, F.-A. (2016). Motivations for leaving gangs in the USA: A qualitative comparison of leaving processes across gang definitions. In C. L. Maxson & F.-A. Esbensen (Eds.), *Gang transitions and transformations in an international context* (pp. 139–155). Switzerland: Springer.

Chin, K. (1990). *Chinese subculture and criminality: Non-traditional crime group in America*. Westport: Greenwood Press.

Cloward, R., & Ohlin, L. (1960). *Delinquency and opportunity: A theory of delinquent gangs*. New York: The Free Press.

Cohen, A. K. (1955). *Delinquent boys: The culture of the gang*. New York: The Free Press.

Connell, R. W. (2005). *Masculinities*. Cambridge: Polity Press.

Decker, S. H., Pyrooz, D., & Moule, R. K., Jr. (2014). Disengagement from gangs as role transitions. *Journal of Research on Adolescence, 24*(2), 268–283.

Densley, J. (2013). *How gangs work: An ethnography of youth violence*. London: Palgrave Macmillan.

Densely, J. A. (2015). 'We'll show you gang': The subterranean structuration of gang life in London. *Criminology and Criminal Justice, 15*(1), 102–120.

Deuchar, R. (2009). *Gangs, marginalized youth and social capital*. Stoke on Trent: Trentham.

Deuchar, R. (2013). *Policing youth violence: Transatlantic connections*. London: Trentham Books/IOE Press.

Flores, E. O. (2014). *God's gangs: Barrio ministry, masculinity and gang recovery*. New York: New York University Press.

Fraser, A. (2015). *Urban legends: Gang identity in the post-industrial city*. Oxford: Oxford University Press.

Gadd, D., & Farrall, S. (2004). Criminal careers, desistance and subjectivity. *Theoretical Criminology, 8*(2), 1362–4806.

Giordano, P. C., Cernkovich, S. A., & Rudolph, J. L. (2002). Gender, crime, and desistance: Toward a theory of cognitive transformation. *American Journal of Sociology, 107*(4), 990–1064.

Goodey, J. (1997). Boys don't cry: Masculinities, fear of crime, and fearlessness. *British Journal of Criminology, 37*(3), 401–418.

Hagedorn, J. M. (2004). Gang. In M. S. Kimmel & A. Aronson (Eds.), *Encyclopedia of men and masculinities* (pp. 329–330). Santa Barbara: ABC-CLIO.

Hagedorn, J. (2008). *A world of gangs: Armed young men and gansta culture*. Minneapolis: University of Minnesota.

Hallsworth, S. (2011). *Street crime*. Oxon: Routledge.

Harding, S. (2014). *The street casino: Survival in violent street gangs*. Bristol: Policy Press.

Hayward, K., & Ilan, J. (2011). Deviant subcultures. In C. D. Bryant (Ed.), *The Routledge handbook of deviant behavior* (pp. 233–239). New York: Routledge.

Healy, D. (2012). *The dynamics of desistance: Charting pathways through change*. New York: Routledge.

Holligan, C., & Deuchar, R. (2015). What does it mean to be a man? Psychosocial undercurrents in the voices of incarcerated (violent) Scottish teenage offenders. *Criminology and Criminal Justice, 15*(3), 361–377.

Honkatukia, P., Nyqvist, L., & Tarja, P. (2007). Violence talk and gender in youth residential care. *Journal of Scandinavian Studies in Criminology and Crime Prevention, 8*, 56–76.

Joe-laidler, K., & Hunt, G. (2012). Moving beyond the gang–drug–violence connection. *Drugs: Education, Prevention and Policy, 19*(6), 442–452.

Keddie, A. (2003). Little boys: Tomorrow's macho lads. *Discourse: Studies in the Cultural Politics of Education, 24*(3), 289–306.

Kersten, J. (2001). Groups of violent males in Germany. In M. Klein, H.-J. Kerner, C. Maxson, & E. Whitekamp (Eds.), *The Eurogang pardox: Street gangs and youth groups in the U.S. and Europe* (pp. 247–255). London: Kluwer Academic Publishers.

Klein, M. (1971). *Street gangs and street workers*. Englewood Cliffs, NJ: Prentice Hall.

Klein, M. (2008). Foreword. In F. Van Gemert, D. Petersen, & I. L. Lien (Eds.), *Street gangs, migration and ethnicity* (pp. xi–xv). Collumpton: Willan.

Laub, J. H., & Sampson, R. J. (1993). Turning points in the life course: Why change matters to the study of crime. *Criminology, 31*(3), 301–325.

Laub, J. H., & Sampson, R. J. (2003). *Shared beginnings, divergent lives: Delinquent boys to age 70*. Cambridge, MA: Harvard University Press.

Liebregts, N., van der Pol, P., de Graafb, R., van Laar, M., van den Brink, W., & Korf, D. J. (2015). Persistence and desistance in heavy cannabis use: The role of identity, agency, and life events. *Journal of Youth Studies, 18*(5), 617–633.

Lien, I.-L. (2005). Criminal gangs and their connections: Metaphors, definitions and structures. In S. H. Decker & F. M. Weerman (Eds.), *European street gangs and troublesome youth groups* (pp. 31–50). New York: Altamira Press.

Lo, T. W. (2010). Beyond social capital: Triad organized crime in Hong Kong and China. *British Journal of Criminology, 50*, 851–872.

Maruna, S. (2001). *Making good: How ex-convicts reform and rebuild their lives*. Washington, DC: American Psychological Association.

Maruna, S., & Farrall, S. (2004). Desistance from crime: A theoretical reformulation. *Kolner Zeitschrift fur Soziologie und Sozialpsychologie, 43*, 171–194.

McNeill, F. (2004). Desistance, rehabilitation and correctionalism: Developments and prospects in Scotland. *The Howard Journal, 43*(4), 420–436.

McNeill, F., & Maruna, S. (2008). Giving up and giving back: Desistance, generativity and social work with offenders. In G. McIvor & P. Raynor (Eds.), *Developments in social work with offenders* (pp. 224–339). London: Jessica Kingsley.

Messerschmidt, J. (1993). *Masculinities and crime: Critique and reconceptualization of theory*. Lanham, MD: Rowman & Littlefield.

Messerschmidt, J. (2005). Men, masculinities and crime. In M. S. Kimmel, J. Hearn, & R. W. Connell (Eds.), *Handbook of studies on men and masculinities* (pp. 196–212). London: Sage.

Miller, W. (1958). Lower class culture as a generating milieu of gang delinquency. *Social Issues, 14*(3), 5–19.
Palasinski, M., & Riggs, D. W. (2012). Young British men and knife-carrying in public: Discourses of masculinity, protection and vulnerability. *Critical Criminology, 20*(4), 463–476.
Patrick, J. (1973). *A Glasgow gang observed*. London: Eyre Muthuen.
Phoenix, A., Frosh, S., & Pattman, R. (2003). Producing contradictory masculine subject positions: Narratives of threat, homophobia and bullying in 11–14 year old boys. *Journal of Social Issues, 59*(1), 179–195.
Pitts, J. (2008). *Reluctant gangsters: The changing face of youth crime*. Devon: Willan.
Pyrooz, D. C. (2014). Book review: God's gangs: Barrio ministry, masculinity and gang recovery, by Edward Orozco Flores. *Crime, Law and Social Change, 62*, 621–624.
Pyrooz, D. C., & Decker, S. H. (2011). Motives and methods for leaving the gang: Understanding the process of gang desistance. *Journal of Criminal Justice, 39*, 417–425.
Pyrooz, D. C., & Decker, S. H. (2013). Delinquent behavior, violence, and gang involvement in China. *Journal of Quantitative Criminology, 29*(2), 251–272.
Sampson, R. J., & Laub, J. H. (2005). A life-course view of the development of crime. *The ANNALS of the American Academy of Political and Social Science, 602*(1), 12–45.
Sandberg, S., & Pedersen, W. (2011). *Street capital: Black cannabis dealers in a white welfare state*. Bristol: Policy Press.
Scott-Samuel, A., Stanistreet, D., & Crawshaw, P. (2009). Hegemonic masculinity, structural violence and health inequalities. *Critical Public Health, 19*(3–4), 287–292.
Shaw, C. R., & McKay, H. D. (1942). *Juvenile delinquency and urban areas*. Chicago: University of Chicago Press.
Søgaard, T. F., Kolind, T., Thylstrup, B., & Deuchar, R. (2016). Desistance and the micro-narrative construction in a Danish rehabilitation centre. *Criminology and Criminal Justice, 16*(1), 99–108.
Thrasher, F. (1927). *The gang: A study of 1313 gangs in Chicago*. Chicago: University of Chicago Press.
Van Gemert, F., & Stuifbergen, J. (2008). Gangs, migration and conflict: Thrasher's theme in The Netherlands. In F. Van Gemert, D. Peterson, & I.-L. Lien (Eds.), *Street gangs, migration and ethnicity* (pp. 79–96). Cullompton: Willan.

Van Gemert, F., Esbensen, F.-A., & Maxson, C. L. (2011). Five decades of defining gangs in The Netherlands: The Eurogang paradox in practice. In F.-A. Esbensen & C. L. Maxson (Eds.), *Youth gangs in international perspective: Results from the Eurogang progam of research* (pp. 69–83). London: Springer.

Van Gemert, F., Roks, R., & Drogt, M. (2016). Dutch Crips run dry in liquid society. In C. L. Maxson & F.-A. Esbensen (Eds.), *Gang transitions and transformations in an international context* (pp. 157–172). Switzerland: Springer.

Vigil, J. D. (1988). *Barrio gangs: Street life and identity in Southern California*. Austin: University of Texas Press.

Weitekamp, E. G. M., Reich, K., & Kerner, H.-J. (2005). Why do young male Russians of German descent tend to join or form violent gangs? In S. H. Decker & F. M. Weerman (Eds.), *European street gangs and troublesome youth groups* (pp. 81–104). New York: Altamira Press.

White, R. (2013). *Youth gangs, violence and social respect: Exploring the nature of provocations and punch-ups*. Basingstoke, UK: Palgrave Macmillan.

Whyte, W. F. (1943). *Street corner society*. Chicago: University of Chicago Press.

Yablonsky, L. (1967). *The violent gang*. Middlesex: Pelican.

3

Religious and Spiritual Desistance From Gangs

In this chapter, I explore the evidence that suggests that religious and/or spiritual engagement can support masculinity identity reconstruction among offenders in such a way as to stimulate the desistance process. The process of faith conversion and the emergence of redemption scripts (Maruna 2001) is critically analysed, and I consider the potential salience of the way in which faith-based contexts may enhance some men's ability to publically project stories of change about their values, attitudes and priorities. I also examine the existing insights that suggest that engagement in wider, more holistic spiritual practices may also play a role in the type of identity and behaviour change that stimulates progression towards desistance.

Introduction: Religion, Spirituality and Desistance

As the previous chapter indicated, there are complexities associated with the way masculine identity is often constructed and embodied by male gang members. This suggests that intervention strategies designed to nurture desistance from gang-related crime must incorporate a range of elements. As I have argued, it is important to be mindful of the fact that desistance is best viewed as an 'ongoing work in progress' (McNeill and Maruna 2008, p. 225), and that the turning points that may stimulate personal identity change often unfold over time. Carlsson (2012, p. 4) highlights that certain transition processes may be salient enough to nurture offenders' initial and continuing 'progression towards desistance'.

It is these processes and these types of progressive steps that are of most interest to me in this book, particularly within the context of early-stage desisters' experiences of gang disengagement. As discussed in Chapter 1, over the years my interest in this area has led me to study gang intervention programmes and initiatives across the globe. In particular, I have become most interested in exploring religious and spiritual elements of programmes and interventions. I have begun to explore the potential that these initiatives may have in stimulating the types of early transitions and turning points that encourage the most marginalised to begin to shift their emphasis away from 'hypermasculine' gang behaviour, while also preventing feelings of emasculation (Flores 2014, p. 150; Deuchar et al. 2016b).

In doing so, I have of course recognised the need to cast a critical eye over some interventions and practices. For example, it is important to reflect upon the extent to which some patriarchal religious beliefs might encourage men to justify violence and abuse. On the other hand it is also important to consider whether some faith-based or spiritual practices might facilitate wider views of masculinity, where offenders begin to see expressing fear, 'backing down' from conflict and seeking social support as signs of confidence and maturity rather than weakness (Levitt et al. 2008).

To set the context for the discussion in this chapter, it is important to acknowledge that religion and spirituality are generally considered to be separate concepts (Nardi et al. 2011). Accordingly, careful distinctions need to be made between them. Religion has been described as a 'system of transcendent beliefs which has been manifested in diverse practices, customs, denominational and institutional formations' (Whitehead 2013, p. 1). Religious participation is viewed as a social experience that involves established 'rules, practices, beliefs and values' (Tanyi 2006, p. 288) and 'a system of worship and doctrine that is shared within a group' (Schroeder and Frana 2009, p. 720). On the other hand, spirituality goes beyond religion (Nardi et al. 2011). It is often viewed as a transcendent experience (Hall et al. 2011), seen to be concerned with 'addressing ultimate questions about life's meaning' in a more holistic sense (Fetzer Institute [1999] 2003, p. 2; see also Thomas and Zaitzow 2006). Some have argued that spirituality is focused on a 'search for purpose and meaning and having a moral dimension which reflects a concern with relationships to others ... and to some transcendental being or force' (Lindsay 2002, pp. 31–32); or just simply any subjective experience that 'results in greater knowledge and love' or 'precipitates comprehension of new meanings in life which enhances growth' (Hall et al. 2011, p. 207).

In the following sections, I review some of the existing evidence related to the impact of interventions focused around these broadly-defined views of both religion and spirituality.

Religion, Social Control and Social Capital

Emile Durkheim (1915) was among the first scholars to recognise that religion could be a mechanism for social integration and positive behaviour change (see Schroeder and Frana 2009). He viewed religion as a 'crucial, integrative mechanism for maintaining social order and fostering a common set of values and beliefs' (Clear and Sumter 2002, p. 127). Much scholarship has drawn upon control theory perspectives to argue that practising religion can provide offenders with a stake in conformity (Giordano et al. 2008; Schroeder and Frana 2009; Hallett and McCoy 2014). Functionalists have often claimed that religious beliefs provide a strong foundation for moral behaviour, thus enabling offenders to express remorse for previous activity. At the same time, they argue that religious engagement can help to prevent deviation from societal norms in the future (Clear and Sumter 2002; Jensen and Gibbons 2002).

In Laub and Sampson's (2003) seminal longitudinal analysis of desistance processes, the role of religion was not emphasised; however, a small number of the Glueck respondents did report having benefited from religiously-involved self-help groups (Bakken et al. 2014). In wider terms, there has been an increasing body of empirical evidence that has indicated an inverse relationship between religion and offending behaviour (for reviews, see Whitehead 2013; Giordano et al. 2008; Hallett and McCoy 2014). The most rigorous systematic review of existing international research in this area was conducted by Johnson (2011), who identified that 90% of studies reported a beneficial relationship between religion and disengagement from criminality (Whitehead 2013). However, other scholars have remained sceptical about the potential of religion to inhibit offending (Clear and Sumter 2002). Giordano et al. (2008) draw attention to the claims emerging from several research studies that there is no apparent difference between religious and nonreligious youth in criminal offending (see, for instance, Hirschi and Stark 1969; Krohn et al. 1982; Evans et al. 1996).

Among the studies that do point towards positive effects, Giordano et al. (2008) draw upon differential association theory to argue that religious practice can introduce offenders to strong social bonds which can subsequently generate the social capital that supports gradual disengagement from crime (Hallett and McCoy 2014). Putnam (2000) believes that social capital is a collective asset with a common good. He concentrates upon the interaction of capital between the individual and a given community, while Coleman (1988) argues that social capital is 'embodied in relations among people' (see also Deuchar 2009, p. 98). Recognised indicators of social capital include high levels of social interaction and networking, information-sharing and obligations to others (Coleman 1988; Leonard and Onyx 2004; Deuchar 2009).

Putnam (2000) argues that social capital arises within the context of civic community networks, and includes a sense of belonging to a civic community and the emergence of norms of reciprocity and trust. Some authors (Barry 2006; Deuchar 2009, 2013) have highlighted that giving offenders opportunities to accumulate social capital can aid them in making the transition out of crime. Some have also highlighted the way in which members of the clergy can enmesh offenders in compassionate, trusting and reciprocal relationships, characterised by unconditional support. In so doing, they can enable these offenders to develop an impulse towards generative motivations where they begin to support others (Maruna 2001; Barry 2006; Deuchar 2013; Deuchar et al. 2016a).

Some research suggests that the black church, in particular, can be an important source of social capital whereby social connections are fostered and collective agency established (Coleman 1988; Putnam 2000; Field 2003; Deuchar 2009). For instance, against the backdrop of the Boston Ceasefire in the 1990s members of the black clergy engaged in important advocacy work for young gang members via probation officers. They mobilized other community organisations, police departments and neighbourhood residents to develop programmes and initiatives and acted as 'brokers' in order to connect young people with a range of social service agencies (Pegram et al. 2016). Similarly, my own previous research (Deuchar 2013, p. 150) illustrates the way in which African American Street Advocates played an integral role within the Cincinnati Initiative to Reduce Violence (CIRV) from 2006 onwards, offering gang-involved young men social support. They liaised with wider agencies for education, training and employment opportunities while also fostering in them a desire for 'lasting accomplishments' and an impulse to expend social capital onto others through generative action.

Almost all prisons have religious chaplains, and it has been argued that religious involvement is one of the most common forms of 'programming' in prisons (O'Connor and Perreyclear 2002, p. 12; see also Sundt and Cullen 2002; Thomas and Zaitzow 2006; Liebling 2014; for further discussion, see Chapter 7, this book). Some research has suggested that, through its dual focus on supporting and enabling social control and social capital, religious practice in prisons helps offenders to adjust to prison life more easily. In turn, offenders begin to avoid disciplinary confinement for violating prison rules and experience greater levels of post-prison adjustment in the community following release (Clear and Sumter 2002; O'Connor and Duncan 2011).

In his ethnographic research in Rio de Janeiro, Johnson's (2017, p. 111) exploration of Pentecostal Christianity in a Brazilian prison suggests that male gang members who engage in the Pentecostal church increasingly begin to use different criteria to judge what it means to be a 'successful man'. Aggression, violence and pride is thus replaced by a focus on peace seeking, humility, self-restraint and re-orientation of priorities away from street and onto domestic roles. However, some studies also contain criticism against prison religion and, indeed, prison religiosity (Bonner and Rich 1990; Thomas and Zaitzow 2006). For example, some have questioned the 'sincerity' of prison conversion, arguing that while there could be some genuine 'conversions', the fact that in many cases prisoners become involved with religion soon after incarceration lends hand to the view that many such conversions are directly related to the deprivation of liberty and conditions of prison life (Deuchar et al. 2016a; for further insights, see Chapter 7).

Accordingly, although sceptical voices abound, there is clearly a body of scholarship and empirical evidence that suggests engaging in religious practices, interventions and groups in the community or in prison can have beneficial outcomes for those involved in offending. While functionalist perspectives stress the potential for enhanced moral codes, adherence to social norms and conformity, interactionist perspectives highlight the impact of enhanced social bonds and capital that can support disengagement from crime. However, as I discussed in Chapter 2, some have argued that cognitive transformations are also crucial in nurturing desistance. In particular, it is important for offenders to develop an openness for change as well an ability to envision new identities or representations of 'possible selves' they would like to become (or may be afraid of becoming) (Paternoster and Bushway 2009, p. 1113). Of particular interest to me is the potential relationship between these types of current and projected cognitive and identity reconstructions and religious participation.

Identity Reconstruction, Emotional Transitions and 'Stories of Change'

It has been argued by some that not only can religion be viewed as a source of external control over individual behaviour, but also as a 'catalyst for new definitions of the situation and as a cognitive blueprint for how one is to proceed as a changed individual' (Giordano et al. 2008,

p. 102). Whether offenders engage with religion via formal pastors, in an organisation like the church or simply through personal experiences, some scholars suggest that it can facilitate identity reconstruction and change.

For instance, in Hallett and McCoy's (2014, p. 4) work with male ex-offenders who had become active Christians, they suggest that the participants weighed up the costs of offending against the backdrop of a 'chrystallisation of discontent'. They drew upon the notion of the 'feared self'—an image of what they did not want to become—as a motivator for self-change, holding this image in sharp contrast to their 'new self in Jesus' (ibid, p. 14, and see also Healy 2012). Importantly, these reformed offenders highlighted identity change as an important resource for embellishing their new Christian behaviour, while also stressing the importance of the meaningful social support they experienced within the context of their faith practice.

Other studies have drawn attention to the way in which religious engagement can stimulate painful confrontations among some individual offenders with negative characteristics of real or projected self-images. In turn, this provides a catalyst for offenders to abandon 'old selves' and adopt 'new selves' which build on and elaborate their new Christian (or other religious) identities (Hallett and McCoy 2014, p. 14, and see also Healy 2012). Some have also identified the way in which faith-oriented programmes may have an indirect effect on desistance efforts by simply increasing offenders' willingness to confront issues of addiction or trauma through accessing relevant services—thus reducing criminogenic factors (Maruna et al. 2006; Mears et al. 2006).

In their own research, Giordano et al. (2008, p. 102) argue that acquiring new perspectives on the self often involves emotional as well as cognitive changes, and that religion provides a resource for 'emotion-coping'. Indeed, Schroeder and Frana's (2009) research in a halfway house in the American Midwest suggests that emotion-coping was the main repercussion to emerge from practicing religion; the emergence of positive feelings such as peace, tolerance, and love ultimately helped inmates to alleviate feelings of anger, anxiety and depression. Similarly, Baker's (2011) work with Muslim offenders found that the emergence of spiritual capital through the discipline of daily prayers brought an increased sense of responsibility to pass on religious ideals to others, while also stimulating feelings of well-being, support and fulfillment (Deuchar et al. 2016a).

Some evidence suggests that engaging in religious practices and communities and beginning to believe in a higher power such as God can enable some offenders to experience feelings of strength, comfort, inner peace and harmony. This provides resilience against the mental health issues and feelings of trauma that participating in or being exposed to violent crime can bring about (Huculak and McLennan 2010). In turn, it can help offenders to gain a sense of hope and motivation to change, and begin to construct 'stories of change' that become central to an altered sense of self (Hallett and McCoy 2014, p. 2; see also O'Connor and Perreyclear 2002).

It seems, then, that participating in faith-based programmes, organisations and contexts may benefit some offenders through nurturing positive emotional changes that create a space for personal reflection and introspection (Deuchar et al. 2016a). Opportunities then arise to weigh up the costs of crime, and the emergence of new faith-oriented identities may begin to trump violent and criminal identities and support a greater impulse to carve change narratives. However, in considering the potential that religious interventions may hold, cognisance needs to be given to the increasingly secular nature of many western societies and the tendency to favour more traditional, non-religious techniques (Hall et al. 2011). With male gang-affiliated offenders there is also the particular challenge associated with the need to problematize their perceptions and performance of hyper-masculinity, while also preventing them from experiencing feelings of emasculation (Deuchar et al. 2016b; Søgaard et al. 2016).

Masculinity, Gangs and Religion

As I have argued, gang membership often provides a potent context for the re-assertion of marginalised masculinity through violent physicality and criminal behaviour (Pitts 2008; Melde et al. 2016). Interventions designed to help disadvantaged males to begin to desist from gang-related offending clearly need to support them in constructing reformed masculine positions. In Flores' (2014) analysis of gang intervention programmes, he found that faith-based rehabilitation enabled Chicano gang members to begin to desist from gang violence through supporting them in reformulating fundamental masculine ideals. The men regularly engaged in verbal rituals where they renounced substance misuse and violence; they expressed regret and began to view this as a sign of strength rather than weakness. In addition, these reforming offenders were encouraged to discuss gang masculinity in negative terms, while the image of the family-oriented male breadwinner was celebrated. They gradually re-aligned their masculine identities and created 'distance between the former and current self' through public interactions with others (Pyrooz 2014, p. 623).

Religiosity has often been seen as a hook that helps offenders to create an evolving self-narrative that can assist them in acquiring enough agency to create a redemptive path (Hallett and McCoy 2014). For male offenders associated with gangs, the experience of finding religion can represent a salient turning point that, over time, can help them to transition from being angry, anxious or depressed to being calmer, more tolerant and peaceful and generally experiencing a greater sense of wellbeing (Thomas and Zaitzow 2006; Giordano et al. 2008; Schroeder and Frana 2009). In turn, this new sense of peaceful wellbeing may be conducive to facilitating agentic self-narratives characterised by a sense of empowerment and self-mastery (Healy 2012). However, it is clear that the challenge of encouraging violent male gang members to initially begin practicing religion may be no mean task. Brenneman (2012) poses the legitimate question: 'what makes a gang member trade in his gun for a Bible?'

In his research with gang members in Guatemala, El Salvador and Hondurus, Brenneman identifies the way in which the 'good feeling' experienced through participation in violent offending tends to wear off and can become a source of shame for some men. Combined with the knowledge that those who report a conversion may often be extended a 'pass' by gang leaders, this may be the hook that first leads these men to seek out religious engagement (Densley 2013). In addition, Brenneman (2012) highlights the way in which many male gang members he worked with reported a range of other benefits for religious participation, such as the support offered to them by church members to find employment, the networks of trust and new healthy routines they were able to establish. Further, he draws attention to the way in which several men reported emotional experiences where they were encouraged to publicly express remorse for prior lifestyles. Accordingly, Brenneman (2012, p. 237) argues that emotional conversions played a role in 'reintegrative shaming', and enabled many of the men to exit the 'shame-rage' spiral that may often fuel gang violence and wider criminality. Engaging with religious ideas and networks, Brenneman argues, can thus set the stage for a change in course that would not have occurred otherwise.

Thus, over time religious engagement can evidently bring about opportunities for male gang members to gradually re-align their views on masculinity through taking on and celebrating alternative roles, supporting each others' creation of conversion narratives and encouraging public expressions of remorse within the context of new, supportive networks. In so doing, the peer support they experience in re-formulating masculine ideals may prevent perceptions of demasculinization (Deuchar et al. 2016b). However, similar types of conversion narratives and 'redemption scripts' have been found among those who participate in secular programmes. Maruna (2001, p. 87) found that many of the self-narratives of offenders he worked with included a tendency to find meaning in their experiences of crime and a desire to 'give something back', especially to young people in trouble (see also Maruna et al. 2006). In subsequent analyses, Maruna et al. (2006) identified that the religious self-narratives of male offenders who had been converted to Christianity could clearly be understood as a 'subtype' of these more generic self-narratives. An additional stimulus for nurturing narrative changes and redemption scripts is engagement in wider, more holistic spiritual practices.

Spirituality, Cognitive Change, Psychosocial Processes and Desistance

As discussed earlier, spirituality tends to be concerned with the transcendent. It is underpinned with an assumption that there is 'more to life than what we see or fully understand' (Fetzer Institute [1999]

2003, p. 3; see also Bakken et al. 2014), and is focused on notions of deeper meaning, purpose and connection to others (Alburquerque et al. 2014). Although some research suggests that spiritual involvement does not necessarily predict long-term desistance, it has been found by some to be mentioned as a potential 'hook' that can initiate behaviour change away from crime (Giordano et al. 2008; Bakken et al. 2014). Some evidence has also implied that positive relationships between spirituality and mental health may be more robust in males than in females (Pandya 2015).

In particular, evidence suggests that creative and ascetic-spiritual practices such as yoga and meditation can play a valuable part in fostering wellbeing and positive identity change among offenders that can support engagement with the desistance process (Parkes and Bilby 2010; Bilderdeck et al. 2013; Deuchar et al. 2016a). Yoga has been practiced in India for thousands of years, and over the past 30 years has grown in popularity in the western world (Derezotes 2000). It includes the use of physical exercises, particular dietary practices and belief systems and has been shown to support patients in managing and reducing a variety of physical and mental ailments (Derezotes 2000). Meditation is a 'self-directed method used to help quiet the mind and relax the body' by enabling participants to develop subtle experience of conscious attention and support the development of restful physiological conditions (Derezotes 2000, p. 100; Himelstein 2011). Although originating in India, China and Japan it has also been used by followers of some western religious traditions for many years (Derezotes 2000).

There are many types of meditative practices, including the use of Transcendental Meditation (TM), popularized in the western world by Maharishi Mahesh Yogi (Walsh 1996). TM has been defined as a 'wakeful condition of alertness' (Himelstein 2011, p. 648), where a mantra is recited and participants return to this mantra whenever the mind wanders. Mindfulness meditation dates back to the fifth Century to the teachings of Buddha, and has been defined as the 'nonreactive attention to one's ongoing mental processes' (Himelstein 2011, p. 648). Mindfulness practice usually comprises participants' enhanced awareness of the breath during sitting meditation, body scanning while lying down and Hatha yoga postures (Kabat-Zinn 2013).

It has been suggested that the regular practicing of mindfulness has the capacity to 'enhance cognitive change, self management, relaxation and acceptance' (Himelstein 2011, p. 648). Research has suggested that meditation-based programmes may provide significant contributions to enhancing overall mental health and wellbeing (Tanyi 2006; Pandya 2015). They may increase positive psychological states such as hopefulness, optimism and happiness as well as decreasing negative states such as rumination, obsessive compulsive behaviour, anxiety and stress (for review, see Himelstein 2011).

Particularly relevant to Criminologists is the evidence that suggests that meditative practices have the potential to address psychosocial processes that are clearly related to recidivism. For example, some research has highlighted that some practices have been found to be helpful in the control of anger that can often lead to violence, as well as in the reduction of substance dependency (Howells et al. 2010; Bakken et al. 2014). The work of Rucker (2005) shows that the combined use of meditation and yoga enabled male prisoners in a US mid-western maximum security prison with convictions for violence to gain a sense of self-mastery which led on to increased self-value and an ability to take control of their own emotions in a peaceful environment (see, also Parkes and Bilby 2010).

Wider research conducted in prisons around the world has also found that the combination of yoga and meditation has led to positive outcomes that may be conducive to criminal desistance. These include an enhanced ability among inmates to engage in personal reflection and acquire greater coping skills (Pham 2013); an increased ability to engage in self-control (Parkes and Bilby 2010); and a greater sense of empathy towards and compassion for others (Duncombe 2004).

Although treatment and rehabilitation of offenders has largely been based on cognitive behavioural models and therapies in the past, Howells et al. (2010, p. 4) argue that 'third wave' creative and ascetic-spiritual practices, strongly influenced by spiritual and contemplative traditions such as Buddhism, have come more to the fore during the last decade. They highlight that, rather than focusing on assisting participants to change particular thoughts or emotions, the goal of these interventions tends to focus on 'encouraging them to observe and accept rather than react' (p. 4). Howells et al. refer to several pre-post differences on measures of mood disturbance, hostility and self-esteem among inmates engaged in mindfulness programmes in US prisons. However, they also draw attention to the fact that 'inwardness, reflection and introspection … are not widely valued or practiced in many western societies' and may meet resistance against the dominant backdrop of punishment-oriented criminal justice systems (ibid, p. 7). Embedded within the existing social work literature on spirituality, although some evidence suggests a growing interest among practitioners in drawing on holistic spiritual practices in recent years (Zapf 2005), others suggest that spirituality as a tool is currently often underused to support clients since many practitioners view it as potentially oppressive or judgemental (Gilligan and Furness 2006; Hall et al. 2011).

Of most significance to this book's focus on masculinity and gang-related criminality is the evidence discussed in Chapter 2 that suggests that men's (particularly young men's) motivations for group and gang-related offending are often guided by strong moral and ethical precepts (White 2013). These include a strong commitment and loyalty towards brotherhood and a focus on reciprocity within gang environments (Anderson 1999; de Haan and Loder 2002; Arsovska and Craig 2006; Boyle 2010; Lo 2010; Flores 2014). Also highly significant is the additional evidence—also discussed in Chapter 2—suggesting that gang members' prolonged involvement in violent criminality and other types of offending can leave them carrying a range of 'stigmata' into their futures, including fear of reprisal, prolonged substance dependency and a range of mental health conditions (Densley 2013, p. 139). Clearly, this can lead to a greater propensity towards recidivism.

Some research suggests that engagement in holistic spiritual practices such as rhythmic breathing, meditation and yogic postures may help to steer offenders' natural proclivity towards moral and ethical precepts and values in positive, non-criminal directions. In addition, it may help them to manage the negative repercussions of prolonged criminal lifestyles more effectively, thus supporting progression towards desistance (Murthy et al. 1998; Brown and Gerbarg 2005a, b; Agte and Chiplonkar 2008; Carlsson 2012).

Concluding Discussion

Given the evidence that suggests that male offenders' disengagement from gangs, violence and crime may be dependent on their ability to reconstruct and reformulate their sense of masculine identity, in this chapter I have argued that it is important for us to understand the extent to and ways in which religion and spirituality may support this process.

I have explored and examined the potential for religious engagement as a 'turning point' to enhance offenders' moral codes, generate social bonds and social capital as well as nurturing an openness for lifestyle change. I have acknowledged the evidence that suggests that participating in faith-based programmes, organisations and contexts may benefit some men through nurturing a sense of emotional wellbeing that is conducive to problematizing their perceptions and performance of hyper-masculinity, and through supporting them to take on alternative roles. The process of faith conversion and the emergence of redemption scripts has been critically analysed, and I have considered the potential salience of the way in which faith-based contexts may enhance some men's ability to publically project stories of change about their values, attitudes and priorities. These new narratives may be characterised by openly rejecting gang masculinity, embracing enhanced male family roles and upholding masculine honour by viewing vulnerability as strength. In turn, the persistent projection of the narratives may nurture greater desistance efforts.

Further, I have also examined the existing insights that suggest that engagement in wider, more holistic spiritual practices may also play a role in the type of identity and behaviour change that stimulates progression towards desistance. I have touched on the potential role of ascetic-spiritual practices such as yoga and meditation, and the emerging insights that suggest the way in which engagement with these practices may enhance positive psychological states that in turn help to steer male gang members' and offenders' moral principles in non-criminal directions. I have also considered the evidence that suggests that these practices may enable them to manage the prolonged negative repercussions of criminal behaviour that often stimulate re-offending.

Parts II–IV of the book present insights from my own empirical research that explores and examines the experiences and perspectives of male gang members and offenders who inhabited a liminal space. Against the backdrop of three different Continents of the world, the data outlined in the chapters draw attention to the common reasons that the majority of these men joined gangs and participated in violence and crime during their formative and (in some cases) adult years. They also illustrate the role that programmes and interventions saturated by spiritual perspectives, meditative practices as well as faith-based religious approaches played in helping these men to begin to redefine masculinity and take initial steps to leave gang-related criminality behind. While highlighting positive illustrations and initial successes, the chapters also highlight the challenges, obstacles and uncertainties that often still characterised the lives of the men during the liminal phase. The insights I provide ultimately enable me to draw conclusions about the men's pathways into and out of gang membership, violence and criminality, drawing on Bourdieusian field analysis combined with theoretical perspectives on hegemonic masculinity in the final chapter.

As an introduction to the empirical section of the book, Part II places the spotlight on the USA, where gangs have been part of the cultural fabric for over 300 years. I focus specifically on Los Angeles, the city that gave America the modern street gang, and consider the way in which issues of race, segregation and discrimination have combined to create communities that have spawned gang formation there (Vigil 2007; Alonso 2010). Insights from life history interviews with Latino men from Los Angeles provide evidence of the social barriers they came across during their early lives, and how this led on to gang membership and offending. Further insights from participant observation of intervention strategies implemented within *Homeboy Industries* (one of the biggest and most renowned gang intervention programme in the world) and from follow-up interviews with the Latino men also illustrate the impact that spiritual interventions were having on changing their perceptions about masculinity and nurturing greater commitment to criminal desistance.

References

Agte, V. V., & Chiplonkar, S. A. (2008). Sudarshan Kriya Yoga for improving antioxidant status and reducing anxiety in adults. *Alternative and Complementary Therapies*, April, 96–100.

Albuquerque, I. F., Cunha, R. C., Martins, L. D., & Sá, A. B. (2014). Primary health care services: Workplace spirituality and organisational performance. *Journal of Organizational Change Management, 27*(1), 59–82.

Alonso, A. (2010). Out of the void: Street gangs in black Los Angeles. In D. Hunt & A. C. Ramon (Eds.), *American dreams and racial realities* (pp. 140–167). New York: New York University Press.

Anderson, E. (1999). *Code of the street*. New York: W. W. Norton and Co.

Arsovska, J., & Craig, M. (2006). 'Honourable' behaviour and the conceptualisation of violence in ethnic-based organised crime groups: An examination of the Chinese Triads. *Global Crime, 7*(2), 214–246.

Baker, C. (2011). The one in the morning knock: Exploring the connections between faith, participation and wellbeing. In J. Atherton, E. Grahamand & I. Steedman (Eds.), *The practice of happiness: Political economy, religion and wellbeing* (pp. 169–183). London: Routledge.

Bakken, N. W., DeCamp, W., & Visher, C. A. (2014). Spirituality and desistance from substance use among reentering offenders. *International Journal of Offender Therapy and Comparative Criminology, 58*(11), 1229–1321.

Barry, M. (2006). *Youth offending in transition: The search for social recognition*. London: Routledge.

Bilderdeck, A. C., Farias, M., Brazil, I. A., Jakobowitz, S., & Wikholm, C. (2013). Participation in a 1-week course of yoga improves behavioural control and decreased psychological distress in a prison population. *Journal of Psychiatric Research, 47*, 1438–1445.

Bonner, R., & Rich, A. (1990). Psychosocial vulnerability, life stress, and suicide ideation in a jail population: A cross-validation study. *Suicide Life Threat Behavior, 20*(3), 213–224.

Boyle, G. (2010). *Tattoos on the heart: The power of boundless compassion*. New York: Free Press.

Brenneman, R. (2012). *Homies and hermanos: God and gangs in central America*. Oxford: Oxford University Press.

Brown, R. P., & Gerbarg, P. L. (2005a). Sudarshan Kriya yogic breathing in the treatment of stress, anxiety, and depression: Part I neurophysiologic model. *The Journal of Alternative and Complementary Medicine, 11*(1), 189–201.

Brown, R. P., & Gerbarg, P. L. (2005b). Sudarshan Kriya yogic breathing in the treatment of stress, anxiety, and depression: Part II—Clinical applications and guidelines. *The Journal of Alternative and Complementary Medicine, 11*(4), 711–717.

Carlsson, C. (2012). Using 'turning points' to understand processes of change in offending. *British Journal of Criminology, 52*, 1–16.

Clear, T., & Sumter, M. (2002). Prisoners, prison, and religion. *Journal of Offender Rehabilitation, 35*(3/4), 125–156.

Coleman, J. (1988). Social capital and the creation of human capital. *American Journal of Sociology, 94*, S95–S120.

De Haan, W., & Loader, I. (2002). On the emotions of crime, punishment and social control. *Theoretical Criminology, 6*(3), 243–253.

Densley, J. (2013). *How gangs work: An ethnography of youth violence*. London: Palgrave MacMillan.

Deuchar, R. (2009). *Gangs, marginalised youth and social capital*. Stoke on Trent: Trentham.

Deuchar, R. (2013). *Policing youth violence: Transatlantic connections*. London: Trentham/IOE Press.

Deuchar, R., Morck, L., Matemba, Y. H., McLean, R., & Riaz, N. (2016a). 'It's as if you're not in jail, as if you're not a prisoner: Young male offenders' experiences of incarceration, prison chaplaincy, religion and spirituality in Scotland and Denmark. *The Howard Journal of Criminal Justice, 55*(1–2), 131–150.

Deuchar, R., Søgaard, T. F., Kolind, T., Thylstrup, B., & Wells, L. (2016b). 'When you're boxing you don't think so much': Pugilism, transitional masculinities and criminal desistance among young Danish gang members. *Journal of Youth Studies, 19*(6), 625–742.

Derezotes, D. (2000). Evaluation of yoga and meditation trainings with adolescent sex offenders. *Child Adolescent Social Work Journal, 17*(2), 97–113.

Duncombe, B. (2004). Compassion is at the core of prison program in Hawaii. *Offender Programs Report, 8*(1), 1–6.

Durkheim, E. (1915). *The elementary forms of the religious life*. New York: Free Press.

Evans, D., Cullen, F., Burton, V. S., Jr., Dunaway, R. G., Payne, G. L., & Kethineni. S. K. (1996). Religion, social bonds, and delinquency. *Deviant Behavior, 17*, 43–70.

Fetzer Institute and National Institute on Aging Working Group [1999] (2003). *Multidimensional measurement of religiousness/spirituality for use in health research*. Kalamazoo, MI: Fetzer Institute.

Field, J. (2003). *Social capital*. New York: Routledge.

Flores, E. O. (2014). *God's gangs: Barrio ministry, masculinity and gang recovery*. New York: NYU Press.

Gilligan, P., & Furness, S. (2006). The role of religion and spirituality in social work practice: Views and experiences of social workers and students. *British Journal of Social Work, 36*, 617–637.

Giordano, P. C., Longmore, M., Schroeder, R., & Seffrin, P. (2008). A lifecourse perspective on spirituality and desistance from crime. *Criminology, 46*(99), 1–132.

Hall, R. E., Livingston, J. N., Brown, C. J., & Mohabir, J. A. (2011). Islam and Asia Pacific Muslims: The implications of spirituality for social work practice. *Journal of Social Work Practice, 25*(2), 205–215.

Hallet, M., & McCoy, J. S. (2014). Religiously motivated desistance: An exploratory study. *International Journal of Offender Therapy and Comparative Criminology, 59*(8), 855–872.

Healy, D. (2012). *The dynamics of desistance: Charting pathways through change*. New York: Routledge.

Himelstein, S. (2011). Meditation research: The state of the art in correctional settings. *International Journal of Offender Therapy and Comparative Criminology, 55*(4), 646–661.

Hirschi, T., & Stark, R. (1969). Hellfire and delinquency. *Social Problems, 17*, 202–213.

Howells, K., Tennant, A., Day, A., & Elmer, R. (2010). Mindfulness in forensic mental health: Does it have a role? *Mindfulness, 1*, 4–9.

Huculak, S., & McLennan, D. (2010). The lord is my shepherd: Examining spirituality as a protection against mental health problems in youth exposed to violence in Brazil. *Mental Health, Religion and Culture, 13*(5), 467–484.

Jensen, K. D., & Gibbons, S. G. (2002). Shame and religion as factors in the rehabilitation of serious offenders. *Journal of Offender Rehabilitation, 35*(3–4), 209–224.

Johnson, A. (2017). *If I give my soul: Faith behind bars in Rio de Janeiro*. Oxford: Oxford University Press.

Johnson, B. R. (2011). *More god, less crime: Why faith matters and how it could matter more*. Philadelphia: Templeton Press.

Kabat-Zinn, J. (2013). *Full catastrophe living: Using the wisdom of your body and mind to face stress, pain, and illness*. New York: Bantam.

Krohn, M. D., Akers, R., Radosevich, M. J., & Lanza-Kaduce, L. (1982). Norm qualities and adolescent drinking and drug behavior: The effects of norm quality and reference group on using and abusing alcohol and marijuana. *Journal of Drug Issues, 12,* 343–359.

Laub, J. H., & Sampson, R. J. (2003). *Shared beginnings, divergent lives: Delinquent boys to age 70.* Cambridge, MA: Harvard University Press.

Leonard, R., & Onyx, J. (2004). *Social capital and community building: Spinning straw into gold.* London: Janus Publishing Co Ltd.

Levitt, H. M., Swanger, R. T., & Butler, J. B. (2008). Male perpetrators' perspectives on intimate partner violence, religion and masculinity. *Sex Roles, 58,* 435–448.

Liebling, A. (2014). Moral and philosophical problems of long-term imprisonment. *Studies in Christian Ethics, 27*(3), 258–273.

Lindsay, R. (2002). *Recognizing spirituality: The interface between faith and social work.* Crawley: University of Western Australia Press.

Lo, T. W. (2010). Beyond social capital: Triad organized crime in Hong Kong and China. *British Journal of Criminology, 50,* 851–872.

Maruna, S. (2001). *Making good: How ex-convicts reform and rebuild their lives.* Washington, DC: American Psychological Association.

Maruna, S., Wilson, L., & Curran, K. (2006). Why god is often found behind bars: Prison conversions and the crisis of self-narrative. *Research in Human Development, 3*(2–3), 161–184.

McNeill, F., & Maruna, S. (2008). Giving up and giving back: Desistance, generativity and social work with offenders. In G. McIvor & P. Raynor (Eds.), *Developments in social work with offenders* (pp. 224–339). London: Jessica Kingsley.

Mears, D. P., Roman, C. G., Wolff, A., & Buck, J. (2006). Faith-based efforts to improve prisoner reentry: Assessing the logic and evidence. *Journal of Criminal Justice, 34,* 351–367.

Melde, C., Esbensen, F.-A., & Carson, D. C. (2016). Gang membership and involvement in violence among US adolescents: A test of construct validity. In C. L. Maxson & F.-A. Esbensen (Eds.) *Gang transitions and transformations in an international context* (pp. 33–50). Switzerland: Springer.

Murthy, P. J. N. V., Janakiramaiah, N., Gangadhar, B. N., & Subbakrishna, D. K. (1998). P300 amplitude and antidepressant response to Sudarshan Kriya Yoga (SKY). *Journal of Affective Disorders, 50,* 45–48.

Nardi, D., & Rooda, L. (2011). Spirituality-based nursing practice by nursing students: An exploratory study. *Journal of Professional Nursing, 27*(4), 255–263.

O'Connor, T. P., & Duncan, J. B. (2011). The sociology of humanist, spiritual and religious practice in prison: Supporting responsivity and desistance from crime. *Religions, 2,* 590–610.
O'Connor, T. P., & Perreyclear, M. (2002). Prison religion in action and its influence on offender rehabilitation. *Journal of Offender Rehabilitation, 35*(3–4), 11–33.
Pandya, S. P. (2015). Adolescents, well-being and spirituality: Insights from a spiritual program. *International Journal of Children's Spirituality, 20*(1), 29–49.
Parkes, R., & Bilby, C. (2010). The courage to create: The role of artistic and spiritual activities in prison. *Howard Journal, 49,* 97–110.
Paternoster, R., & Bushway, S. (2009). Desistance and the feared self: Toward an identity theory of criminal desistance. *Journal of Criminal Law and Criminology, 99*(4), 1103–1156.
Pegram, K., Bruson, R. K., & Braga, A. A. (2016). The doors of the church are now open: Black clergy, collective efficacy and neighbourhood violence. *City and Community, 15*(3), 289–314.
Pham, K. H. (2013). *Outcomes of a recreation therapy yoga meditation intervention on prison inmates' spiritual wellbeing.* Unpublished master's thesis paper 4307. San Jose State University.
Pitts, J. (2008). *Reluctant gangsters: The changing face of youth crime.* London: Willen Publishing.
Putnam, R. (2000). *Bowling alone: The collapse and revival of American community.* New York: Simon and Schuster.
Pyrooz, D. C. (2014). Book review: God's gangs: Barrio ministry, masculinity and gang recovery, by Edward Orozco Flores. *Crime, Law and Social Change, 62,* 621–624.
Rucker, L. (2005). Yoga and restorative justice in prison: An experience of 'response-ability to harms'. *Contemporary Justice Review: Issues in Criminal, Social, and Restorative Justice, 8*(1), 107–120.
Schroeder, R. D., & Frana, J. F. (2009). Spirituality and religion, emotional coping, and criminal desistance: A qualitative study of men undergoing change. *Sociological Spectrum, 29,* 718–741.
Søgaard, T. F., Kolind, T., Thylstrup, B., & Deuchar, R. (2016). Desistance and the micro-narrative construction of reformed masculinities in a Danish rehabilitation centre. *Criminology and Criminal Justice, 16*(1), 1–99.
Sundt, J. L., & Cullen, F. T. (2002). The correctional ideology of prison chaplains: A national survey. *Journal of Criminal Justice, 30,* 369–385.

Tanyi, R. A. (2006). Spirituality and family nursing: Spiritual assessment and interventions for families. *Journal of Advanced Nursing, 53*(3), 287–294.
Thomas, J., & Zaitzow, B. H. (2006). Conning or conversion? The role of religion in prison coping. *The Prison Journal, 86*(2), 242–259.
Vigil, J. D. (2007). *The projects: Gang and non-gang families in east Los Angeles.* Austin: University of Texas.
Walsh, R. (1996). Meditation research: The state of the art. In J. R. Battista, A. B. Chinen, & B. W. Scotton (Eds.), *Textbook of transpersonal psychiatry and psychology* (pp. 175–267). New York: Basic Books.
White, R. (2013). *Youth gangs, violence and social respect: Exploring the nature of provocations and punch-ups.* Basingstoke, UK: Palgrave Macmillan.
Whitehead, P. L. (2013). Touching the void: Community chaplaincy as an ethical-cultural agency in criminal justice re-formation in England and Wales. *Social and Public Policy Review, 7*(1), 40–54.
Zapf, M. K. (2005). The spiritual dimension of person and environment: Perspectives from social work and traditional knowledge. *International Social Work, 48*(5), 633–642.

Part III
Los Angeles, USA: From Gangs and Guns to Love and Compassion

4

Amplified Masculinity Among Los Angeles Homeboys

As an introduction to the empirical section of the book, the next two chapters draw upon insights from the country where gangs have been part of the cultural fabric for over 300 years—the USA. They focus specifically on Los Angeles, the city that gave America the modern street gang. In this chapter, I begin by considering the way in which issues of race, segregation and discrimination combined to create communities that spawned street gang formation in Los Angeles. I also discuss the way in which wider social marginalisation has sustained this. In the main body of the chapter, I share insights from life history interviews conducted with male Latino gang members from the most socially disadvantaged areas of the city, all of whom were in the early stages of transition and change when I met them. I discuss the social barriers that they came across during their early lives, the profound lack of love and hope they experienced, their perceptions about masculinity and described involvement in gang-related offending. I also consider what motivated their initial desire to change and begin to move away from violent criminality.

© The Author(s) 2018
R. Deuchar, *Gangs and Spirituality*,
https://doi.org/10.1007/978-3-319-78899-9_4

Racial Oppression, Multiple Marginality and Gangs in Los Angeles

In his seminal work, James Diego Vigil (1988) draws attention to the links between *multiple marginality* and Los Angeles gangs. He argues that inter-related variables are at the root of gang formation, such as mother-centred homes, lack of male guidance and economic disadvantage. He discusses the way in which street violence often emerges against the backdrop of overcrowded living conditions, dysfunctional relationships, domestic violence, drug addiction and low educational attainment. However, Alonso (2004) argues that we need to move beyond the *multiple marginality* lens in order to understand the roots of gang formation in Los Angeles. Street-oriented 'clubs' were formed in the 1930s as a means of enabling men of colour to protect their neighbourhoods from the effects of exclusion emerging from legally-enforced, racially restrictive covenants designed to bring about residential segregation and maintain social and racial homogeneity (Alonso 2004; Unnever and Gabbidon 2011). Sustained exploitation and white violence by agents of social control later led to the collapse of the Black Power movement at the end of the 1960s. This stimulated a self-destructive reaction, whereby young men of colour formed gangs and became instruments of their own oppression (Alonso 2010). Crips, Bloods and a range of Latino gangs emerged, with members unleashing decades or nihilistic violence on one another (Alonso 2004, 2010; Leap 2012).

Accordingly, the African American and Latino gangs that emerged in Los Angeles became 'etched into an already existing racialized geography' (Alonso 2004, p. 671). Rather than being the cause of the gang issues, characteristics of *multiple marginality* (such as deindustrialisation, mother-centred households and difficult family lives) exacerbated the already-existing problems (ibid.). Wacquant (2008) draws attention to the way in which similar processes of spatial dispersal, residential segregation and State oppression of communities of colour have taken place in other US cities such as Chicago, leading to what Unnever and Gabbidon (2011, p. 7) have described as 'American apartheid'. By the 1970s, an 'urban colour line between blacks and whites had effectively been redrawn along a class fracture' (Wacquant 2008, p. 59) and—unsurprisingly—gang activity became prevalent at the heart of American ghettos.

Los Angeles has been dubbed a 'traditional' gang city, in as much as it has an established gang history that stretches beyond the 1980s (for further discussion, see Decker et al. 1998; Pyrooz et al. 2011). In the past, it was dubbed the 'gang capital of America', although evidence suggests that more recently the city of Chicago has inherited this distinction (LAPD 2017). At its peak period in the late-1990s official Los Angeles Police Department (LAPD) statistics suggest that there were 64,429 gang members in the city, that this figure had dropped to 38,974 by 2006 but currently sits at around 45,000 today (Flores 2014; LAPD 2017). Further, the National Drug Intelligence Center (2000) estimated that there were 152,000 gang members in Los Angeles County at the turn of the twenty-first century. At that time, this was the highest figure for any city in the USA (Flores 2014). According to LAPD (2017), during the three years leading up to 2016 there were over 16,000 verified violent gang crimes in the City of Los Angeles including over 400 gang-related homicides.

Historically, both the Latino and African American population in Los Angeles were relegated to racially-defined neighbourhoods to the east and the south of the city. Their mutual oppression, combined with the huge influx of additional immigrants of Mexican-descent as well as those with other Latin American origins into the city in recent years, has led to inter-racial tension within the context of gang conflict (Weide 2015). Accordingly, ethnic fighting between inter-cultural gangs exists in several areas of the city and in the jails (Alonso 1999; Flores 2014). Much of this is characterised by territorial conflict over the illicit drug markets, but is stimulated by despair, trauma and an absence of hope (Boyle 2010).

It is, of course, beyond the scope of this book to be able to consider the potential solutions to the deep-rooted issues of racial oppression or, indeed, all of the issues related to *multiple marginality* (Vigil 1988;

Alonso 2004; Vigil 2007). However, it *is* possible to consider the extent to which problematic issues of masculine identity construction that arise as symptoms of oppression often maintain and exacerbate the gang offending problems in Los Angeles. By drawing on empirical data gathered in the city, in this chapter I attempt to do just that before moving on in the next chapter to explore the role that spirituality may potentially play in beginning to address some of these issues.

Insights into the Experiences of Male Latino Gang Members in Los Angeles

The remainder of this chapter and the next will focus on insights gained from small-scale qualitative research I conducted in Los Angeles in the spring of 2015. The site for the data collection was *Homeboy Industries*—an internationally recognised and much emulated non-profit organisation focused on offering rehabilitative and employment-related services for formerly incarcerated and/or gang involved persons across an 18-month period (for further detail on the organisation and its intervention programmes, see Chapter 5). In this chapter, I report on the insights from life history interviews, before drawing on wider data in order to explore the impact of the *Homeboy Industries* interventions in the next chapter.

In total, I conducted in-depth life history interviews with eleven men who could be described at the time of the data collection process taking place as 'reforming' gang members on the threshold or early stages of change (Healy 2012). The age-ranges of the men spanned between early twenties and late thirties at the time that the interviews took place, and they were each at different stages in the 18-month *Homeboy Industries* programme when I met them (some near the beginning, others further on or near completion). All of them had been born and raised in the most socially disadvantaged communities of Los Angeles, and all were Latino. More specifically, when asked how they would describe their ethnicity most of the participants referred to themselves as being of Mexican descent. Table 4.1 provides an overview of the eleven main

4 Amplified Masculinity Among Los Angeles Homeboys

Table 4.1 The research participants in Los Angeles

Name	Age	Neighbourhood
Emilio	23	Long Beach
Dylan	27	South Los Angeles
Lucas	33	Northeast Los Angeles
Bruno	29	Boyle Heights
Marcos	36	Long Beach
Francisco	39	East Los Angeles
Diego	28	North Hollywood
Sergio	28	Boyle Heights
Benjamin	32	Lincoln Heights
Juan	25	Lincoln Heights
Daniel	29	El Sereno

research participants: their names (pseudonyms), ages and the areas of the city that they denoted as the backdrop for their previous gang-related offending.

I was initially introduced to all the staff and reforming gang members (employed as 'trainees' within the *Homeboy Industries* programme) during one of the organisation's daily early-morning meetings. I subsequently met with the programme mentors and their assigned trainees and sought volunteers to participate in interviews. Individual interviews lasting between 60–70 minutes were then conducted in small meeting rooms within the *Homeboy Industries* complex. In the sections that follow, the emerging themes are presented and key quotations emerging from life history interviews highlighted. As a further layer of insight into the issues related to gang membership and criminality within Los Angeles, I also refer briefly to perceptions emerging from some follow-up semi-structured interviews with staff members from *Homeboy Industries* (most of whom were also reformed gang members, and are reported on more fully in the next chapter). Furthermore, I refer to some supplementary insights gained from an informal interview with Dr Robert Weide, a former gang member who is now Assistant Professor of Sociology at California State University, Los Angeles (and who consented to his real name being used during data reporting). With the exception of Weide, pseudonyms are used when referring to participants throughout.

Multiple Disadvantage, Marginalisation and Gang Involvement

The men had lived their relatively young lives against the backdrop of cultural and social oppression and marginalisation (as described above). Although racial issues were not specifically the intended focus of the interviews I conducted with them, without being prompted some reflected openly on the way in which they had been racially profiled and oppressed:

> We're profiled, racially profiled ... if you're bald-headed, you're Hispanic, you're immediately gang, labelled as a gang member – even if you're not. (Dylan)

During an informal interview with Dr Robert Weide, former gang member and Assistant Professor at California State University, he elaborated on this. He highlighted that the racial oppression that blacks and Latinos had experienced for over a Century in Los Angeles was now being strengthened by further state control that resulted in increased poverty and social exclusion:

> Now we have the reverse of 'white flight', where white people are coming back into the deprived neighbourhoods and the areas are being gentrified. This pushes rents up and so destroys the neighbourhoods. Blacks and Latinos need to move to even poorer areas – it's a form of ethnic cleansing, I call it 'hipster colonianism'; these new Bohemians - white, middle to upper class people - are moving into the neighbourhoods, pushing the rents up ... I guess I have this nefarious conspiracy that suggests that police departments focus suppression tactics on the areas that will become gentrified in preparation for these Bohemians to move in. (Robert Weide, Sociologist)

Against this oppressive backdrop, the men also described a range of difficult family circumstances they encountered while growing up. These were very often characterised by missing father figures or fathers who were addicted to alcohol or drugs and/or were violent within the family home:

4 Amplified Masculinity Among Los Angeles Homeboys 69

My mom and dad separated when I was five years old, my dad was an alcoholic – he would drink too much, and then he would cheat on my mom, he would sleep around with other women … so my mom ended up leaving him. So my mom basically was the one who raised us. (Bruno)

My childhood was rough out there, you know? I was raised by a single parent … single mother. My father was addicted to crack, so he was outta the picture. (Dylan)

I left home at nine and I remember thinking … there was more hatred for my father 'cause he had a drinking problem, there was violence inside the home, you know? … He was abusive to [my mother], abusive to me - for the smallest offence he would beat me. (Emilio)

Against the historical backdrop of racial oppression (Alonso 2004, 2010), it seemed that issues of *multiple marginality* characterised these Latino men's formative years (Vigil 2007, p. 197). Box 4.1 illustrates the particular forms of disadvantage experienced by Sergio, and the impact this had in terms of the emotional baggage he carried with him and the criminal acts he became involved in.

> **Box 4.1:** *Sergio's Story*
>
> Sergio was born into a family of Mexican descent in one of the most socially deprived areas in South Central Los Angeles in the mid-1970s. During his early childhood, his father was in and out of prison several times for drug-related and violent crimes. When he was at home, his father was addicted to heroin and following a serious drug-related crime, he eventually became sentenced to 20 years in prison. When he was aged nine, Sergio was raped by his older brother. His mother eventually divorced his father and re-married, and the family moved from South Central to another disadvantaged neighbourhood in Boyle Heights in East Los Angeles. Sergio's older step-brother was later sent to jail when he was a young teenager for violent crimes.
>
> Sergio grew up supressing his emotional anguish that emerged as a result of having been raped, and kept it in the back of his head because he couldn't understand why it had happened to him and didn't know how to deal with it. As he grew a little older, he found that he was having more and more aggressive and violent outbursts in the house, a great deal of which was stimulated by emotional distress and a fear about telling his mother about the rape in case she did not believe him. He was also violent

> to teachers in his school. In time, he gravitated more and more towards the streets and found that every block in his neighbourhood in Boyle Heights had a different gang. Most of them were of Mexican descent, and Sergio identified with the older guys he met out on the street. At age 12, the older guys on the block introduced him to marijuana and he quickly became addicted to smoking it. When his mother found out, she threw him out of the house because she could not cope with Sergio's behaviour.
>
> During his early teens, Sergio initially slept in the local cemetery and would waken up nearly every morning and go round to the house of one of his 'homeboys' and shower there. Because he increasingly found that he was unable to sleep, he began taking methamphetamine after being introduced to it by the older men on the street. By using meth, he found that he didn't get tired or hungry, and he soon became addicted to it. At age 14, he began dealing to try and make money for clothes, but slowly found that he smoked a great deal of the drugs himself. He always ensured that he had a plentiful supply of marijuana on his possession so that some of the guys in the street would invite him to take refuge in their homes. He would often spend several weeks in the gang members' houses where they would smoke marijuana balls and this would ensure that Sergio did not need to sleep or eat for long periods. His school attendance diminished, and Sergio eventually ended up being a leading member of his local Latino street gang, dealing drugs to fund his own habit and shooting rival gang members.

In response to his own empirical research findings in Los Angeles, Sanders (2012, p. 990) concludes that 'gang membership is an indicator of chronic substance use'. While Sanders found that gang members tend to normalise marijuana use, he also found that drugs like methamphetamine, heroin and crack cocaine are often stigmatised. However, the above case study illustrates that the combined effects of Sergio's own father's heroin addiction, his early exposure to family-based sexual abuse and the resulting emotional distress and anger he expressed through violence and gang membership led to meth dependency and addiction issues. Sergio's continuing issues of addiction, abandonment and homelessness led to increasing involvement in gang-related drug offences to feed his own drug habit and to cope with the crippling emotional and psychological trauma he had carried around with him since childhood (Vigil 2007).

In his own work, Vigil (2007) highlights the way in which conflictual or dysfunctional home relationships that are often characterised by domestic violence and abuse may further the allure of gang membership. In addition to Sergio (above) the other men that I interviewed talked about the way in which they slowly began to regard the older men in the local gangs as 'homeboys' and members of surrogate families during their formative years:

> I don't know, something just snapped in me and I left and it wasn't hard for me to step out and find the people that were in the neighbourhood, in the street. (Emilio)

> I started hanging around people that would be in the streets ... like I wouldn't come home until like 12, or I wouldn't come home ... it was alright, you know, to be in the streets and ... basically the people in the streets are gang members. (Lucas)

> I was basically looking for family, looking for some type of father-figure, you know? And then my older 'homies' were father figures. (Marcos)

Accordingly, the interviewees had in many senses been pushed into gang membership as young men as result of disadvantaged family circumstances and against the wider backdrop of social and cultural disadvantage. The additional influences of peers out on the streets, who had also suffered social and cultural marginality, added weight to the process (Vigil 2007). In turn, the men described the way in which gang membership and the weapons, money and reputation associated with it had provided them with a form of masculine status that was seen as their ultimate validation (Pitts 2008; Densley 2013).

Guns, Money, Violence and Amplified Masculinity

The interviewees talked at length about the way in which they initially had to engage in very physical initiation processes in order to prove their sense of masculinity and become recognised as gang members. This partly reflected earlier insights about the 'blood in, blood out' mantra of gangs (Pyrooz and Decker 2011, p. 419). For example, Bruno talked about the way in which he had had to stand up and fight a rival gang member in public to prove his credentials. He then had to defend himself against the physical violence from three older members of the gang he wished to become part of before he was accepted as a member. Further, Marcos also talked about being 'jumped in' by five older gang members when he was just nine years old, and how his reward was being presented with a gun and a set of territorial 'guidelines':

> I was nine years old when I got jumped into my gang ... like five guys from the neighbourhood got together. Since I was the youngest one – everybody else was like fifteen – so they whooped my ass ... for about 15 seconds, then we got up ... and celebrated and they give you a gun and say 'OK, these guys are your enemy now'. (Marcos)

Once initiated, as young men they rapidly became immersed into a hyper-masculine world. The gang environment was centred around 'toxic' masculinity, focused on the need to dominate others and be continually ready to resort to violence (Kupers 2005, and see also Deuchar 2013). As Diego, Lucas and Bruno explained, carrying and using guns as part of the street action they were involved in became a key focus. This was ultimately an addictive source of adrenaline rush, and a perceived means of status, power and protection (see also Deuchar 2013; Bergen-Cico et al. 2014):

> Broad daylight and we used to just chase 'em and 'boom, boom', they'll be passing their cars ... we used to just chase their cars and just try shooting. It kinda just hit me, like I like doing it 'cause it gave me ... like, yeah, I liked carrying a gun and just pulling the trigger, just because once I pull that one time it's just like I feel good. (Diego)
>
> Being in a gang you've gotta have a gun, you know? ... Over time, people start ... shooting at me. At first I was questioning like 'damn, why are they shooting at me?' But, to be honest, it kinda excited me, you know, getting shot at ... the thrill of getting away with it and honestly a depressive state of mind, like 'fuck it, if I die who gives a fuck?' (Lucas)
>
> I love guns, I always had guns ... I just like the way they look, the way they fire ... I used to carry it in my car all the time ... it made me feel safer, powerful and safer. (Bruno)

Benjamin, who had been initiated into a Latino gang at age eleven, talked about how he was quickly encouraged by fellow 'homeboys' to begin engaging in drive-by shootings of rival gang members. Initially describing this as a reluctant transition (as in Pitts 2008), in time he found it addictive and he ultimately became habituated to it:

> By eleven years old, I was already doing drive-bys ... I kinda was pressured into doing it. I didn't want to let ('homies') down ... after I did it, it was like it broke my barriers and I was like, 'it was on' ... I wanted to keep doing it ... after a while it seems like nothin', you know what I mean? (Benjamin)

Benjamin's experiences of becoming de-sensitised to gun violence was not uncommon. Robert Weide described the way in which many male gang members begin shooting to try and gain a sense of status. Although they may be initially nervous, once they become used to it they come to enjoy the power and prestige that firearms use gives them:

> People commit violence because, you know, a loss of status would mean that they would become the victim of violence ... the first time you shoot someone you're really scared and you're jittery and you're sweaty and, you know, your heart's beating fast and all that but after you do it a few times and you don't get caught ... some of those people that make that transition end up, you know, enjoying the power and prestige of doing that so they do it regularly. (Robert Weide, Sociologist)

Citing Goffman (1959), Stretesky and Pogrebin (2007) argue that guns offer gang members important tools of impression management. They are often connected in some way to masculine attributes, and used to project gang members' reputation and/or to gain (or reclaim) respect. Drawing on gun crime as a resource to enact amplified forms of 'hyper' or 'toxic' masculinity had clearly been widespread in the lives of the 'homeboys' I interviewed (Kupers 2005; Messerschmidt 2005; Hagedorn 2008; Baird 2012). Box 4.2 outlines the particular forms of violence and serious crime that Diego engaged in over a prolonged period. It illustrates how the 'tough guy' image he worked so hard to cultivate was a product of both socio-economic marginality and gender insecurity (Hagedorn 2008; Pitts 2008).

Box 4.2: *Diego's Story*

Growing up in an extremely socially deprived area of North Hollywood, Diego became initiated into a Latino gang at the age of 14, after the older members noticed that he had a good ability to sell marijuana and make money quickly. He began carrying a gun and shooting rival gang members. The shootings were purely about territory and about upholding respect out on the street. Diego became immersed in the lifestyle because he was motivated by the 'easy' money he could make from selling drugs. At age 16, he was arrested for drug offences and gun sales and ended up in jail for three years. When he was released, he very quickly became involved in all the same things again. In his early twenties, he participated in drive-by shootings, and he felt that owning and using a gun as well as engaging in drug dealing gave him an enhanced reputation and status among the other men. Diego related his desire to earn a violent, criminal reputation to a feeling of needing to be seen as the 'tough guy', who was devoid of any emotion or feeling:

I was actually kinda involved in the end because I wanted to be the tough guy. I wanted to be that guy who actually didn't have any feelings and didn't care.

Diego related this intense desire to separate himself from any type of emotional expression to his childhood experiences. He had never known his father, and his mother and all of his uncles were unemployed and had been involved in selling marijuana while Diego was growing up. He felt that his mother had never shown any love or emotion towards him, and that this had impacted on his desire to develop as tough a reputation out on the streets as possible:

I mean it [mother's love] was there but she never actually showed me that ... she always got stuck on selling, doing drugs, selling drugs.

The lack of emotional support from his mother combined with a missing father-figure meant that Diego looked towards his 'homeboys' for attachment. Once immersed fully into the gang lifestyle, he got several gang tattoos on his head, face and neck in order to further promote his violent, gang-involved reputation. This reputation was enhanced further after he had served time in prison for gang offences. As a result, Diego finally managed to gain the male attachment he had always been looking for within the family, when his uncles made him feel important by asking him if he could supply them with guns for the drug-related violence they continued to be involved in.

4 Amplified Masculinity Among Los Angeles Homeboys

Flores (2014) argues that acculturation into street gangs and drugs is often a by-product of strained family ties, while Vigil (2007) highlights that the reasons for young men engaging in violent criminality often hinge on an inability to deal with childhood distress. Against the backdrop of economic, social and cultural marginality as a young Latino male living in a ghetto community, Diego had experienced the trauma of rejected family life. Accordingly, issues of attachment and loss were clearly drivers of his gang involvement and violence. He compensated for both the father-to-son and mother-to-son alienation he suffered through adhering to the locally dominated street codes centred around 'respect', territorial dominance and accumulation of fast, easy money. In the process, he built up a tough and heartless reputation and adopted a putatively detached emotionality associated with a macho identity (Holligan and Deuchar 2015).

When interviewing Diego and many of the other men in Los Angeles, I became increasingly conscious that hegemonic forms of masculinity within their neighbourhoods had become amplified within the context of gang involvement. The tough gang images they became attracted to and the violent identities they had tried to cultivate for themselves were often a means of coping with the combined impact of social and cultural marginalisation and troubled inner worlds. Kevin, a former Latino gang member who was now a personal mentor (known as 'navigator') at *Homeboy Industries* and Hugo, who was Associate Director of the organisation, summed this up for me during follow-up interviews. They talked about the way in which many young men projected tough façades and carved out violent reputations as a means of expressing the hurt and pain that they felt:

> A lot of us are brought up to believe that a man ... doesn't cry, that a man doesn't show weakness ... if a man is hurt and he's in pain but he can't cry, how's he gonna act out? In violence ... a lot of these gang members, that's how they think. And now the next thing you know it becomes, as we grow up from one generation to the next, now this is what a man is. (Kevin, *Homeboy Industries* 'navigator')

> Toughness is survival, you know behind every tough person is a crying little boy ... that's just neglected and feels left out. (Hugo, *Homeboy Industries* Associate Director)

In addition to street gangs, prison had also provided a further stimulus for the men I interviewed to 'act out' in violence. It is to this context that I now turn.

Prison Gangs, Criminal Credentials and Elevation of Masculine Status

The men all talked about having been incarcerated on several occasions during their young lives. Often they were sent to Juvenile Hall, a youth detention centre in Los Angeles, when they were teenagers. Later, some served further sentences in County or State jails or even Federal prisons after they had continued to reoffend. While incarcerated, they often engaged in prison gang membership, and the violence that went with it. Fleisher and Decker (2001, p. 3) draw attention to the prevalent behaviour of prison gang members: violent behaviour is 'customary' and can be used to move a member upward in the prison hierarchy, and the focus is often on drug trafficking and dealing. Among those I interviewed, prison violence had been a common feature of their criminal trajectory. Daniel, who was from El Sereno in the Eastside Los Angeles region, admitted that 'even in Juvenile Hall, there's fighting'. Once in prison, on some occasions the violence they engaged in had become more centred on racial divisions as opposed to territorial ones, as Bruno described:

> I was in with this group of Mexicans, you know? And there was a couple of times that, if one Mexican and one black would get into a fight or something – we would all get in, and it would cause a big old riot. (Bruno)

For some, engaging in prison gang violence led to solitary confinement and extended sentences. Marcos's gang-related offences inside prison eventually led to him being sent to long-term confinement in Pelican Bay State Prison. Pelican Bay is the only 'supermax' prison in California and has been described as the 'last stop in California's penal system', where inmates are confined to small cells for twenty-two and a half hours a day in the prison's Security Housing Unit (SHU) (Ramano 1996, p. 1089):

> I was 18 and I got sentenced to 39 years to life, and I went to prison ... I served 18 years ... the only thing I know how to do is muscle my way through, so I went to prison and tried to get into prison politics and gangs ... I joined the other gangs in there and we were part of organising people in there and I was in an organiser's role ... it came natural to me ... I started runnin' yards ... and not caring, and I ended up in a lot of trouble in prison ... they stuck me in the SHU, which is like the hole ... I was in, like the hardest prison in California ... that's where I grew up. (Marcos)

Griffin and Hepburn (2006) argue that violent misconduct in prisons is often related to the attitudes, values and prior experiences that some inmates bring with them. For Marcos, involvement in running the prison yards through gang involvement reflected his earlier experiences and established values and attitudes. His family had been part of drug dealing cartels in Mexico and his grandfather had taught him to shoot. As a teenager, he had developed masculine status on the streets by shooting a rival gang member in the head. Accordingly, he was able to bring the norms and experiences he acquired within his family life and as a street gang member into the prison to attempt to 'muscle' his way through his sentence and establish social status among other inmates through becoming a yard leader. Ultimately this led to further disciplinary sanctions, which in turn cemented his status within the prison further (Griffin and Hepburn 2006). Like Marcos, Francisco was also a Mexican gang member and admitted that he had engaged in prison gang violence. Having been given a life sentence for a charge of armed robbery and multiple shootings, he participated in prison gangs to accumulate highly masculinised forms of social status, but also to acquire economic capital:

> I felt 'well, this is going to be my house, you know, I'm not going to be just anybody – I'm going to be somebody'. So I started doing things and I started picking up charges ... (for) assault and it was with a sharpened

object which was a razor … it was good for me, I didn't have to worry about coffee, I didn't have to worry about nothin' like because I was taken care of … (Francisco)

Johnson's (2017, p. 110) ethnographic research within a Brazilian prison led him to conclude that prison gangs promoted an 'archetype of masculinity' that was an 'extra-strength version of *machismo*'. Gang affiliation in prisons is often rewarded with social support, personal security and access to material goods including contraband (Griffin and Hepburn 2006). Evidence suggests that, in American prisons, Mexican-oriented gangs are often associated with the Mexican Mafia, which uses threats to acquire resources (Vigil 2007; Skarbek 2011). Francisco implied that he was 'taken care of' as an inmate, having demonstrated his affiliation with a potent form of gang masculinity by engaging in prison violence (Skarbek 2011; Johnson 2017). Ultimately, the men explained that extending their time inside by controlling the yards via prison gangs had helped them to gain a sense of enhanced authority on the streets once released:

> I spent more than half my life in jail … so that even gave me more empowerment cause I would get out and you know, 'this guy just got out of jail' and now there's a certain 'he's been to jail' type of thing, you know 'he's done things for the gang' … you know, that's where you get your stamp and you come out and you're going to be able to do whatever you want on the streets. (Francisco)

> When you go to prison you become … you're still a member of your gang outside but then you become a member of something else in there, you become a member of pretty much the gang that runs them … so it's like twice you're a care-giver … (to) your gang out on the streets. (Emilio)

Drawing on signalling theory (Gambetta 2009), Densley (2013) observes that crime conveys information, and that violent reputations combined with criminal credentials allows male gang members to signal their elevated masculine status to each other (see also Storrod and Densley 2017). Several of the men I talked to had clearly enhanced their credentials in jail and used this as a form of impression management. However, in some cases they had realised that serving time in State prison alongside their enemies ultimately defeated the purpose of gangbanging:

> As an adult I went to State prison. And State prison is ... different, you know? ... There's a different structure, a different set of rules. Basically you had to get along with everybody, your enemies included ... and that's like well I (decided) I'm not gonna come to jail and serve a lot of time to chill with my enemies, and go on the streets to be against them ... it didn't make sense. It's stupidity, you know? ... Why risk doing life in prison to hurt somebody or take somebody out, just to be with their 'homies' which are your enemies ... it kinda defeats the purpose of gangbanging. (Lucas)

As I discussed in Chapter 2, previous research has drawn attention to *push* or *pull* factors for leaving the gang (Pyrooz and Decker 2011; Carson and Esbensen 2016). It has been found that the most common *push* factor is disillusionment (Carson and Esbensen 2016). Lucas clearly reached the stage where he wanted to make a change in his life, due to the weariness he felt with the lifestyle and the realisation that serving time was counter-productive. Among the sample, there were many other retrospective references to turning points that were viewed as salient enough to enable the men to develop an awareness that change was both desirable and needed (Giordano et al. 2002; McNeill et al. 2012; Carson and Esbensen 2016). However, these initial 'hooks for change' were often accompanied by ongoing obstacles and challenges (Giordano et al. 2002, p. 1000).

Initial Turning Points, Transitions and Challenges

As McNeill et al. (2012, p. 6) have argued, a period of 'reflection and reassessment of what is important to the individual' is a common feature of the initial process of desistance. During interviews, the men indicated that *push* factors (such as weariness, fatigue or disenchantment) had sometimes led them to reflect upon and reassess their lifestyles. Taken on their own, we could perhaps draw upon rational choice perspective to understand these personal reassessments in response to *push* factors (Cusson and Pinsonneault 1986).

However, there were also intertwining *pull* factors that emerged in many of the interviews (Carson and Esbensen 2016). While Lucas had become disillusioned with the gang lifestyle and recognised the ludicracy of some aspects of it, he had also become a father around the time when he went back to prison for the final time. This clearly increased his commitment not to reoffend. Juan, who had been a Latino gang member in Lincoln Heights, also talked about picking up a felony that led to his children being taken away from him. This motivated him to move away from violent crime. Indeed, entry into parenthood was a recurring theme within the interviews, and some men felt that fatherhood was the driving 'hook for change' that enabled them to begin looking for opportunities to try and change their lifestyles (Giordano et al. 2002, p. 1000):

> Mostly what drove me was my kids ... I started thinking about my kids, like 'wow, how about if I get killed ... my kids are not gonna have a father'. (Bruno)
>
> It was my daughter, you know? I don't wanna be that bad example to her, like I didn't have a role model ... my father wasn't around. So, to me, I don't think she has to go through that ... it's not just about me no more, you know? And I don't wanna have her having her communication with her dad through some jail cell or letters, you know what I mean? (Benjamin)

Maruna (2001) argues that the generative commitment associated with parenthood can be an important *pull* factor and can often act as a turning point that stimulates dedication towards desistance. It could be argued that Benjamin's (above) overwhelming *pull* factor was related to his 'feared self' concerning parenthood (Paternoster and Bushway 2009, p. 1103). He was clearly beginning to realise that continued imprisonment would have an adverse effect on his daughter, and feared becoming a bad example to her and the type of absent father he had been exposed to himself as a child. However, as I discussed in Chapter 2, initial commitment to desistance actions among gang members can also be related to accompanying *push* factors such as witnessing violent incidents, becoming a victim of violence or suffering the trauma of real or potential loss (Pyrooz and Decker 2011; Deuchar 2013; Decker et al. 2014). In Dylan's case, hearing about his closest 'homeboy' from his neighbourhood gang being killed over a drug deal while he was in prison was an initial trigger, while for Sergio it was the fear of dying in prison:

> I got a call that my friend, my partner, got killed – over $46,000. So after that, I just lost it. I lost it. And that's when I just decided that it was the time for a change. (Dylan)
>
> My biggest fear was to die in prison … that was my biggest fear. (Sergio)

Accordingly, the men described making early, fledgling attempts to desist based on the initial hooks for change that included taking on new personal responsibilities and commitments and experiencing emotional transitions (Deuchar 2013). Hence, they often articulated what might be described as 'morality-based' reasons for wishing to try and give up their gang and criminal lifestyles (McNeill and Farrall 2013, p. 150).

However, as I alluded to in Chapter 2 much scholarship has drawn attention to the difference between *primary* and *secondary* desistance: whereas *primary* desistance is seen as a 'lull or crime-free gap' in a criminal career, *secondary* desistance occurs when offenders experience a fundamental change in self-identity and assume the role of a 'changed person' (McNeill and Maruna 2008, p. 226). Initial decisions to desist are not always seen through, and offenders thus frequently oscillate between periods of offending and long gaps between them, often experiencing progress but also setbacks and disappointments (McNeill 2009; Deuchar 2013; McNeill and Farrall 2013). For instance, following the multiple challenges that Sergio had faced during his formative years and the prolonged periods of violence he had engaged in (see Box 4.1), he finally formed a steady relationship with a woman who subsequently became pregnant with his child. At this point, his commitment to the relationship combined with his fear of returning to prison and dying there (above) led him to want to change his lifestyle. However, during the pregnancy he fell back into taking drugs and engaging in violent crime again to try and make a decent living and he was eventually sent back to prison before his daughter was born.

Flores (2014, p. 169) discusses the way in which many recovering Los Angeles gang members still bear elements of 'masculine gang embodiment'. As I discussed in Chapter 2, this can include everything from a continued dependency on or urge for drugs, to shaved heads, gang tattoos, particular ways of walking or gesturing or even permanent disabilities from gun wounds. As I also mentioned in Chapter 2, Densley (2013, p. 139) describes these as 'stigmata', since they often prevent access to employment, lead to continued harassment from the police and ultimately hinder progression towards secondary desistance (see also Deuchar 2013). As the extracts above illustrate, at a certain point in their lives many of the men began striving towards gang recovery and desistance. However, they realised that the range of gang embodiment issues they carried around, combined in some cases with their continuing tendency towards viewing masculinity as being synonymous with street status, held them back. Lucas, who had a string of felonies and also a permanent disability from gang violence, perhaps most strikingly summed up the collective impact of the 'stigmata' that gang members can often experience (Densley 2013, p. 139):

> You know what, I have Federal felonies, State felonies. I have tattoos on my face. You know, that's gonna hold me back a lot. And then sometimes I have problems walking 'cause when they put a pole in my leg they … measured it, they're off by like … an inch. And it's been like ten years. So these ten years is, they catch up to me, you know … because of a gunshot wound … it's like really I can't work construction, I can't work hard labour. You know, I can't really be on that … sometimes it hurts so much, you know? But I just gotta deal with it and and go on, you know? (Lucas)

Against this backdrop, the men had all begun to seek out additional support to nurture their transitions and deal with their continued challenges. That support ultimately came their way via *Homeboy Industries*, where they entered into a liminal phase characterised by deeper introspection, personal transformation and growth (Healy 2012).

Concluding Discussion

In this chapter, I have explored the historical evidence that suggests that racial oppression was an initial driving force for gang formation in Los Angeles. Through drawing largely on the work of Alonso (2004, 2010), I have documented the way in which conservative white backlash against the Civil Rights Movement eventually led to young black and Latino men becoming instruments of their own oppression through the type of street violence and criminality that still plagues the city today. Flores (2014, p. 192) discusses the way in which the later re-casting of racial stereotypes of blacks and Latinos as marked by 'cultural pathologies' set the stage for a 'retreat from overt state-sanctioned structures of racist domination to covert, neoliberal racist expressions that blame the individual and promote a retreat of big government'.

Accordingly, as in many other American cities the existence of low-income racial enclaves, the continuing increase of mass incarceration of young men of colour combined with the rise of neoliberalism set the context for one of the symptoms of racial oppression—*multiple* and *advanced marginality* (Vigil 1988, 2007; Wacquant 2008). Poverty, lack of education, domestic violence, stressed single parent homes and drug addiction have maintained and exacerbated the gang issues among marginalised men in the city, which are often focused on territorial and racially-motivated violence (Alonso 2004; Vigil 2007).

In the main body of the chapter, I presented insights from life history interviews with a small group of male gang members I met while engaged in programmes and interventions within *Homeboy Industries*. It was clear to me that, against the backdrop of social and cultural disadvantage these men had become attracted to gang membership during their formative years because of challenging family circumstances, prolonged issues of neglect and trauma and the lure of being able to re-assert masculine status out on the streets. The weapons and 'easy' money from drug dealing had provided them with a form of masculine respect (Anderson 1999; Vigil 2007; Flores 2014; Holligan and Deuchar 2015). Locally-dominated forms of hegemonic masculinity focused on toughness and machismo had thus became amplified within the context of street gangs, often as a means of dealing with troubled inner worlds.

Once incarcerated, the men had often accumulated additional violence capital and criminal credentials through both serving time for their gangs and (in some cases) through further engagement in prison gangs. Towards the end of the life history interviews, they often described the way in which they had made fledgling attempts to desist from gang criminality and violence based on initial hooks for change (Giordano et al. 2002). However, they were often limited in their success due to continuing issues related to gang embodiment and the 'stigmata' that held them back (Densley 2013, p. 139; Flores 2014).

While Decker et al. (2014) suggest that gang members cannot always rely on service agencies for adequate support over the course of their desistance trajectory, some studies have found evidence of the potential effectiveness of gang intervention programmes in nurturing gang desistance (Flores 2014; Deuchar and Weide 2018). In Los Angeles, *Homeboy Industries* has progressively evolved from its modest routes in a non-profit employment referral agency into the biggest and most renowned gang intervention initiative in the world (Choi and Kiesner 2007; Boyle 2010). As a result of various trigger points, the men in my sample had found their way there; they engaged in programmes and practices rooted in 'eclectic spirituality' and group therapy (Flores 2014, p. 184). In the next chapter, I place the spotlight on these programmes and practices, and examine the transitions that the men were experiencing during the time that I engaged with them.

References

Alonso, A. A. (1999). *Territoriality among African American street gangs in Los Angeles*. Unpublished master's thesis, Department of Geography, University of Southern California.
Alonso, A. (2004). Racialized identities and the formation of black gangs in Los Angeles. *Urban Geography, 25*(7), 658–674.
Alonso, A. (2010). Out of the void: Street gangs in black Los Angeles. In D. Hunt & A-C. Ramón (Eds.), *Black Los Angeles: American dreams and racial realities* (pp. 140–167). New York: New York University Press.
Anderson, E. (1999). *Code of the street*. New York: W. W. Norton & Company.

Baird, A. (2012). The violent gang and the construction of masculinity amongst socially excluded young men. *Safer Communities, 11*(4), 179–190.
Bergen-Cico, D. K., Haygood-El, A., Jennings-Bey, T. N., & Kane, S. D. (2014). Street addiction: A proposed theoretical model for understanding the draw of street life and gang activity. *Addiction Research & Theory, 22*(1), 15–26.
Boyle, G. (2010). *Tattoos on the heart: The power of boundless compassion.* New York: Free Press.
Carson, D. C., & Esbenson, F.-A. (2016). Motivations for leaving gangs in the USA: A qualitative comparison of leaving processes across gang definitions. In C. L. Maxson & F.-A. Esbensen (Eds.), *Gang transitions and transformations in an international context* (pp. 139–155). Switzerland: Springer.
Choi, D. Y., & Kiesner, F. (2007). Homeboy Industries: An incubator of hope and business. *Entrepreneurship Theory and Practice, 31*(5), 769–786.
Cusson, M., & Pinsonneault, P. (1986). The decision to give up crime. In D. B. Cornish & R. V. Clarke (Eds.), *The reasoning criminal: Rational choice perspectives on offending* (pp. 72–82). New York: Springer.
Decker, S. H., Bynum, T., & Weisel, D. (1998). A tale of two cities: Gangs as organized crime groups. *Justice Quarterly, 15*, 395–425.
Decker, S. H., Pyrooz, D., & Moule, R. K., Jr. (2014). Disengagement from gangs as role transitions. *Journal of Research on Adolescence, 24*(2), 268–283.
Densley, J. (2013). *How gangs work: An ethnography of youth violence.* London: Palgrave Macmillan.
Deuchar, R. (2013). *Policing youth violence: Transatlantic connections.* London: Trentham Books/IOE Press.
Deuchar, R., & Weide, R. (2018). Journeys in gang masculinity: Insights from international case studies of interventions. *Deviant Behavior*, 1–15. https://doi.org/10.1080/01639625.2018.1443761.
Fleisher, M. S., & Decker, S. H. (2001). An overview of the challenge of prison gangs. *Corrections Management Quarterly, 5*, 1–9.
Flores, E. O. (2014). *God's gangs: Barrio ministry, masculinity and gang recovery.* New York: New York University Press.
Gambetta, D. (2009). *Codes of the underworld: How criminals communicate.* Princeton, NJ: Princeton University Press.
Giordano, P. C., Cernkovich, S. A., & Rudolph, J. L. (2002). Gender, crime and desistance: Toward a theory of cognitive transformation. *American Journal of Sociology, 107*, 990–1064.

Goffman, E. (1959). *The presentation of self in everyday life*. Garden City, NY: Doubleday.

Griffin, M. L., & Hepburn, J. R. (2006). The effect of gang affiliation on violent misconduct among inmates during the early years of confinement. *Criminal Justice and Behavior, 33*(4), 419–466.

Hagedorn, J. (2008). *A world of gangs: Armed young men and gansta culture*. Minneapolis: University of Minnesota.

Healy, D. (2012). *The dynamics of desistance: Charting pathways through change*. New York: Routledge.

Holligan, C., & Deuchar, R. (2015). What does it mean to be a man? Psychosocial undercurrents in the voices of incarcerated (violent) Scottish teenage offenders. *Criminology and Criminal Justice, 15*(3), 361–377.

Johnson, A. (2017). *If I give my soul: Faith behind bars in Rio de Janeiro*. Oxford: Oxford University Press.

Kupers, T. A. (2005). Toxic masculinity as a barrier to mental health treatment in prisons. *Journal of Clinical Psychology, 61*(6), 713–724.

Leap, J. (2012). *Jumped in: What gangs taught me about violence, drugs, love and redemption*. Boston: Beacon Press.

Los Angeles Police Department (LAPD). (2017). *Gangs*. Available at: http://www.lapdonline.org/get_informed/content_basic_view/1396. Accessed 20 February 2017.

Maruna, S. (2001). *Making good: How ex-convicts reform and rebuild their lives*. Washington, DC: American Psychological Association.

McNeill, F. (2009). What works and what's just? *European Journal of Probation, 1*(1), 21–40.

McNeill, F., & Farrall, S. (2013). A moral in the story? Virtues, values and desistance from crime. In M. Cowburn, M. Duggan, A. Robinson, & P. Senior (Eds.), *Values in criminology and community justice* (pp. 147–164). Bristol: Policy Press.

McNeill, F., Farrall, S., Lightowler, C., & Maruna, S. (2012). *How and why people stop offending: Discovering desistance*. Glasgow: Institute for Research and Innovation in Social Services.

McNeill, F., & Maruna, S. (2008). Giving up and giving back: Desistance, generativity and social work with offenders. In G. McIvor & P. Raynor (Eds.), *Developments in social work with offenders* (pp. 224–339). London: Jessica Kingsley.

Messerschmidt, J. (2005). Men, masculinities and crime. In M. S. Kimmel, J. Hearn, & R. W. Connell (Eds.), *Handbook of studies on men and masculinities* (pp. 196–212). London: Sage.

National Drug Intelligence Center. (2000). National drug threat assessment 2001: The domestic perspective. US Department of Justice. Available at: https://babel.hathitrust.org/cgi/pt?id=pur1.32754070201052;view=1up; seq=2. Accessed 29 December 2017.

Paternoster, R., & Bushway, S. (2009). Desistance and the feared self: Toward an identity theory of criminal desistance. *Journal of Criminal Law and Criminology, 99*(4), 1103–1156.

Pitts, J. (2008). *Reluctant gangsters: The changing face of youth crime*. Devon: Willan.

Pyrooz, D. C., Decker, S. E., & Spohn, C. (2011). Gang-related homicide charging decisions: The implementation of a specialized prosecution unit in Los Angeles. *Criminal Justice Review, 22*(1), 3–26.

Pyrooz, D. C., & Decker, S. H. (2011). Motives and methods for leaving the gang: Understanding the process of gang desistance. *Journal of Criminal Justice, 39*, 417–425.

Romano, S. M. (1996). If the SHU fits: Cruel and unusual punishment at California's Pelican Bay State Prison. *Emory Law Journal, 45*, 1089.

Sanders, B. (2012). Gang youth, substance use patterns, and drug normalization. *Journal of Youth Studies, 15*(8), 978–994.

Skarbek, D. (2011). Governance and prison gangs. *American Political Science Review, 105*(4), 702–716.

Storrod, M. L., & Densley, J. (2017). 'Going viral' and 'going country': The expressive and instrumental activities of street gangs on social media. *Journal of Youth Studies, 20*(6), 677–696.

Stretesky, P. B., & Pogrebin, M. R. (2007). Gang-related gun violence: Socialization, identity and self. *Journal of Contemporary Ethnography, 36*(1), 85–114.

Unnever, J. D., & Gabbidon, S. L. (2011). *A theory of African American offending: Race, racism, and crime*. New York: Routledge.

Vigil, J. D. (1988). *Barrio gangs: Street life and identity in Southern California*. Austin: University of Texas Press.

Vigil, J. D. (2007). *The projects: Gang and non-gang families in East Los Angeles*. Austin: University of Texas Press.

Wacquant, L. (2008). *Urban outcasts: A comparative sociology of advanced marginality*. Cambridge: Polity.

Weide, R. D. (2015). *Race war? Racial relations and racial conflict between black and Latino gangs in Los Angeles County*. Unpublished PhD thesis, California State University, Los Angeles.

5

Love, Compassion and Therapeutic Communities in *Homeboy Industries*

Following on directly from the previous chapter, in this chapter I share insights from participant observation of intervention strategies implemented within *Homeboy Industries*, Los Angeles. I draw on ethnographic fieldnotes to provide illustrations of the holistic culture within the organisation, and the nature and potential impact of coaching and mentoring strategies and group therapy sessions. In addition, insights from follow-up interviews and informal interactions with the male reforming gang members I described in the previous chapter illustrate the main factors that led to their motivation to engage with *Homeboy Industries*, and the perceived impact that it was having on them during the liminal phase (Healy 2012). Further, data gathered via semi-structured interviews with mentors, coaches and staff provide deeper insights into the ways—and extent to which—the structured programmes were providing an initial mechanism for changing perceptions about masculinity and nurturing greater commitment to criminal desistance.

Background to and Focus of *Homeboy Industries*

Since its founding in 1988 under the name, *Jobs For a Future*, a modest non-profit employment referral organisation for gang members, *Homeboy Industries* has evolved into the biggest and most renowned gang intervention programme in the world (Choi and Kiesner 2007; Boyle 2010). Founded by Father Gregory (Greg) Boyle, a former Jesuit Priest, *Homeboy Industries* has progressively launched a series of ambitious business ventures. Rather than focusing on creating profit, these businesses have had the aim of providing stable employment and job training for gang members and/or former prison inmates. They include but are not limited to: the Homeboy Bakery, Homeboy Silkscreen, Homeboy Merchandise, Homegirl Café, Homeboy Grocery, Homeboy Solar Panel Installation Training and Certification, as well as Maintenance Services (Choi and Kiesner 2007). In addition, *Homeboy Industries* offers a plethora of services and education programmes including group and individual counselling and therapy, employment placement, tattoo removal, parenting classes, anger management classes, computer literacy classes and substance abuse meetings (Choi and Kiesner 2007; Leap 2012). Evidence suggests that its education programmes have facilitated the entry of dozens upon dozens of formerly incarcerated and/or gang involved 'homeboys' and 'homegirls' into local colleges and universities (Choi and Kiesner 2007).

In his memoirs *Tattoos on the Heart*, Boyle (2010, p. 8) discusses the way in which *Homeboy Industries* simultaneously offers gang members jobs but also access to a 'therapeutic community'. Boyle describes the initiative as the 'United Nations' of gangs, where former enemies work with one another over an 18-month period and barriers are broken down. He constantly strives to build a supportive and compassionate environment and draws upon his own deep personal faith to project an ethos characterised by his experience of the 'no matter whatness' of God (Boyle 2010, p. 52). But, as Flores (2014, p. 184) has argued, although informed and inspired by Boyle's religious perspective, *Homeboy Industries* primarily supports gang members and offenders to move away from violent crime through a focus on integrative, inclusive practices rooted in 'eclectic spirituality'.

Participant Observation and Follow-up Interviews in *Homeboy Industries*

As I described in the previous chapter, during my early visits to *Homeboy Industries* I met with groups of gang members enrolled on its programmes as 'trainees' as well as their mentors and trainers during one of the organisation's morning meetings. I described my intention to actively participate alongside them during intervention programmes. In addition to seeking volunteers for life history interviews (as described in Chapter 4), I sought the consent of the wider cohort of trainees to observe them informally and record observational insights as well as fragments of discussions and conversations that emerged during classes, workshops and group therapy sessions.

Building on the insights from life history interviews outlined in the previous chapter I later conducted follow-up semi-structured interviews, and engaged in continuing informal conversations with, the eleven reforming male gang members who were the focus for Chapter 4 (see Table 4.1). Finally, I conducted semi-structured interviews with a small sample of six staff members (including Directors, mentors, coaches and trainers). In so doing, I was able to explore the potential social, emotional and spiritual engagement that *Homeboy Industries* initiated among gang members through its programmes. I was also able to consider the extent to—and ways in which—this engagement supported them in beginning to reconstruct their views on masculinity in a way that supported their early and continuing desistance efforts.

Although my observations of intervention initiatives within *Homeboy Industries* included the participation of both male and female gang members, continuing with my key interest in masculinity identity construction and desistance I focused closely on the emerging themes that were most pertinent to the experiences of male participants in my analysis of fieldnotes and interviews. In the sections that follow, these themes will be presented and key extracts from fieldnotes and quotations emerging from follow-up interviews and informal interaction highlighted. Similarly to Dr Robert Weide (referred to in the previous chapter), Father Greg Boyle consented to his real name being used during data reporting. Otherwise, pseudonyms are used as in the previous chapter for the main sample members and also for additional, supplementary participants.

Recruitment, Supervision and Mentoring

In the previous chapter, I described the way in which the men I worked with had begun to make fledgling attempts to desist from gang violence based on initial hooks for change before engaging with *Homeboy Industries* (Giordano et al. 2002). However, early desistance efforts were often restricted or thwarted by continuing issues related to gang embodiment and the structural and interpersonal barriers and 'stigmata' that held them back (Healy 2012; Densley 2013; Flores 2014). During follow-up interviews, they talked about how they had come to seek additional support within *Homeboy Industries*. In some cases, they had initially met Father Greg Boyle while incarcerated in Juvenile Hall, County or State jail. In other cases, they had heard about the work of *Homeboy Industries* from other friends, relatives or fellow inmates or had earlier benefited from Father Greg's help within their neighbourhoods:

> I had met Father G. a long time ago in Juvenile Hall … throughout my (time in) Juvenile Hall, I always thought of *Homeboys,* it was always there even when I was in jail. Somebody brought it to me – another inmate that was … here before and I always thought of coming. (Lucas)

> When I was doin' all my shit, I had a friend and relative who worked here. I had my brother, my younger brother used to work here … I met Father Greg while I was in jail, and I knew him from my church as well … my friends … told me that he was someone who only wants the best for people. (Dylan)

> I used to go and help out since I was like eight, nine years old … where I used to live at, it was maybe like five blocks away from my house… the

old *Homeboys*... and Father G. would like go buy us shoes and he would buy us clothes and stuff like that. (Bruno)

During my initial visits to *Homeboy Industries*, I was able to observe the recruitment process for gang members (who, once registered onto programmes, became referred to as 'trainees'). I noted how they were informed about the nature of the support classes and employment opportunities on offer, the regular narcotics tests they would be subjected to and the inclusive nature of the 18-month programme that was geared towards those with a history of gang-related offending.

During my subsequent visits, I observed the trainees working in a variety of contexts. They would begin by doing maintenance work, cleaning and washing windows, and then progress to working in the bakery, the café, merchandising or a variety of other industries before then gaining experience of administrative and clerical work. All the while, they were enrolled on a schedule of support classes. The organisation thus focused on a careful blend of introducing the trainees to employment opportunities while also offering them personal support with anger management, addiction problems and/or mental health challenges. Throughout, personal mentors supported the trainees to maintain their commitment and motivation and to avoid retreating into gang mindsets. While case managers guided the trainees to engage with essential administrative systems and create personal service plans, personal 'navigators' had practical supervision roles.

While offering the gang members paid employment was empowering, it was the personal support that was seen to be the biggest priority in the minds of the staff since this would be where the healing would take place:

> You see them in the (industries) and they stand and look you in the eye, it's empowerment because they feel part of it now – they have something to offer ... they feel valued ... and throughout the time they're gonna always be in therapy. And ... the priority here is to work on yourself. (Kevin, *Homeboy Industries* 'navigator')

> In the old days we would get a job and we'd send them, 'hey, they're hiring over there, good ... next!' ... But they hadn't healed. And the world

would throw at them what it would, and they'd be toppled by it. They'd run right back to the old things and it didn't work, because they weren't healing. A job is nice, but the healing is forever. (Father Greg Boyle, *Homeboy Industries* founder and Director)

In *Tattoos on the Heart,* Boyle (2010, p. 89) highlights that 'gang members form an exclusive club of young people who plan their funerals not their futures'. At *Homeboy Industries*, there was a focus on giving the trainees their futures back. Members of the team encouraged them to set goals, but were also alert to any potential to regress and strove to maintain their focus and motivation:

Around here we say 'we gotcha!' You know, we're gonna catch ya' if you're colouring outside the lines – you know, if your car is going in a different lane. 'We gotcha'… so the 'navigator' mainly does that, you know? And we try to make sure that folks are cooperating 100 per cent. (Father Greg Boyle, *Homeboy Industries* founder and Director)

It's explained to them, there's gonna be enemies here from the street … if anything happens we'll put a stop to it. Like what we say is 'we're like water, man, instead of fire' … and it'll take another 'homeboy' to come up and be like, 'hey, my boy, what's goin' on man?' if somebody is getting agitated or upset. (Javier, *Homeboy Industries* 'navigator')

Against the backdrop of personal supervision, nurturing and role modelling, I found that *Homeboy Industries* exuded an ethos of inclusion and social justice. It was not only about offering practical and social support to those enrolled on its programmes. As the following sections illustrate, the organisation sought to be a community of 'unconditional love', since community was seen to 'trump' gang any day (Boyle 2010, p. 94).

Community-Building, Compassion and Mutual Transformation

Homeboy Industries was originally founded by Father Greg Boyle as a means of eliminating gang criminality by rooting out its cause—namely,

5 Love, Compassion and Therapeutic Communities ...

the lack of hope arising from lack of opportunities (Choi and Kiesner 2007). Accordingly, the organisation continually tries to support those at the margins to become valued, 'contributing members' of their communities (ibid., p. 777). During my observations, I found that one of the principal means of doing this was through publically celebrating the trainees' achievements during the morning 'thought for the day' sessions. This included anniversaries associated with getting 'clean' from drugs, gaining driving licences or coming back from relapses, as my fieldnotes illustrate:

> A sea of faces surrounds me in the reception area early in the morning, and as I gaze around me I realise that something important is about to happen as people crowd together to make room for others just arriving. A female American staff member steps up to the microphone: 'Ok, today is a very special day because Aretha is two years clean today!' she announces beamingly, at which point Aretha, one of the trainees, steps up and receives a small cake with a candle on the top. All at once, the whole room bursts into a recital of 'happy birthday to Aretha' and I realise that these achievements are of monumental importance. Other announcements follow – one young man has just received his driving licence, while another is being 'welcomed back'. No matter where people are or where they have been, the *Homeboy Industries* community is always ready to welcome them back. (Researcher's fieldnotes)

Several of the staff members indicated that the morning 'thought for the day' meetings were the most important parts of the day. They were seen as a time that nurtured the building of a community of 'unconditional love' (Boyle 2010, p. 94):

> It's the most important 15 min of the day ... because, you know, with all the things we have in here at *Homeboys*, the one that trumps gangs is community. And that is a therapeutic community ... so the morning meeting pushes that, that we're all one community. We're all gonna stop, we're all gonna, you know, welcome each other into this morning, we're gonna do announcements and we're gonna see that this person has been sober for a year and this person got their licence, driver's licence, and this

person has their birthday and this one got their children back. (Hugo, *Homeboy Industries* Associate Director)

That's the most important part of the day because ... I would say it almost dictates the flow of your day. Like, if you're in tune with it, if you're in the moment and you're present and you're receiving it, the thought for the day is beautiful. I've used what they've said in the thought for the day so many times when I'm working with my mentees. (Ryan, *Homeboy Industries* 'senior navigator')

The focus on community-building was also evident in the support classes on offer (Leap 2012). For instance, in the 'Criminals and Gang Members Anonymous' class, trainees were able to collectively explore emotions and triggers through intense discussion. Box 5.1 illustrates an extract of the content of one of the sessions I observed. In this case, male trainees were encouraged to reflect upon the common stimuli for anger, the links with temptation, shame and pride and the positive emotions that can emerge as a result of personal accomplishments.

> **Box 5.1:** *Exploring Personal Triggers and Emotions in 'Criminals and Gang Members Anonymous'*
>
> The room is filled full of trainees—around 40 in total. The class leader is Kevin, who is a 'navigator' but also a trainer and class facilitator in *Homeboy Industries*. He is a small but tough-looking guy who has the remains of gang tattoos on the back of his head which are now becoming increasingly difficult to see as his hair has grown in thick. He stands in the middle of the room with trainees sitting in a circle around him. The session is focused on finding alternative approaches to dealing with anger within the context of gangs. 'Ok, you remember the skits we came up with last week – Adam came up with one, where he had a partner, he's low on rent, they've just had a baby – he couldn't provide money, so how do you think he felt?' One young man calls out, 'temptation'. 'Ok, temptation,' Kevin repeats. Others respond with words like 'shame' and 'less than'. 'You might feel "less than", that's a good one homeboy,' Kevin acknowledges.
>
> 'OK, so those of you who have issues with anger, how do you deal with it?' Kevin enquires. One older white male trainee, calls out, 'well you need to take more time – instead of just goin' at it ... and not let a temporary temptation affect a long-term decision,' he answers. 'That's a good one top dog, but how often do we go through shit and we don't talk to no one?' Kevin prompts further and I become aware of

> the audience nodding in agreement. 'So when things come our way out there, and they will come our way, how are we gonna deal with them … why can't we make those choices we need to make, what stops us?' Miguel, a tall trainee of Mexican descent, puts his hand up and says the simple word, 'pride'. 'Pride – that's it, dop dog, it's pride,' Kevin responds. 'OK, and how does it make you feel if you're doin' it right top dog?' he asks as he looks directly at one of the young Latino men in the room. 'It makes me feel good, proud of myself,' the young man answers. 'Exactly, we all have choices and that's empowerment. It is ultimately your own choice,' Kevin concludes. (Researcher's fieldnotes)

Wallace and Nosko (2003) argue that personal feelings of shame often produce stigmatism and humiliation. The subsequent anger that often emerges (particularly in already-marginalised men) becomes a means of by-passing and containing shame but can also increase recidivism (Healy 2012). For men, encountering situations that confront traditional male socialisation by evoking 'dependency needs, powerlessness or vulnerable emotions such as shame will potentially trigger an experience of failed masculinity' (Wallace and Nosko 2003, p. 55). During the class I observed, Kevin explored these emotions with the reforming gang members and explored the additional links between anger, temptation and pride. Through focusing on a social group work model, he carefully nurtured the male trainees' ability to consider their capacity for making more informed choices by drawing on collective discussion and reflection. In so doing, the men were simultaneously mentored and also encouraged to collectively identity non-violent means of responding. They were encouraged to begin to view the seeking of social support (Cullen 1994) as a sign of maturity rather than weakness, and to exit the 'shame-rage' spiral that was often at the core of their gang-related behaviour (Levitt et al. 2008; Brenneman 2012, p. 237).

Decker et al. (2014, p. 13) discuss the way in which successful interventions must be able to 'discern and document the doubts, concerns and needs' expressed by gang members, and enhance the 'natural social processes working to push and pull individuals out of their gang'. Sessions like the one outlined in Box 5.1 enabled the staff in *Homeboy Industries* to build upon the triggers and turning points that had brought the gang members into its programmes by enabling them to collectively support each other in weighing up the costs and benefits of continued transition away from violent crime (Decker et al. 2014). The social group work model led by Kevin, who was himself a reformed gang member and thus exuded a sense of credibility among the trainees, provided a framework for the trainees to discuss and think through their situations and dilemmas. In doing so, therapeutic spaces were created that helped to support the men to open up in conversation with Kevin and with other trainees for the first time about problems, emotions and feelings and to consider future choices and consequences.

During follow-up interviews and informal discussions with the sample of men I discussed in Chapter 4 (see Table 4.1), they indicated that 'navigators', case workers and therapists were important sources of motivation to them. However, their narratives suggested at times that it was the other trainees who ultimately became the most powerful source of help and support. Flores (2014) highlights the importance of public talk performed through the use of the 'podium' as a means of shaping and supporting recovery from addictive and destructive behaviour. Several men drew attention to the process of story-telling about damaged pasts and current struggles. They felt that this helped them to understand themselves and others more deeply (Leap 2012) and to build a sense of mutual support and recovery:

> The stories that you hear in a lot of the classes, the interaction … you start building friendships when they tell you what they're going through. (Emilio)

> All the groups we go to, it gives me the chance to … like I used to be a real personal person. I didn't wanna talk to no one, or express myself. I didn't want anyone to know nothin' about my life … now all these groups are helping me, you know, like open up, talk about my story. We are similar, you know we all have similar stories so I'm glad I'm here and able to bond with other people that have been through and feel the same shit I have … the way I see it is we all help each other, whether we know it or not. (Benjamin)

Maruna (2001) argues that the catalyst for change among offenders often comes from within. The 'looking glass recovery' process means that someone else believing in them makes them realise that they have personal value and enough self-worth to choose a new destiny. In *Homeboy Industries*, the ethos of unconditional love and support that was generated by Father Greg cascaded through all mentors, participants and classes. This spawned a strong feeling of empathy and shared understanding. It nurtured a sense of tenderness that was often the stimulus for an enhanced change and recovery process:

> One of the things that I love about this place is that, you know, we're not judged ... and the reasons they let you express yourself, this is what I think, is because how can you give a person feedback if you're not real with yourself? If I go on an anger management class and say 'yeah, I was going to kick this dude's ass' ... they start breaking it down, and they let you analyse it, let you think it out ... in most classes you gotta say what they want to hear ... right here you can be you, you know? (Franciso)

> You become that kinda person that we want because of the love that he (Father G.) has for us. So we feel it and we reflect it in other people because how can I not reflect it towards you when it's being reflected towards me? You understand what I'm saying? How can I not love you as a brother when you're loving me as a family member? (Sergio)

Indeed, Father Greg himself made it very clear that everyone in *Homeboy Industries* was on a journey. Rather than focusing on 'reaching' or 'fixing' gang members, it was about staff, trainees and anyone else involved in the organisation reaching and supporting each other in a process of mutual transformation:

> Around here, if somebody says 'how do you reach them?' then around here we would say 'stop trying to reach them'. So the real question around here we always ask is 'can you be reached by them?' Which turns the whole thing on its head ... If love is the answer, community is the context and tenderness is the methodology ... tenderness is the connective tissue that gives you to this other place, where you enter into exquisite mutuality with each other ... a reporter asked me 'how's it feel to have saved thousands of lives?' And I go, 'I don't know what you're talking about – but the only thing I know for sure is my life is saved here every day.' (Father Greg Boyle)

Accordingly, the true meaning of compassion at *Homeboy Industries* was not related merely to serving those on the margins, but about a willingness for everyone to see themselves in kinship with each other (Boyle 2010; Leap 2012). Within this context, I found that holistic and eclectic forms of spirituality were prominent (Flores 2014).

Spirituality, Meditation, Group Therapy and Healing

As I discussed in Chapter 3, spirituality is a 'multifaceted concept' and tends to be concerned with the transcendent (Fetzer Institute 2003 [1999], p. 3; Bakken et al. 2014). Griera (2016, p. 83) argues that the term 'holistic spiritualities' refers to a broad range of beliefs and practices that are oriented towards 'the attainment of wholeness, health and wellbeing of body, mind and spirit'. At *Homeboy Industries*, creative and ascetic spiritual practices were drawn upon during classes such as 'Alcoholics Anonymous' and also during 'thought for the day' sessions. In particular, there was an emphasis on mindfulness meditation:

> As the class begins a young white woman in her early forties begins to speak about her own personal struggle with alcohol. I feel the room grow silent. The woman describes how she has been clean for three years, but had been free of alcohol for eleven years before and then 'went back out'. She describes the way in which her personal sensitivity had led her to think too much and get anxious – and so alcohol had been a way of self-medicating. But just because she has been clean for several years is no guarantee that she won't mess up again, she says, and each day is a new day and one where her battle continues. The woman describes the role of meditation in her life, and how it has helped her to breathe again … and the way in which focusing on the 'here and now' without trying to change what is in front of her has given her more peace. (Researcher's fieldnotes)
>
> At the daily morning meeting this morning, a middle-aged white woman who works as part of the marketing team leads the 'thought for the day.' 'Today I'm gonna share with you the secret of love - and you know, I'm 58 years of age and it's taken me until now to figure this. And that is – that the only thing to do is to be mindful. It's been found that

mindfulness has a positive effect on numerous illnesses, including depression. It decreases the brain's smoke detectors and so we react less to incidents. So how does this work?' she asks, looking around the room. 'Well can anyone in the room breathe?' To this, everyone nods and there are a few smiles. 'OK, it's the one thing that all of us do every single day – so when I give the signal, I want you to breathe into a count of four and then breathe out to a count of eight ... OK, let's go.' As she gives the signal, I along with everyone else in the room begin to breathe slowly ... As we all breathe out, the female facilitator asks us to repeat the action. 'You see,' she says, drawing the session to a close, 'we all have this amazing tool that we can use anytime, anywhere.' (Researcher's fieldnotes)

As I alluded to in Chapter 3, it has been suggested that the regular practicing of mindfulness has the capacity to enhance cognitive change and enable non-judgemental acceptance and relaxation (Himelstein 2011). Among the staff members, there was a strong feeling that meditation was an important form of spiritual practice that helped the trainees to slow down, focus on quieting the mind and relaxing the body. In so doing, it generated peaceful physiological conditions that helped to facilitate positive relationships, even among rival gang members:

> I think it is absolutely spiritual ... I think everyone has it inside of them ... we're hard wired to look for something bigger than us ... meditation ... it's just slowing things down, slowing things down and aligning things with what is right – peace, love, joy and abundance. (Hugo, *Homeboy Industries* Associate Director)
>
> This place kinda becomes the sanctuary. You know ... if there was no spiritual aspect to it ... it would be war here ... to see all these different gang members come from different rival neighbourhoods, and to see the minimal chaos that there is, it's amazing. (Ryan, *Homeboy Industries* 'senior navigator')

Some of the men I interviewed saw the benefit of meditation as a means of personal reflection and developing a non-judging, accepting, beginner's mind (Kabitt Zinn 2013). However, others felt it could be a double-edged sword that could at times encourage them to fixate more on their challenges, obstacles and temptations:

On Monday mornings we have what's called Monday morning meditation. You're coming off the weekend ... we just close our eyes and just meditate ... just reflect on our weekend, reflect on our past. Think about the future, what we're trying to accomplish ... that can be a double-edged sword. Because you're sitting in a room with about 20 people and if you're going through something in your life and you're tryin' to meditate... that may be the only thing you're focusing on. And that gives you a whole hour of thinking about the same thing. So if that's what you're thinking about the whole time, it's gonna bug you the rest of the day. (Dylan)

Preliminary evidence from clinical trials has suggested that mindfulness meditation is a potentially safe and valuable form of intervention for treating addictive, obsessive and destructive behaviour, although conclusive data are still lacking (Zgierska et al. 2009). In *Homeboy Industries*, meditation was just one form of spiritual intervention that was used alongside a wider range of strategies. Indeed, Father Greg viewed the organisation's programmes as being 'soaked' in spiritual practices. This manifested through the holistic focus on building a loving and supportive place of discovery, characterised by mutual acceptance, growth and fulfilment (Lindsay 2002; Boyle 2010; Hall et al. 2011):

> You know, a lot of people wanna say 'we'll talk about the spiritual part' as if it's something separate from what just happened right now ... it's really about the whole thing is soaked in spirit ... you know, this is a place of discovery, where people discover the truth of who they are ... everybody is being returned to themselves ... if you don't welcome your own wounds, then you're going to despise the woundedness in others. (Father Greg Boyle, *Homeboy Industries* founder and Director)

Viewing spirituality as focused on searching for meaning and purpose and returning to a place where body, mind and spirit connect was a recurring feature (Lindsay 2002; Griera 2016). During a follow-up interview with one of the participating men, Marcos, he described the way in which he had begun to return to his Native American roots through participating in a 'sweat lodge' (a traditional Native American faith ritual of cleansing) within *Homeboy Industries* (see also Flores

2014). This had enabled him to connect his energy with other trainees of Mexican descent (Alburquerque et al. 2014), and led to a greater ability to manage difficult patterns of thinking and experience deeper peace:

> When I got into a sweat lodge, we're praying in connection to everybody around and all our energies connect … I finally got my mind to clear everything, my mind to stop thinking … just peace. And when I found peace I knew that's where I belonged. (Marcos)

In addition to responding to culture-specific spiritual yearnings, through participant observation I also noted that interventions such as group therapy and creative poetry writing classes had an underpinning focus on eclectic spirituality (Flores 2014). Box 5.2 provides some insight into this.

Box 5.2: *Confronting and Sharing Emotions and Transitional Experiences Through 'Healing Circles' and Poetry Writing*

Early on Thursday morning I participate in the 'Healing Circle', which today is being led by a middle-aged white woman named Anna. There are 12 of us in the room sitting on the floor. Anna lights up a candle and what looks like some incense in a half shell in front of her. As she passes the shell and a short wooden stick around the room I begin to become aware of the strong aroma emanating from it. Anna explains that the shell contains a particular type of Californian herb with healing qualities. 'Ok so as I pass round the shell and the talking stick, each of you just say a little bit about your highs and lows.'

As the stick and the incense moves around the room, each person says something slightly different. 'Hi, my name is Fernando and I'm pretty good today,' one Latino young man says. 'Hi, my name is Mick and I'm generally good,' another young black man adds. 'My name is Martha and there's still some shit going on but I'm getting there,' one of the Latino young women responds. 'Hi, I'm Jack and I've just got visiting rights to my son which is good. He's still a little shy with me but at least he's getting to know me,' adds a slightly older Latino man who looks as if he is in his early thirties. 'Hi, last week I found out that I lost my rights to see my kids. I'm beginning to get there now, but I just wanna thank Miguel and Heidi for all their support because I know I was a mess last Friday and I wouldn't have got through it without them.' As this young Latino woman makes this statement, I notice that Miguel and Heidi are sitting on the floor beside her and smile and nod kindly.

> Now the incense is passed to me. 'Hi, I'm Ross and I'm from Scotland ... I'm a Criminologist in a university there. I've had a wonderful time here and it's just been a privilege to meet you all and hear about your challenges and some of the wonderful stories of transformation. I've learned a lot from you on this, the way you share and give to each other – that makes a tremendous difference.' Anna then takes the stick and the incense and continues, 'you know what Ross said is so important – it's that sharing, that talking and healing that is so important. We can talk openly here – we can cry if we want.'
> The next day I participate in the 'Street Poetry' class. Each of the 'homeboys' and 'homegirls' share poems and narratives they have written, expressing their personal emotions, struggles and feelings. Two men from Street Poets are facilitating. Street Poets is a 'non-profit poetry-based peace-making organisation dedicated to the creative process as a force for individual and community transformation' (Street Poets Inc., 2017). The poets talk to the participants about choices – the harder choice, they explain, is to be here in this class sharing insights and engaging in personal development: 'You're all trying to re-educate yourselves, and that's harder than being on the block.'
> The facilitators ask if anyone else feels ready to share their work. One young Latino man in his late twenties, whose name is Jesus, reads out a thought-provoking poem about his deepest emotions and challenges. The description is amazing, and it is clear that this young man has a talent for writing. One of the street poets snaps his fingers in approval. 'You know you got a beautiful mind, man – now you have this gift, you need to look for the cracks of light to come in because once we write things down, the process begins... as street poets, we have this identity as wounded healers – not getting away from the wounds but getting closer to them. You know, brother, we live in a city with millions of people in it – but every one of us is lonely ... but by sharing that piece, you are beginning to create a community ... you were in prison for 18 years, but now you're back, man, and you should share your gifts ... these gifts can be like medicine to a sick culture. It's like you have been in prison – you have experienced the poison ... but in doing so you have something with which to heal others.'
> At this point, we all stand up and we bow our heads to say the serenity prayer. Once again, I feel the strong feeling of kinship in the room that I have felt many times over the course of my visit. As I leave the room, I am fascinated by the continual focus on personal and mutual affirmation that emerges from these therapy sessions. (Researcher's fieldnotes)

Bregman (2004, p. 160) argues that the concept of spirituality is ambiguous and 'hard to pin down'. It tends to be focused on a number of non-theological concerns regarding the significance and meaning of life and avoids the specifics of what religious observance might connote (Mandhouj et al. 2014; see also Lindsay 2002; Fetzer Institute 2003 [1999]; Hall et al. 2011). Flores (2014) discusses *Homeboy Industries'* ecumenical leanings that allow therapeutic models of rehabilitation to be used, including healing circles that end with the serenity prayer (suggesting no religious preference), Native American practices and verbal testimonies. The experiences of Marcos combined with my own observation of and participation in group therapy sessions and poetry classes illustrated to me the way in which the trainees were continually encouraged to confront their own feelings and emotions. They connected with each other as well as with mentors, facilitators and group leaders (Alburquerque et al. 2014). They shared and discharged issues of 'chronic shame' and transitional experiences in public settings and gave and received positive affirmation within the context of therapeutic communities (Brenneman 2012, p. 17).

Some of the men I interviewed disclosed to me that they had religious beliefs, while others admitted that they had none. By avoiding 'religious particularism' but focusing instead on eclectic approaches that nurtured a sense of inclusive community-building and kinship, Father Greg and the other *Homeboy Industries* staff encouraged trainees to use the 'podium' to discuss their deepest personal battles (Pyrooz 2014, pp. 622–623). In doing so, the trainees each began to engage in the generative role of the 'wounded healer' through sharing their narratives characterised by damaged and shameful pasts as well as their current struggles and turning points as moral tales to help guide others 'in the right direction' (Maruna 2001, p. 11). As the next section illustrates, these eclectic spiritual and therapeutic practices encouraged the men to begin to reject conventional gang-oriented perspectives and re-align their personal definitions of masculinity (Parkes and Bilby 2010; Flores 2014).

Dismantling Gang Masculinity and Nurturing Broader Versions of Manhood

As the previous sub-sections have illustrated, the overarching focus on creating a community of unconditional love within *Homeboy Industries* was stimulated by nurturing an atmosphere of 'endless acceptance' amongst everyone within the organisation (Boyle 2010, p. 145). Senior staff talked to me about their strong convictions that exposing the male trainees to supportive, therapeutic communities characterised by an holistic and eclectic spiritual focus helped to break down external façades characterised by *machismo* (Johnson 2017). The tough images the men had projected within the context of gangs, often created as a form of armour against feelings of disadvantage, trauma and pain, were thus dismantled and new 'possible selves' embraced and accepted (Paternoster and Bushway 2009, p. 1113; see also Healy 2012):

> The toughness is just a thick layer … we gotta get under that, we gotta expose it for what it is. It's a survival mechanism … (so) let's go to where the pain really is. Let's expose the pain, let's talk about that pain, and let's open up and release it from ourselves. And then your toughness starts to fade away and it feels good just to kind of like not care about having my heavy shield in front of me that's trying to block all the craziness … I'm renewing my mind and life is starting to follow. (Hugo, *Homeboy Industries* Associate Director)

> You come in and you're embraced by this community and there's no judgement, they embrace you as you are. And most of us have never been embraced or accepted by our own families, so when this happens you feel loved, you feel beautiful and you're not afraid to be yourself because there is no judgement, there is no condemnation … you're able to be who you are, you're able to speak in front of people, do poetry in front of people, something you would never do amongst your 'homies' … because that would be considered 'soft'. So this community, it returns you to the true essence of who you are … (Ryan, *Homeboy Industries* 'senior navigator')

Building on the initial turning points and 'hooks for change' that had brought them to *Homeboy Industries* to begin with (Giordano et al. 2002, p. 1000), the men in my main sample indicated that the feelings of love, kinship and mutual support they experienced there had begun to have a transformative impact on them. They had increasingly begun to contest gang masculinity and to embrace new types of 'countercultural' masculine identity (Johnson 2017, p. 112; see also Brenneman 2012; Flores 2014):

Before … guns gave me the power. Now my kids give me the power. (Juan)

When I was younger a lot of people would be offering me 2000 bucks and I was like 'what do you want me to do?' … (now) I can sit down and be calm and humble and wait for those little pay cheques and actually live day by day … it's just tryin' to be a man and fight for like what's right for like kids … (Diego)

Before I'd be like, 'man, fuck you' you know what I mean? … but I guess you could say … it's time to be a man now … to me, being a man is being responsible … taking care of your family … I'm taking a decision to man up to my shit. (Benjamin)

Accordingly, as trainees within *Homeboy Industries* these men were learning to confront and problematize deeply engrained socially and culturally-influenced attitudes and values. Their personal narratives were beginning to reject gun possession and use, violence and the earning of 'fast' money as indicators of masculinity and to focus instead on earning an honest living, being good parents and family men. Thus, their emerging narratives were simultaneously characterised by a rejection of their criminal pasts and emerging aspirational identities centred on 'conventional adults pursuits' (Healy 2012, p. 124). Towards the end of my interviews with them, they each expressed some very focused ambitions for the future that did not involve gang membership or violence. In addition to their strong commitments to family responsibilities and domestic roles (above), these ambitions were also centred on career goals that *Homeboy Industries* had helped to nurture (Flores 2014; Johnson 2017):

I want to be a college graduate some day … I wanna have a career. I wanna be able to finally get off my lazy ass and become the person I wanna become. (Sergio)

I'm about to start solar panel training that they offered me … I really wanna make that a career … that's gonna help me get myself an apartment and provide more for my daughter, you know what I mean? So, I mean this is only the beginning, it's only gonna get better – that's what I tell myself every day. (Benjamin)

The participating men recognised that they were on the early part of a desistance journey and regarded themselves as 'works in progress' taking 'baby steps' forward. Even among those who had almost reached the end of the 18-month programme when I interviewed them, it was evident that some still struggled with gang embodiment issues. This included injuries emerging from earlier gang violence, particular ways of walking and gesturing that were still associated with their gangs and the remaining facial and bodily gang tattoos they still adorned (although several were in the process of having the latter removed through the free tattoo removal service within *Homeboy Industries*) (Leap 2012; Flores 2014). Further, some admitted that they still experienced 'urges' to return to alcohol, drugs or the fast lifestyles they had previously known but were now beginning to step away from. Importantly, for some who had not gained sufficient credibility as members of street and prison gangs there was the added pressure of continually being given a hard time by former 'homies' who tried to pull them back into gang life, violence and crime.

However, when these trials and temptations arose, all of the men were reassured that they could call up their personal 'navigators' or other trainees and they would have access to personal support to help guide them back in the right direction. Supporting earlier insights from Flores (2014), it was evident that the strength that they had gained from the therapeutic and eclectically spiritual community in *Homeboy Industries* was increasingly helping them to resist being pulled back into gang life. At the same time, they were actively envisioning new 'possible selves' (Paternoster and Bushway 2009, p. 1113) they wished to become and constructing new ideas of manhood centred on 'domestic life rather than the streets' (Healy 2012, p. 169; see also Johnson 2017).

Concluding Discussion

In this chapter, I have drawn upon and extended earlier insights from Flores (2014) into the culture and practice within, and impact of, *Homeboy Industries* in Los Angeles. I have illustrated the ways in which I found the focus of the intervention programmes and the nature of the relationships amongst mentors and trainees enabled the male gang members I worked with to begin to problematize subcultural constructions of gang masculinity and strengthen their desistance efforts (Flores 2014). In particular, I have drawn attention to the role of holistic forms of spirituality in nurturing their transitional journeys.

Maruna (2001, p. 87) refers to the life stories of desisting offenders, where they connect negative past experiences to the present. The process of 'making good' thus often involves offenders in sharing redemption scripts with each other in order to 'rewrite a shameful past into a necessary prelude to a productive and worthy life' (ibid.). I found that the opportunity to enact this story-sharing process was a crucial aspect of the *Homeboy Industries* initiative. In the midst of this, a mutually supportive community was enacted wherein a range of transformative experiences continually emerged among male gang members who were in the liminal phase (Healy 2012; Leap 2012). In addition to personal issues of despair, trauma and hopelessness being addressed, in the process territorial and racial barriers were subtly being broken down among previous gang-related enemies who now openly supported each other (Boyle 2010).

Stefanakis (2008, p. 658) argues that interventions for violent male offenders based on compassion help to build 'therapeutic alliances', which in turn keep such men in treatment longer and help to reduce the risk of recidivism. This is consistent with Cullen's (1994, p. 527) earlier contention that the presence of social support 'reduces criminal involvement', and Leap's (2012, p. 212) earlier observation that a community-based approach represents the 'best of all the "answers"' in terms of crime prevention. The compassionate and mutually sympathetic ethos in *Homeboy Industries* was clearly expressed in the form of practical and social support. However, it was also soaked in eclectic spirituality characterised by unconditional love, personal search for true purpose and meaning and kinship, all of which was nurtured through group therapy, personal mentoring and positive affirmation (Lindsay 2002; Flores 2014).

It was clear to me that the men I worked with were still very much in transition. Even after prolonged engagement in *Homeboy Industries*, some still struggled with similar gang embodiment issues and personal temptations and urges that had been present in their lives when they entered its programmes (Flores 2014). However, it was also evident that they were beginning to problematize caustic subcultural constructions of masculinity (Deuchar and Weide 2018). Their narratives suggested that they were starting to emasculate gang life and masculinise recovery, desistance and future, non-criminal, family-oriented lifestyles (Flores 2014). They were also able to access 24/7 personal support from navigators and other trainees when temptations became strong. Importantly, when they reached the end of their time at *Homeboy Industries* I learned that many of the trainees were referred on to wider education, training and employment opportunities through Father Greg's numerous contacts out in the field with inclusive organisations who were willing to recruit ex-felons. This clearly provided them with a greater sense of hope for the future.

However, as with all intervention programmes *Homeboy Industries* relies on funding for its continued operationalisation. Although the profits from the organisation's own social enterprises combined with modest government funds, donations from public and private foundations and those emerging from fundraising events largely maintain its sustainability, budget shortfalls can and do emerge. As I have documented elsewhere (Deuchar and Weide 2018), this has in the past led to trainees being paid off and subsequently increased their vulnerability to revert back to criminal lifestyles.

Weide (2015) argues that substantive social programmes that transcend racial and territorial boundaries, embrace social justice and encourage mutual understanding among the most marginalised are an obvious remedy for gang violence and crime. However, he also highlights that the dominant political focus in the USA has often been on investing in the dramatic expansion of the carceral state as generations of ghetto and barrio youth have been sent to prisons. The insights in this chapter suggest that initiatives like *Homeboy Industries*, with its focus on eclectic spirituality and therapeutic community-building, may play a valuable part in nurturing non-violent attitudes, steering male offenders' already strong moral and ethical principles in non-criminal directions and helping them to manage the negative repercussions of prolonged violent lifestyles more effectively.

Rather than forefronting a focus on repressive criminal justice polices that advance discipline, containment, exclusion and punishment, perhaps American criminal justice policy-making needs to focus on advancing intervention and prevention initiatives centred around holistic forms of spiritual engagement and mutual compassion across targeted, vulnerable cities and States. In so doing, adequate State funding needs to be made available to ensure the interventions remain sustainable. Consequently, wider groups of gang members may begin to experience the type of turning points, identity and behaviour change conducive to initiating *primary* desistance as well as a greater commitment to prospective *secondary* desistance that I witnessed in *Homeboy Industries*.

In Part III, the spotlight moves from the USA to northern Europe. In particular, I engage in a comparative exploration of the nature and impact of gang culture and violent criminality in Scotland and Denmark. I then move on to examine the role that religious and spiritual interventions in prisons and in the community can have on challenging ingrained views about masculinity that are often conducive to gang-related and wider forms of offending there. In Chapter 6, I begin by sharing insights from life history interviews with Scottish and Danish men and their retrospective reflections on their experiences of and motivations for offending.

References

Albuquerque, I. F., Cunha, R. C., Martins, L. D., & Sá, A. B. (2014). Primary health care services: Workplace spirituality and organisational performance. *Journal of Organizational Change Management, 27*(1), 59–82.
Bakken, N. W., DeCamp, W., & Visher, C. A. (2014) Spirituality and desistance from substance use among reentering offenders. *International Journal of Offender Therapy and Comparative Criminology, 58*(11), 1321–1229.
Boyle, G. (2010). *Tattoos on the heart: The power of boundless compassion.* New York: Free Press.
Bregman, L. (2004). Defining spirituality: Multiple uses and murky meanings of an incredibly popular term. *Journal of Pastoral Care and Counselling, 58*(3), 157–167.

Brenneman, R. (2012). *Homies and hermanos: God and gangs in central America*. Oxford: Oxford University Press.

Choi, D., & Kiesner, F. (2007) Homeboy Industries: An incubator of hope and businesses. *Entrepreneurship: Theory and Practice, 31*(5), 769–790.

Cullen, F. T. (1994). Social support as an organizing concept for criminology: Presidential address to the Academy of Criminal Justice Sciences. *Justice Quarterly, 11*(4), 527–559.

Decker, S. H., Pyrooz, D., & Moule, R. K., Jr. (2014). Disengagement from gangs as role transitions. *Journal of Research on Adolescence, 24*(2), 268–283.

Densley, J. (2013). *How gangs work: An ethnography of youth violence*. London: Palgrave Macmillan.

Deuchar, R., & Weide, R. (2018). Journeys in gang masculinity: Insights from international case studies of interventions. *Deviant Behavior*, 1–15. https://doi.org/10.1080/01639625.2018.1443761.

Fetzer Institute and National Institute on Aging Working Group (2003) [1999]. *Multidimensional measurement of religiousness/spirituality for use in health research*. Kalamazoo, MI: Fetzer Institute.

Flores, E. O. (2014). *God's gangs: Barrio ministry, masculinity and gang recovery*. New York: NYU Press.

Giordano, P. C., Cernkovich, S. A., & Rudolph, J. L. (2002). Gender, crime and desistance: Toward a theory of cognitive transformation. *American Journal of Sociology, 107*, 990–1064.

Griera, M. (2016). Yoga in penitentiary settings: Transcendence, spirituality, and self-improvement. *Human Studies, 40*(1), 77–100.

Hall, R. E., Livingston, J. N., Brown, C. J., & Mohabir, J. A. (2011). Islam and Asia Pacific Muslims: The implications of spirituality for social work practice. *Journal of Social Work Practice, 25*(2), 205–215.

Healy, D. (2012). *The dynamics of desistance: Charting pathways through change*. New York: Routledge.

Himelstein, S. (2011). Meditation research: The state of the art in correctional settings. *International Journal of Offender Therapy and Comparative Criminology, 55*(4), 646–661.

Johnson, A. (2017). *If I give my soul: Faith behind bars in Rio de Janeiro*. Oxford: Oxford University Press.

Kabat-Zinn, J. (2013). *Full catastrophe living: Using the wisdom of your body and mind to face stress, pain, and illness*. New York: Bantam.

Leap, J. (2012). *Jumped in: What gangs taught me about violence, drugs, love and redemption*. Boston: Beacon Press.

Levitt, H. M., Swanger, R. T., & Butler, J. B. (2008). Male perpetrators' perspectives on intimate partner violence, religion and masculinity. *Sex Roles, 58*, 435–448.

Lindsay, R. (2002). *Recognizing spirituality: The interface between faith and social work*. Crawley, Australia: University of Western Australia Press.

Mandhouj, O., Aubin, H., Amirouche, A., Perroud, N., & Huguelet, P. (2014). Spirituality and religion among French prisoners: An effective coping resource? *International Journal of Offender Therapy and Comparative Criminology, 58*(7), 821–834.

Maruna, S. (2001). *Making good: How ex-convicts reform and rebuild their lives*. Washington, DC: American Psychological Association.

Parkes, R., & Bilby, C. (2010). The courage to create: The role of artistic and spiritual activities in prison. *Howard Journal, 49*, 97–110.

Paternoster, R., & Bushway, S. (2009). Desistance and the feared self: Toward an identity theory of criminal desistance. *Journal of Criminal Law and Criminology, 99*(4), 1103–1156.

Pyrooz, D. C. (2014). Book review: God's gangs: Barrio ministry, masculinity and gang recovery, by Edward Orozco Flores. *Crime, Law and Social Change, 62*, 621–624.

Stefanakis, H. (2008). Caring and compassion when working with offenders of crime and violence. *Violence and Victims, 23*(5), 652–661.

Street Poets Inc. (2017). Available online. http://streetpoetsinc.com/. Accessed 24 April 2017.

Wallace, R., & Nosko, A. (2003). Shame in male spouse abusers and its treatment in group therapy. *Journal of Aggression, Maltreatment and Trauma, 7*(1–2), 47–74.

Weide, R. D. (2015). *Race war? Racial relations and racial conflict between black and Latino gangs in Los Angeles County*. Unpublished PhD thesis, California State University, Los Angeles.

Zgierska, A., Rabago, D., Chawla, N., Kushner, K., Koehler, R., & Marlatt, A. (2009). Mindfulness meditation for substance use disorders: A systematic review. *Substance Abuse, 30*(4), 266–294.

Part IV

Scotland and Denmark: From Violence, Offending and Prison Life to Religiosity, Yoga and Breathing

6

Masculinity, Morality and Offending in Scotland and Denmark

In the next three chapters, I move the focus of attention across the Atlantic from the USA to northern Europe. Continuing with the prominent focus of the book, I firstly draw upon a comparative perspective to explore and examine the issues relating to gangs and masculinity in Scotland and Denmark, highlighting the key similarities and differences. In the following two chapters I then move on to explore the perceived impact of religious-oriented and ascetic-spiritual interventions in terms of supporting small samples of male offenders in both countries to begin to move away from embracing violent and criminal identities.

In this chapter, I draw upon insights gathered from life history interviews conducted not only with gang members but also with several other types of offenders (such as drug dealers, armed robbers and sex offenders). These participants were mostly residing in Scottish and Danish prisons (or had recently been released) at the time of fieldwork. As in Part II, I explore the links between the interviewees' socially-constructed views of masculinity, their involvement in gangs and (in some cases) wider criminality. Towards the end of the chapter, I highlight the way in which the motivation for violence and crime among many of the Scottish and Danish men I interviewed often also seemed to be guided by strong moral and ethical codes, as were their initial attempts to desist.

Scotland and Denmark: A Comparative Perspective

In this section of the book I focus on Scotland and Denmark because both countries are on the north-west of Europe, have comparable populations of 5.3 million and 5.6 million respectively and similar levels of life expectancy. However, the two countries differ in terms of overall class and welfare distribution levels. While Scotland tends to have high levels of class and income inequality and poverty, Denmark (like other Scandinavian countries) generally has a high standard of living and is characterised by relatively low levels of class and income inequality and low poverty rates (Von Hofer et al. 2012).

In terms of crime, both locations have similar reoffending patterns among males. For instance, in Scotland young men aged under 21 years are most likely to reoffend (Audit Scotland 2012; Deuchar et al. 2016). In Denmark, young males aged less than 25 years also reoffend the most (Deuchar et al. 2016). However, key differences between the violent crime profiles in each country also make Scotland and Denmark interesting sites for comparison. For instance, although levels of violent crime have fallen significantly across Scotland in recent years (Anderson et al. 2016; Scottish Government 2017), statistics suggest that there were just over 1100 police recorded common assaults per 100,000 population in Scotland during 2016/17, and a total of 61 homicides (Scottish Government 2017). In Denmark there were much fewer cases recorded on both measures (142 common assaults per 100,000 population and a total of 33 homicides) (*CPHPost Online* 2017; Statistica 2017). Finally, while concern about street gangs is a relatively new phenomenon in Denmark, it has been prominent for many years in Scotland (Davies 2013; Mørck et al. 2013).

Background to Gang Issues in Scotland and Denmark

In Chapter 2, I explored some links that have been established between marginalisation, gang violence, criminality and masculine identity construction within previous research conducted across Europe. Before exploring these more closely from a Scottish and Danish perspective, a brief review of existing insights into gang culture in both counties follows.

Scotland

The earliest recorded gangs in Scotland date back to the late nineteenth Century, and included the emergence of the *Penny Mobs* in Glasgow (Scotland's largest city) (Deuchar 2016). Gangs in the west of Scotland were formed following the large-scale Irish migration that resulted from the famines of the mid-nineteenth Century. By the early twentieth Century, smaller gangs had converged and the formation of two notorious gangs in the city—the *Billy Boys* (a Protestant gang) and the *Norman Conks* (from Norman Street in Bridgeton, where many Roman Catholics lived)—characterised the sectarian divisions within Glasgow at the time (Davies 2013).

As I referred to in Chapter 2, research into Scottish gangs was first carried out by James Patrick (1973). Patrick's ethnographic fieldwork identified the presence of numerous territorial gangs in Glasgow in the 1960s that were centred primarily on violence. As I have previously argued (Deuchar 2016, p. 71), against the historical backdrop of a city that was once dominated by heavy industry and overcrowded tenements many working-class men from deprived neighbourhoods in Glasgow have traditionally been driven by a 'culture of honour'. But the demise of male-dominated heavy industry in Glasgow over the past 40 years and the resulting inequality has led to a crisis of masculinity in socially disadvantaged housing estates (or 'schemes' as they are commonly referred to) (Deuchar 2009; Fraser 2015; Deuchar 2016). Accordingly, the social construction of masculinity characterised by violent identities has come even more to the fore (ibid.).

It is commonly recognised that a disproportionate number of street gangs have historically been located in the west of Scotland (including Lanarkshire, Dunbartonshire and Inverclyde as well as Glasgow) (Deuchar 2016). Unlike in other parts of the world where I collected data, it has long been recognised that male street gang members in Glasgow and other parts of Scotland tend to be particularly young, with a peak age-range of 12–16 years (Deuchar 2009). Although the UK Government has made clear links between street gang activity and serious organised crime in some parts of England, traditionally no such links have been made in Scotland (McLean 2017). However, although commonly viewed in the modern era as recreational outfits focused on territoriality (as opposed to sectarianism), some more recent evidence suggests that some street gangs (particularly in the west of Scotland) have evolving capabilities. Hence a minority of young men may progress from territorial street violence to involvement in organised criminality, most notably drug dealing (McLean 2017; McLean et al. 2017).

Denmark

In Denmark, historically the main focus has been on outlaw motorcycle gangs such as the *Hells Angels* and *Bandidos*, and over the years several major gang conflicts between these and other gangs have been documented (Pederson and Lindstad 2011). In many ways, these gangs have been inspired by American biker gang culture, whereby members wear jacket emblems and provocative symbols and display aggressive and violent attitudes (ibid.). With the rise of *Bandidos* across Europe during the 1990s, gang conflicts with the *Hell's Angels* and several sub-groups erupted across the Nordic countries. Danish towns and cities subsequently became the sites for three major gang wars between bikers and criminal gangs (Søgaard et al. 2016).

As a result of these high profile gang feuds, the Danish police increasingly focused on gang suppression tactics characterised by intense surveillance and a high volume of stop and search methods (Søgaard et al. 2016). Believing that the biker groups were at the core of organised crime in Denmark, the police collaborated with local bar owners to launch a 'stress strategy' whereby gang members were denied the possibility of frequenting bars and nightclubs (Søgaard 2013). In addition, the police collaborated with tax agencies and social welfare institutions in order to ensure that registered gang members received no welfare benefits unless they were actively seeking work or taking part in 'exit', social enterprise or rehabilitation programmes. The Danish Prison and Probation Service also ensured that those convicted for gang-related offences were segregated in prisons (Mørck et al. 2013; Søgaard 2013).

In addition to the more traditional motorcycle gangs, over the last two decades evidence suggests that a growing number of street communities across Denmark have militarized significantly and demonstrate a new territoriality due to violent conflicts over local drugs markets (Mørck et al. 2013; Søgaard et al. 2016). Some of these territorial street gangs have formed an 'official affiliation' under the banner of 'LTF' (Loyal to Familia). Evidence suggests that gang feuds have intensified in recent years, particularly within the Nørrebro area of Copenhagen, and that membership mainly consists of young ethnic minority men who have felt discriminated against for many years (Mørck et al. 2013; Deuchar et al. 2018).

Insights into the Experiences of Gang Members and Offenders: Scotland and Denmark

In this chapter, I share in-depth insights gained from qualitative research conducted in Scottish and Danish prisons and wider Danish communities over a four-year period between 2012 and 2016. Firstly, I visited Scotland's largest Young Offenders' Institution (YOI) on multiple occasions to conduct initial life history interviews with 11 young male offenders who were between the ages of 17 and 21 years. The young men were predominantly from socially disadvantaged areas in the west of Scotland, but some came from deprived communities in Edinburgh, Dundee and the Scottish Highlands. The majority of the young men had been born and raised in Scotland and were white, although one had been born in Jamaica and then moved to Scotland with his family at the age of 10.

Secondly, during intermittent visits to Denmark I conducted life history interviews with 15 male offenders there. Of these, seven were incarcerated in three different closed prisons during the time of the interviews (having already been sentenced or on remand, awaiting their trials), while a further two had been transferred to open prisons and an additional six had recently been released back into the community. With the Danish sample, the age range was between 23 and 49 years. Thus, I was able to engage not only with reasonably young offenders but with those slightly older who were able to reflect back on their prolonged experiences with violent offending and criminality since their youth. Of the 15 men who participated, eight had been born and raised in Denmark, mostly in and around Copenhagen (Denmark's capital city). The remaining seven were first generation immigrants from Poland, Turkey, Kuwait, Saudi Arabia, Macedonia, Somalia and Uganda.

In both Scotland and Denmark, the interviewees had mostly been involved in gang-related violence or crime at some point during their periods of offending. Some, but not all, of those who were incarcerated at the time of the interviews were in prison for gang-related offences. Most commonly the men's offences were serious assaults, gang-related drug dealing or robbery but in some cases even more serious charges such as attempted murder or murder. In a small minority of cases, the men had been involved in criminal acts that were not connected to gang structures. For example, two participants in Scotland had been convicted for sex offences that were not gang-related. The inclusion of these men as interviewees provided a nuanced and illuminating contrast to the wider sample, but at the same time there were areas of commonality in terms of the nature of their crimes. For instance, the two men's criminal offending (as with many of the reforming gang members in the sample) had been violent in nature. They had evidently used sex as a weapon and violated the physical space of young women as a means of enacting dominant masculinity (Messerschmidt 2000; Johnson 2007), in contrast to gang members who tend to use other types of weapons to assert their masculinity within the context of group struggles (Connell 2005). During interviews, I found that the two men were more reticent about disclosing precise details of their offending behaviour and

6 Masculinity, Morality and Offending in Scotland and Denmark

my access to them was more limited than with other participants due to security protocols in the YOI. Accordingly, the majority of my insights from these men were focused on their difficult childhood experiences and the perceived impact of their exposure to pastoral and religious support in prison (as outlined in the next chapter), rather than the nature of their offending behaviour per se.

In Denmark, one of the participants was *suspected* by the authorities of having been embroiled in gangs; however, he claimed that his drug dealing was conducted on an individual basis and that he had never been involved in gang structures. One other had been convicted for armed robbery and two for individual drug dealing, and all of these three men also claimed that they had never been gang members. However, whether or not these men had been involved in gangs, their offending behaviour was clearly very similar to those in the wider sample of gang members. These participants were more easily accessible and more candid about their offending histories than the two sex offenders in Scotland, and fuller insights about some of their offending behaviour are therefore included in this chapter. Overall, I believe that the inclusion of the slightly wider sample of men enabled me to broaden my analysis slightly, and to explore the links between masculinity and crime and (in particular) between spirituality and desistance outwith a specific gang context.

Each of the interviewees had been in prison for varying lengths of time—while some were only recently incarcerated, others (in Denmark) had been in prison for some time awaiting their trials. Some others in both countries had served a full sentence and were close to release by the time I met them, and some of the Danes had already been released by the time I interviewed them. For those men in Denmark who had either been convicted for or were being held in prisons for charges of gang-related offences, I often interviewed them in segregated areas of the prisons due to the sanctions that had been put upon them as a result of the 'stress strategy' discussed earlier. Similarly, the two young men who were in prison for sex offences in Scotland were located in segregated areas of the YOI due to the nature of their crimes. During follow-up semi-structured interviews, I selected two sub-groups from the wider sample who—for one reason or another—had either sought out contact with prison chaplains or had engaged in particular forms of yoga, meditation and breathing practices, and were willing to engage in further discussion about their experiences. I also engaged in informal discussions with inmates during study groups and recreational activities arranged by prison chaplains in both countries. Finally, I actively participated in yoga, breathing and mediation practices initiated by trained coaches in Denmark (for further detail, see Chapters 7 and 8).

Table 6.1 provides a full list of the 26 participants (using pseudonyms), their ages, countries of origin and residence as well as details of whether they were incarcerated in a YOI and/or closed prison (on remand awaiting trials or already sentenced), in an open prison or recently released from prison during the time that the fieldwork took place.

Table 6.1 The research participants in Scotland and Denmark

Name	Age	Country of birth	Geographical location	Prison/released
Callum	18	Scotland	Scotland	YOI (closed prison)
Andy	20	Scotland	Scotland	YOI (closed prison)
Stevie	17	Scotland	Scotland	YOI (closed prison)
Gregor	18	Scotland	Scotland	YOI (closed prison)
Fergus	20	Scotland	Scotland	YOI (closed prison)
Adam	20	Scotland	Scotland	YOI (closed prison)
Tarone	20	Jamaica	Scotland	YOI (closed prison)
Connor	19	Scotland	Scotland	YOI (closed prison)
Paul	19	Scotland	Scotland	YOI (closed prison)
Keith	21	Scotland	Scotland	YOI (closed prison)
Martyn	20	Scotland	Scotland	YOI (closed prison)
Stefan	24	Poland	Denmark	closed prison
Umar	23	Denmark	Denmark	Closed prison
Yusuf	28	Turkey	Denmark	Closed prison
Ahmed	28	Kuwait	Denmark	Closed prison
Patric	40	Denmark	Denmark	Closed prison
Søren	37	Denmark	Denmark	Closed prison
Abbad	37	Saudi Arabia	Denmark	Released
Jesper	42	Denmark	Denmark	Released
Ivan	47	Macedonia	Denmark	Open prison
Hans	49	Denmark	Denmark	Released
Lasse	37	Denmark	Denmark	Released
Lucas	43	Denmark	Denmark	Released
Damon	34	Denmark	Denmark	Closed prison
Cumar	23	Somalia	Denmark	Open prison
Jamaal	32	Uganda	Denmark	Released

With inmates, interviews were conducted in small meeting rooms within the prisons. For those who had recently been released from prisons in Denmark I interviewed them in the premises of the *Breathe Smart* organisation, having been introduced to them by coaches and instructors of Sadarshan Kriya Yoga (SKY) (for further details on this, see Chapter 8). In this chapter, I report on the insights from life history interviews conducted in prisons or in the community, before drawing on the wider follow-up data with the two sub-groups in the next two chapters (for additional details on methodological approaches used across sample sites, see Chapter 1).

'Products' of Their Environments: Early Disadvantage, Social Exclusion and Trauma

During interviews in Scotland, the men often described in detail the difficult family environments that they had experienced while growing up. These were characterised by loss and bereavement, missing male role models and challenging or abusive relationships with alcohol/drug-dependent and vulnerable parents that in some cases led to them being taken into care:

> I'd lost my dad when I was 11 ... I think it was alcohol-related ...and my mum, when I was 15 she passed away with cancer. (Callum, Scotland)
>
> When I was about nine years of age my dad passed away ... and straight after that my ... my ma' had mental health problems and a' that, so me and my brother went into residential – as soon as we went into a home then that's when we just kinda went off the rails. (Andy, Scotland)
>
> My maw and da', they were on drugs n'that ... my gran had to look after us, and I was a wee terror and my gran couldnae look after us so I got put in ... a home for two year ... you couldnae keep me in, just bouncin' aboot wi' all the older ones. (Fergus, Scotland)

It has been found that the residential care environment can present young people with encounters that reinforce offending behaviour (Hayden 2010). It has also been found that many of those growing up in care homes later become disproportionately represented in the criminal justice system and in prisons (Mellon 2011). Several of the men I interviewed (such as Andy and Fergus) clearly made links between their transition into care at a young age and their subsequent involvement in crime. One interviewee, Connor, also felt that coming into prison for the first time simply reminded him of many of his previous home environments and felt 'pretty much like being back in care'.

The two young men who had been convicted of sex offences in Scotland clearly also had been exposed to challenging family environments during their early years. These were characterised by alcohol problems or the presence of men who had difficulty expressing emotions. With Adam, this led to a phobia about expressing affection, and for Keith his difficulties were compounded when he was also badly treated in residential care environments:

> I grew up around a family where the men, it was sort of the case that men didn't feel kind of thing … as a child you look at what the majority of men are doing … [I had a] fear of affection. (Adam, Scotland)
>
> There was a lot of problems in my house wi' … my dad was drinking, my mum … was kind of an alcoholic … things just spiralled out of control. Eventually I was taken into care at 14 … they dumped me wi' two guys, and they were to supervise me … they treated me like a piece of dirt. (Keith, Scotland)

Combined with these difficult circumstances, the men in Scotland also often experienced living their early lives against the backdrop of extreme poverty and social disadvantage. One interviewee, Tarone, had been born in Jamaica and moved to Scotland when he was aged 10. He summed up the views of many when he described himself as a 'product' of his environment. Like others, he was raised in a family where his father was aggressive and violent and in a community that was characterised by poverty, drugs and violence. In Denmark, the slightly older men also described the multiple forms of disadvantage that had characterised their lives. Although levels of income inequality and poverty rates are less significant in Denmark than in Scotland, the men still experienced relative deprivation compared to other parts of Danish society. As in Scotland, some talked about their experiences of living in challenging neighbourhoods, losing father figures at a young age or growing up in homes where their fathers were involved in gang-related crime. They also described mothers who struggled to cope or were unavailable to them in an emotional sense:

> My father died when I was small … I'm from a part of Copenhagen that is, let's call it 'challenged' – there's a lot of gang concentration and so on. (Jesper, Denmark)

> My father, when I was very young he was in [motorcycle gang] – the bikers. I finished high school and then my father went to jail … he got 15 years. (Stefan, Denmark)

> My mother got divorced from my real father when I was three months old … my dad was drinking and my mother threw him out … my mother was not there for me and I'd like her to be … giving me love and cuddle me and do things with me … because she was working, I missed that. (Ivan, Denmark)

Some of the ethnic minority men talked about the stigmatising nature of the Danish media and the police. Although they thought of their peer group that they offended with as a 'brotherhood' or 'community', they found that the 'gang' label was often placed on them and this then became an image that they started to embrace. The stigma and social exclusion that these men experienced was clearly exacerbated further among those who were imprisoned for specific gang-related offences, since they found themselves segregated and only able to have contact with other gang members. Gang-related and more individualised crime among some ethnic minority men was potentially linked to wider, more traumatic events that had blighted their childhoods. Several had transitioned to Denmark with their families as immigrants when they were children. Abbad described the way in which his father had become violent following his experience of being tortured in Palestine. Further, Yusuf had experienced his mother being shot dead when he was 10 years old because of an honour-related family conflict in Turkey, and

Ivan (who had become a drug dealer but not a gang member) had been exposed to a violent assault during the civil war in Africa, after his family had moved there from Macedonia:

> My father when he was young in Palestine ... had been tortured, so my father was very violent ... when I was a little boy, if I do the wrong thing he hit me, you know? (Abbad, Denmark)
>
> My mother died in 1996, I was 10. She was killed, she was shot ... when I was 10 years old – what you would call an honour-related family conflict ... I needed some security and acknowledgement, and I got that in the street. (Yusuf, Denmark)
>
> My mother got divorced from my father, then we went to Africa and there was a civil war ... I got brutally mugged in the city there, they stamped my head and broke my jaw. (Ivan, Denmark)

Some research has suggested clear links between early *exposure* to violent incidents, the development of stress and later *participation* in violence (Burton et al. 1994). Several other first generation immigrants in the Danish sample also described witnessing traumatic events as children and subsequently experiencing symptoms of post-traumatic stress disorder (PTSD). As in Los Angeles, the different forms of disadvantage, marginalisation and trauma that both the Scottish and Danish participants experienced ultimately led them into gang-related violence and other types of crime. This provided a channel for their anger and re-assertion of masculine status, but also in some cases created a context for expressing morality.

'Like the Premier League': Anger, Morality and Re-asserting Masculinity Through Gangs

The younger Scottish men I met in prison often indicated that they began to spend time out on the streets from a very young age. They quickly became influenced by their older peers and the need to defend key territories in their local housing schemes through gang fighting. Many began carrying knives for self-protection against both real and perceived threats, and as a means of gaining status:

6 Masculinity, Morality and Offending in Scotland and Denmark

You don't know, just people runnin' about wi' knives n'that ... I just started to get really paranoid actually and I started taking it [knife] to make me feel safer. (Gregor, Scotland)

People get a reputation, especially for gang fightin' n'that. 'I'm gonna go stab him 'cos he's hard and I'm gonna stab him just so I get my name up in the ranks' or whatever ... (Callum, Scotland)

Many of the Scottish men often talked about the seductive nature of the violence they engaged in and the enhanced local reputations (or 'street capital') they could gain from being known as good fighters (Deuchar 2009; Harding 2014; Densley and Stevens 2015). Box 6.1 illustrates the insights that Paul provided within the context of interviews I conducted with him during his lengthy period of incarceration.

> **Box 6.1:** *Paul's Story*
>
> Paul was born in one of the most socially deprived and disadvantaged neighbourhoods in the west of Scotland, just east of Glasgow. At the age of six, he was taken into care because of his family situation, where his mother was disabled and unable to look after him and his father had alcohol issues. For the next few years, he moved in and out of different care homes. Eventually, Paul's father died at the age of 12 after suffering from a series of strokes, and from this moment Paul increasingly began to experience intense feelings of resentment and recurring bouts of rage. He looked towards his older brother as a role model, but by this time his brother was very involved in gang-related violence out on the streets and was also actively selling drugs. His brother served several short-term prison sentences for the violent offending and drug dealing he had become involved in, and Paul slowly began to become involved in gang violence and to experiment with alcohol and recreational drugs himself. This ultimately led to addiction and mental health issues:
>
> *I used to take drink and drugs. I used drugs every day ... I was on valium, cocaine, cannabis, ecstasy ... I actually got addicted to drugs, and I ended up wi' mental health problems.*
>
> Over the next few years, Paul picked up charges for violent offences and was sent to several secure units. Each time he was released, he immediately became involved in recreational street violence and drug use again. He eventually experienced a drug-induced psychosis as a result of the cocktail of drugs he was taking. He also suffered from intense feelings of stress, which was later diagnosed as PTSD, as a direct result of some of the violent incidents that he had seen and participated in. In time,

> Paul realised that the incidents he had become involved in were directly related to the absence of a positive male role model in his life and the example that his brother had set for him:
>
> *My da' died so I never had a role model. I looked up to my brother, and my brother used to run the streets selling drug and gettin' the jail n'that. So I thought that was the life to go down.*
>
> At the age of 16, Paul served a short-term sentence in Scotland's largest YOI for gang-related violent offending. Following his release, Paul's girlfriend became pregnant. One evening when they were out together, they bumped into a young man who was a member of a rival gang from another housing scheme. The young man pushed Paul's girlfriend and Paul immediately reacted with anger. He pulled out the knife he had in his pocket and slashed the young man's face with it. He was later charged with serious assault and permanent disfigurement, and sent back to prison for five years.

Agnew et al. (2002) draw upon empirical data to highlight that juveniles high in negative emotionality and low in constraint are often more likely to react to the multiple 'strains' they may experience through violence. Paul clearly experienced early psychological distress relating to lack of positive male attachment as well as his mother's inability to look after him, his experience of being taken into care and his father's subsequent death. As his frustration and rage deepened and his drug dependency grew, increasingly severe forms of violence became a tool for masculine expression. His attack on the rival gang member when the latter pushed his girlfriend represented the wider culture of honour and intense need to uphold and defend a sense of 'heroic' respect as part of a street code that often exists among disadvantaged young men (Deuchar 2009; Harding 2014).

Much research has illustrated that delinquent behaviour tends to be higher among young people who are convicted in their teens than those unconvicted at similar ages, and that that those young people given stiffer sanctions tend to progress to more serious criminality (for review, see Deuchar and Bhopal 2017). The insights from Paul's case study corroborate with this. His experience of being sent to secure units and then to the YOI as a juvenile did not prevent him from reoffending, and the intensity of his violence continued to increase over time. His recurring

6 Masculinity, Morality and Offending in Scotland and Denmark   131

issues with drug addiction led on to mental health problems, which evidently intertwined with his offending behaviour.

In addition to engaging in the type of serious violent incidents that Paul described, several other Scottish interviewees talked about progressing from gang-related territorial behaviour to more serious crimes. For instance, as a teenager Fergus (like Paul) had no positive male role model in his life: his father had been convicted for culpable homicide and sentenced to a seven-year prison sentence when Fergus was aged 10. In his teens, Fergus became involved in heavy drinking, recreational drug use and gang violence, and he eventually served a three-year custodial sentence for serious assault and permanent disfigurement of a rival gang member. Upon his release at age 18, he and his friends had begun to engage in more serious organised forms of criminality when they carried out armed robberies together fuelled by heavy drug use:

> I was full o' drugs … and I'm like, 'let's do it then.' … ended up goin' up and trying to rob a jewellers and we robbed a mad guy and his bird [girlfriend] too, man … I held them up wi' a knife. (Fergus, Scotland)

Within three months of his release, Fergus found himself back in the YOI serving an extended sentence of seven years. Further, Tarone's experience of growing up with a missing father figure combined with his desire to make more money to support his mother led him to progress from gang-related territorial violence onto drug dealing and armed robbery:

> I started selling drugs … I was raised in poverty and so I was thinkin' money would … make shit a lot easier and better for my mum … I'm in [jail] for drugs and armed robbery. (Tarone, Scotland)

In Denmark, the interviewees also referred to the lack of positive role models in their lives and the social, structural and cultural disadvantage they experienced. They often became attracted to emulating those who were seen as the 'tough' and 'bad' guys and who were regarded as powerful and successful. This was the case for gang members (like Hans) but also for those who had been involved in robbery outwith gang contexts (like Lasse):

On the other side of the street there was ... these guys driving Harley Davidsons. They were a little bit older than we were, and a little bit more tough ... and when you are like 18/19/20 years old and some people who are 25 they want to talk to you ... and you are a boy ... then you feel something special. (Hans, Denmark)

I meet some guys and they really made money you know? Older guys, you know ... cool guys ... [I though] 'I can be like that', you know? ... it was money that turned me on. (Lasse, Denmark)

Box 6.2 describes the way in which Jesper's deeply-ingrained need for male attachment and reverence led on to many years of exerting his masculine identity through bodybuilding, steroid use and gang violence.

Box 6.2: *Jesper's Story*

Jesper was born and raised in one of the most disadvantaged areas of Copenhagen, with high levels of unemployment and frequent incidents relating to territorial gang violence out on the streets. His father died when he was small, and he was always searching for alternative male role models. As a young teenager he began to engage in street fighting before eventually joining one of the local street gangs. He admired the older men in the neighbourhood who were more established members of gangs, and who made money from drug dealing and drove nice cars, wore expensive clothes and attracted local girls.

As he slowly began to build his reputation as a street fighter, Jesper found that he got a 'rush' from the idea that people knew who he was, admired him for his violent behaviour but also feared him. His desire to be regarded as overtly masculine also led him to take up bodybuilding—gradually combining frequent heavy weight lifting with steroid use. By age 18, he weighed 125 kilogrammes, and his physical size, muscle mass and older appearance meant that he attracted even more attention from local gang members. He was approached and asked to become a member of a local biker gang and slowly became involved in serious firearms incidents. Following an altercation with one of the other members who had disrespected him, Jesper attacked him violently. His reputation then spread to members of the biker gang's major rivals and Jesper was approached to join the rival gang. He began to feel that he was treated with greater respect by its members as a result of his growing violent reputation, and slowly developed an arrogance associated with being part of what he regarded as the top tier of violent gang members in Danish society:

6 Masculinity, Morality and Offending in Scotland and Denmark   133

> *You begin to get even more of a connection, more ego because before I was looking at [biker gangs] like they were the big gangs ... the mafia, and you say 'wow, this is like the Premier League'.*
>
> As Jesper became more involved with the biker gang he had joined he came into close contact with an older guy called Marc, one of the more senior members of the gang who was very violent and had committed several murders. Jesper looked up to Marc with respect because of his violent credentials, while Marc admired Jesper because he was young, hungry for status, had the physical capital that came from several years of bodybuilding and steroid use and was willing to take on even the most dangerous and violent gang members. The attention that Jesper got from Marc gave him an even greater ego boost. He rose up to the senior ranks within the biker gang and eventually travelled to Finland to engage in drug dealing and to fight in gang wars. Eventually, at the age of 29 Jesper was arrested for the murder of a rival gang member and convicted to a 16-year prison sentence.

As a result of the multiple strains he experienced as a child (Agnew et al. 2002), Jesper became focused on revering the local older men who were respected for their toughness and their possessions. His ego was boosted by establishing a violent reputation, and this was further enhanced through his intense engagement in bodybuilding, fuelled by steroid misuse. Gillett and White (1992, p. 358) argue that the 'hypermasculine body' cultivated by male bodybuilders often symbolizes an attempt to 'restore feelings of masculine self-control and self-worth'. Sculpting a muscular physique with the support of anabolic-androgen steroids (AAS), combined with the increasing accumulation of violence capital, enabled Jesper to continually focus on his body as an instrument of physical performance and thus reassert his gender insecurity (Melki et al. 2015; Ravn and Coffey 2015).

Jesper's growing reputation and personal, physical attributes led him to gain attention from senior biker gang figures like Marc, which in turn boosted Jesper's ego more and eventually led to his positioning within the senior ranks of the biker gang world. The mobility that biker gang membership afforded him enabled him to enter international criminal networks and perhaps to evade law enforcement for longer (Bosmia et al. 2014). In many ways, Jesper's eventual transition to a lengthy prison sentence as a result of a gang-related murder was brought about as a result of his prolonged admiration for and celebration of toughness and hyper-masculinity. This was continually stimulated by an inner need for male attachment in the absence of a father figure or other positive nurturing role models.

Other Danish men I interviewed also suffered from the lack of emotional attachment within their family lives and felt disadvantaged by the lack of positive male role models. For example, both Ivan and Stefan had been (or were being accused of being) involved in dealing drugs (in Ivan's case on an individual basis, and in Stefan's case within a suspected gang context). Ivan described to me how his mother had thrown his father out of the house when he was small, while Stefan (as I referred to earlier) revealed that his father had been a gang member and was involved in drug dealing when he was growing up. In both cases, the men had turned towards bodybuilding and steroid use combined with drug dealing as a means of addressing their own and others' sense of gender insecurity and also gaining enhanced volumes of money and status:

> I started like coming to do weight training ... when you are bigger you feel more masculine ... then things started to roll out and I sell steroids ... [helping guys] getting bigger and bigger. (Ivan, Denmark)

> I got to be like 18 ... I was working out a lot so I didn't really drink alcohol ... but of course I was also taking steroids ... it was also about low self-esteem ... now, of course, I am here in this prison because ... at least the police think I have dealt with hard narcotics. (Stefan, Denmark)

In many other cases, the Danish men talked about the sense of brotherhood they sought and gained from gang membership. This was initially attractive but the loyalty that came from it was conditional on continually being able to display strength and solidarity, particularly among those who were members of biker gangs:

> Of course, it was a brotherhood ... back slapping each other and 'hi, good, cool' everything, like we're brothers, you know? And that's the way the life is when you're in it. (Lucas, Denmark)

6 Masculinity, Morality and Offending in Scotland and Denmark 135

> [I wanted] guys that will be around ... and stick by you and do things for you ... [name of gang], it's like a beautiful rose – it looks nice and it's beautiful but when you come close to the rose and you grab it, you meet the thorns ... and these thorns, they can cut really deep ... if you show any weakness, if you have the wrong opinions. (Damon, Denmark)

In both Scotland and Denmark it was apparent that many of the men's actions did not exist in a moral vacuum. Matthews (2002) discusses the way in which the whole issue of crime is infused with issues of morality, guilt and struggles over identity, while Yablonsky (2000) draws attention to the moral codes associated with gang members. Perhaps more so than in Los Angeles, the described offending behaviour in Scotland and Denmark (with the exception of the two men convicted for sex offences, where it was more difficult to discern) was punctuated throughout by a focus on moral and ethical values. For instance, as described above (in Scotland) Tarone was driven to make money through drug dealing to help his mother who lived in poverty. Gregor (referred to earlier) and also Andy, Martyn and several others explained to me that they carried knives to try and protect themselves, their fellow gang members and their housing schemes from risk. Further, as illustrated in Box 6.1 (above) Paul used violence to protect his pregnant girlfriend from one of his enemies. In addition, (in Denmark) it could be argued that Jesper, Ivan and Stefan viewed steroid use and distribution as a means of improving their own and other men's lifestyles and pursuing 'established' masculinity against the backdrop of marginalisation, as well as gaining economic gain from it (Atkinson 2007). And several of the Danish men such as Lucas and Damon (above) and also Søren made reference to the need for mutual loyalty and brotherhood within the context of biker gangs.

Accordingly, many of the men's offending patterns were a result of rational choices based on 'anticipated costs and benefits' (Cornish and Clarke 2014, p. xviii). Having entered a liminal phase while in prison, often characterised not only by social withdrawal but also personal introspection (Healy 2012), some had begun to reflect upon their behaviour and take initial steps to reorient their rational, moral codes in non-criminal directions.

Striving Towards a 'Normal Life': Reflections on 'Feared' and 'Possible' Selves

Having time to think and reflect while in the liminal carceral space combined with the anticipated generative commitments associated with potential future caring roles within the family were beginning to act as initial hooks for change for some of the interviewees (Giordano et al. 2002; Moran et al. 2013). For instance, in Scotland Keith had been in a segregated area of the YOI for over two years for sex offences when I met him, and realised that he did not want to spend the rest of his life there. Three weeks into his prison sentence, Stevie had also begun to experience strong feelings of regret and a deep awareness of his forthcoming role as an uncle when his sister gave birth:

> I hope to stay out of prison, get on the straight and narrow … the last thing I want to be doing is coming in and out of jail and spending my life in a prison. (Keith, Scotland)

> I just think what a fuckin' prick I've been to be honest …I don't want back in here all the time. I want oot there wi' my family, to see my wee niece or nephew when he's growin' up. (Stevie, Scotland)

Drawing on 'possible selves' theory (Paternoster and Bushway 2009, p. 1113), Healy (2012) draws attention to the way in which offenders' narratives in the liminal phase are often peppered with references to representations of the individuals they would like to become as well as the selves they would like to avoid. As with other men I interviewed, the above extract from Stevie's narrative focused on both his goals and fears; the aspiration to be involved in the life of his niece or nephew (his 'positive possible self') was complemented by his apprehension about becoming a persistent inmate (his 'feared self') (Paternoster and Bushway 2009, p. 1103). In Denmark, several of the men were already fathers when I met them and also expressed regret about their crimes and a desire to see their children grow up and be happy. Ahmed was segregated in prison because of his convictions related to being a senior

6 Masculinity, Morality and Offending in Scotland and Denmark

member of a large immigrant street gang. He had a strong desire not to die in prison and a yearning to see his daughter get married, while Ivan was nearing the end of his first prison sentence and was motivated to stay away from crime because of his young son:

> I would like to see my daughter get married. I want all of them to be happy … if you die what do you take with you? Anything? It's only the coffin that you can take. (Ahmed, Denmark)

> I don't want him [son] to see me in jail no more, this is the first and the last time … I have my kid, my wife, my house. (Ivan, Denmark)

Accordingly, parenthood was carefully intertwined with generativity and the forming of aspirational identities and 'desired selves' (Paternoster and Bushway 2009, p. 1119; see also Healy 2012, p. 111). In Denmark, there was also a tendency for interviewees to express a feeling of simply being tired of their violent lifestyles and developing a desire for a more peaceful and 'normal' life (Healy 2012):

> I want somewhere to go and it is free and there's no violence and there's no gangs. (Umar, Denmark)

> [I want] a good life, a normal life … family and … I dream about a house. (Patric, Denmark)

> When I read the papers of people getting shot all the time, I'm glad that I'm not part of this. I don't want this life with this stress in it any more. (Damon, Denmark)

In a similar way to those I met in Los Angeles, the conversations I had with some of the Scottish and Danish offenders while in the liminal phase were evidently characterised by a subtle, almost spiritual focus on searching for purpose and meaning and morally fulfilling relationships with others (Patel et al. 1998; Lindsay 2002). As illustrated above, several had begun to reassess themselves, to express regret and remorse and to gain an increased desire to give back to others and to live peaceful, non-violent lifestyles (Giordano et al. 2002; Paternoster and Bushway 2009).

Concluding Discussion

Although there are significant differences in terms of poverty rates in Denmark compared to Scotland, it was evident that there were still issues of relative economic inequality as well as social deprivation and disadvantage experienced by the men I interviewed in both countries. They had clearly experienced early marginalisation, emotional insecurity and (in some cases) trauma. Gender insecurity also played a prominent role in their transition into gang membership and (in some cases) criminality aside from gang culture, including (in a small number of cases) sex offences in Scotland and robbery or individualised drug dealing in Denmark. Those who were from ethnic minority groups and first generation immigrants in Denmark clearly experienced feelings of stigmatism at the hands of the Danish media and police, and in some cases this was exacerbated by the lingering impact from traumatic experiences they had had during their childhoods and even further by their segregation in prison.

Some Scottish interviewees drew attention to the way in which knife-carrying often came about as a result of a widespread focus on territoriality and a perceived need for self-protection; that deeply-ingrained anger and aggression was further fuelled by alcohol and drug misuse; and that recreational, territorial violence was seen as a re-assertion of marginalised masculinity. While confined to a minority, some young Scottish males clearly experienced gang violence as an escalator to more serious forms of criminality—mostly focused on drug dealing and armed robbery (Densley and Stevens 2015; McLean 2017; McLean et al. 2017), while two others had evidently become involved in dealing with their sense of disadvantage and marginalisation through sexual offending as opposed to gang violence or organised criminality.

In Denmark, it appeared that bodybuilding and steroid misuse played a more prominent role in the re-assertion of hegemonic masculinity than it did in Scotland; that the accumulation of respect and personal ego through hyper-masculine body images, ruthlessness and toughness and the acquiring of materialistic possessions was very much to the fore; and that building a sense of 'brotherhood' and 'loyalty' was conditional on continued displays of solidarity (Søgaard et al. 2016). Unlike in Scotland it appeared that the Danes I interviewed progressed more quickly and routinely to serious organised forms of criminality. This was particularly the case among those who became involved in biker gang membership and gained the mobility that this afforded them to widen criminal networks and evade law enforcement for longer (Bosmia et al. 2014).

Although it was more difficult to explore and examine the exact details of the offending lifestyles of the two sex offenders in the sample, the insights from interviews conducted with the majority of the men in both counties suggested that their motivations for violence and wider criminality were often guided by rational and moral decision-making. For some, their initial motivations for changing their lifestyles (as in Los Angeles) were characterised by a subtle focus on morality and an almost spiritual yearning for purpose and meaning (Lindsay 2002). Against the backdrop of feeling ready for change while in the liminal carceral space but (in most cases) still limited in their capability to test their capacity to desist due to continued incarceration and/or as a result of wider traumatic circumstances, some of the men in Scotland and all of the men in Denmark had begun to seek out religious or spiritual support. While some sought the support of prison chaplains, others (in Denmark only) became engaged with trained yoga and meditation instructors.

While it was beyond the scope of my research to track the subsequent transitional journeys of those men I had met in Scotland who did not engage in religious/spiritual interventions at all, I was able to explore the experiences of those Scottish and Danish participants who did. Across the pages of the next two chapters I examine the nature of the support this sub-section of men received and the deeper shifts in cognitions, identities and social circumstances that they experienced as a result.

References

Agnew, R., Brezina, T., Wright, J. P., & Cullen, F. T. (2002). Strain, personality traits and delinquency: Extending general strain theory. *Criminology, 40*, 43–72.

Anderson, L. H., Anker, A. S. T., & Anderson, A. H. (2016). A formal decomposition of declining youth crime in Denmark. *Demographic Research, 35*(44), 1303–1316.

Atkinson, M. (2007). Playing with fire: Masculinity, health, and sports supplements. *Sociology of Sport Journal, 24*(2), 165–186.

Audit Scotland. (2012). *Reducing reoffending in Scotland*. Edinburgh: Audit Scotland.

Bosmia, A. N., Quinn, J. F., Peterson, T. B., Griessenauer, C. J., & Tubbs, R. S. (2014). Outlaw motorcycle gangs: Aspects of the one-percenter culture for emergency department personnel to consider. *Western Journal of Emergency Medicine, 15*(4), 523–528.

Burton, D., Foy, D., Bwanausi, J. J., & Moore, L. (1994). The relationship between traumatic exposure, family dysfunction, and post-traumatic stress symptoms in male juvenile offenders. *Journal of Traumatic Stress, 7*(1), 83–93.

Connell, R. W. (2005). *Masculinities*. Cambridge: Policy Press.

Cornish, D. B., & Clarke, R. V. (Eds.). (2014). *The reasoning criminal: Rational choice perspectives on offending*. New Brunswick, NJ: Transaction.

CPHPost Online. (2017). *Steep rise in violent assaults in Copenhagen*. Available at: http://cphpost.dk/news/steep-rise-in-violent-assaults-in-copenhagen.html. Accessed 17 June 2017.

Davies, A. (2013). *City of gangs: Glasgow and the rise of the British gangster*. London: Hodder and Stoughton.

Densley, J., & Stevens, A. (2015). 'We'll show you a gang': The subterranean structuration of gang life in London. *Criminology and Criminal Justice, 15*(1), 102–120.

Deuchar, R. (2009). *Gangs, marginalized youth and social capital*. Stoke on Trent: Trentham.

Deuchar, R. (2016). Youth gangs in Scotland. In H. Croall, G. Mooney, & M. Munro (Eds.), *Crime, justice and society in Scotland* (pp. 67–81). London: Routledge.

Deuchar, R., & Bhopal, K. (2017). *Young people and social control: Problems and prospects from the margins*. Basingstoke: Palgrave MacMillan.

Deuchar, R., Morck, L., Matemba, Y. H., McLean, R., & Riaz, N. (2016). 'It's as if you're not in jail, as if you're not a prisoner': Young male offenders' experiences of incarceration, prison chaplaincy, religion and spirituality in Scotland and Denmark. *The Howard Journal of Crime and Justice, 55*(1–2), 131–150.

Deuchar, R., Friis Søgaard, T., Holligan, C., Miller, K., Bone, A., & Borchardt, L. (2018). Social capital and connectedness in Scottish and Danish neighbourhoods: Paradoxes of a police-community nexus at the front line. *Journal of Scandinavian Studies in Criminology and Crime Prevention*, 1–17. https://doi.org/10.1080/14043858.2018.1448157.

Fraser, A. (2015). *Urban legends: Gang identity in the post-industrial city*. Oxford: Oxford University Press.

Gillett, J., & White, P. G. (1992). Male bodybuilding and the reassertion of hegemonic masculinity: A critical feminist perspective. *Play and Culture, 5*(4), 358–369.

Giordano, P. C., Cernkovich, S. A., & Rudolph, J. L. (2002). Gender, crime, and desistance: Toward a theory of cognitive transformation. *American Journal of Sociology, 107*(4), 990–1064.

Harding, S. (2014). *The street casino: Survival in violent street gangs*. Bristol: Policy Press.

Hayden, C. (2010). Offending behaviour in care: Is residential care a 'criminogenic' environment? *Child and Family Social Work, 15*(4), 461–472.

Healy, D. (2012). *The dynamics of desistance: Charting pathways through change*. New York: Routledge.

Johnson, S. A. (2007). *Physical abusers and sexual offenders: Forensic and clinical strategies*. London: Taylor and Francis.

Lindsay, R. (2002). *Recognizing spirituality: The interface between faith and social work*. Crawley: University of Western Australia Press.

Matthews, R. (2002). *Armed robbery*. Devon: Willan Publishing.

McLean, R. (2017). An evolving gang model in contemporary Scotland. *Deviant Behaviour*, 1–13. https://doi.org/10.1080/01639625.2016.1272969.

McLean, R., Densley, J., & Deuchar, R. (2017). Situating gangs within Scotland's illegal drug market(s). *Trends in Organized Crime*. https://doi.org/10.1007/s12117-017-9328-1.

Mellon, M. (2011). Research: How Scotland is failing young people in residential care. *Community Care*. Available at: http://www.communitycare.co.uk/2011/05/26/research-how-scotland-is-failng-young-people-in-residential-care. Accessed 15 June 2017.

Melki, J. P., Hitti, E. A., Oghia, M. J., & Mufarrij, A. A. (2015). Media exposure, mediated social comparison to idealized images of muscularity, and anabolic steroid use. *Health Communication, 30*(5), 473–484.

Messerschmidt, J. W. (2000). Becoming 'real men': Adolescent masculinity challenges and sexual violence. *Men and Masculinities, 2*(3), 286–307.

Moran, D., Piacentini, L., & Pallot, J. (2013). Liminal transcarceral space: Prison transportation for women in the Russian Federation. In D. Moran, N. Gill, & D. Conlon (Eds.), *Carceral spaces: Mobility and agency in imprisonment and migrant detention* (pp. 109–124). New York: Routledge.

Mørck, L. L., Hussain, K., Møller-Andersen, C., Özüpek, T., Palm, A. M., & Vorbeck, I. H. (2013). Praxis development in relation to gang conflicts in Copenhagen Denmark. *Outlines—Critical Practice Studies, 14*(2), 79–105.
Patel, N., Naik, D., & Humphries, B. (Eds.). (1998). *Visions of reality: Religion and ethnicity in social work*. London: Central Council for Education and Training in Social Work.
Paternoster, R., & Bushway, S. (2009). Desistance and the feared self: Towards an identity theory of criminal desistance. *Journal of Criminal Law and Criminology, 99*(4), 1103–1156.
Patrick, J. (1973). *A Glasgow gang observed*. London: Eyre Methuen.
Pederson, M. L., & Linstad, J. M. (2011). The Danish gang-joining project: Methodological issues and preliminary results. In F.-A. Esbensen & C. L. Maxson (Eds.), *Youth gangs in international perspective* (pp. 239–250). New York: Springer.
Ravn, S., & Coffey, J. (2015). 'Steroids, it's so much an identity thing!' Perceptions of steroid use, risk and masculine body image. *Journal of Youth Studies, 19*(1), 87–102.
Scottish Government. (2017). *Recorded crime in Scotland*. Available at: http://www.gov.scot/Resource/0052/00525055.pdf. Accessed 31 December 2017.
Søgaard, T. F., Houborg, E., & Tutenges, S. (2013). Nightlife partnership policing: (Dis)trust building between bouncers and the police in the war on gangs. *Nordisk Politiforskning, 3*(2), 132–153.
Søgaard, T. F., Kolind, T., Thylstrup, B., & Deuchar, R. (2016). Desistance and the micro-narrative construction in a Danish rehabilitation centre. *Criminology and Criminal Justice, 16*(1), 99–108.
Statistica. (2017). *Number of homicides in Denmark from 2006 to 2016*. Available at: https://www.statista.com/statistics/576114/number-of-homicides-in-denmark/. Accessed 17 June 2017.
Von Hofer, H., Lappi-Seppälä, T., & Westfelt, L. (2012). *Nordic criminal statistics 1950–2010*. Stockholm: Stockholm University.
Yablonsky, L. (2000). *Juvenile delinquency into the 21st Century*. Belmont, CA: Wadsworth and Thomson Learning.

7

Support in Times of Trouble: Chaplaincy in Scottish and Danish Prisons

In this chapter, I draw on insights from follow-up semi-structured interviews that I conducted with one smaller sub-sample of the men in Scottish and Danish prisons, as well as additional interviews with Christian and Muslim prison chaplains. I examine the way in which chaplains conducted religious and spiritual study groups and engaged in recreational pastimes and supportive one-to-one discussions with inmates. I consider the impact that the chaplains and the religious study groups and practices were having on the men's values, attitudes and self-identities while in the liminal phase (Healy 2012). I present case studies that illustrate the turning points and journeys that particular inmates experienced. I then draw conclusions about the way in which prison chaplaincy may provide added value in terms of nurturing a sense of peace, wellbeing, fulfillment and desistance-related attitudes amongst male gang members and offenders.

© The Author(s) 2018
R. Deuchar, *Gangs and Spirituality*,
https://doi.org/10.1007/978-3-319-78899-9_7

The Religious, Spiritual and Pastoral Service of Prison Chaplains

International research evidence illustrates the wide-ranging nature of the prison chaplain's role that goes far beyond simply looking after the religious and spiritual needs of prisoners (Deuchar and Bhopal 2017). Some insights suggest that chaplains often integrate religious and secular beliefs into their counselling of inmates (Sundt et al. 2002). At times, chaplains may help inmates to reflect on the reasons for their incarceration and (in some cases) re-establish connections to an underlying moral (but not necessarily religious) framework (Webber 2014). It has been found that diverse sections of prison populations of various faiths and no faith benefit from the humanitarian, compassionate role of chaplaincy services as an important support mechanism, particularly during times of personal struggle (Tipton 2011; Armstrong 2014).

Research conducted in England and Wales illustrates that chaplains tend to have more time to devote to supporting prisoners compared to other types of care teams. They 'make availability a priority' and offer 'alternative locations' for inmates where they can feel safe and secure (Tipton 2011, p. 4). Other findings also suggest that some chaplaincy services continue to offer intensive levels of support to offenders once they leave custody. They adopt a vision to 'walk with marginalised and excluded ex-prisoners' on difficult journeys because of accumulated problems associated with family issues, disadvantaged employment prospects and vulnerability associated with addiction and/or mental health issues (Whitehead 2011, p. 5).

In addition to their strong person-centred, unconditional pastoral roles, some other research (Johnson and Larson 2003) has demonstrated that chaplaincy services may support and guide inmates in discovering a new religious faith or rediscovering a lost faith from their childhood. Johnson and Larson (2003, p. 28) explore the nature of the 'prison code'—the dominant subculture within male prisons that tends to prioritise displays of machismo and promotes the message that showing love, compassion or affection is a sign of weakness (for further discussion on this, see Deuchar and Bhopal 2017). They discuss the premise that personal transformation and growth through religious faith can provide an antidote to this subculture, and suggest that male prisoners may eventually begin to prioritise their faith and commitment to God over the prison code.

In Maruna et al.'s (2006) work, prisoners who actively experienced religious conversion in prison were also found to articulate conversion narratives that were characterised by perceptions that they were forgiven by God and had optimistic plans for the future. In many ways these narratives shared many similarities with the 'redemption scripts' highlighted in Maruna's (2001) work where offenders found meaning in their experiences of crime and imprisonment combined with a desire to 'give something back' to the wider world (Maruna et al. 2006, p. 181). Further, in Johnson and Larson's (2003) work in Texas, they too found that inmates who participated in Christian-based pre-release programmes felt compelled to 'give back to society' and ultimately reported reduced rates of recidivism.

However, as I alluded to in Chapter 3 there are some sceptical voices regarding the work of prison chaplaincy and prison religiosity. Scholars such as Clear and Sumter (2002) have identified other reasons for inmates' involvement with chaplains and religious participation. These include prisoners using religious participation as a way to 'return' to some normalcy when they interact with outsiders, or to receive refreshments (many chaplaincy services provide tea and coffee) and other contraband (Deuchar et al. 2016). This evidence suggests that, for some inmates, engaging with chaplaincy may simply be a means of gaining personal benefits while incarcerated as opposed to developing authentic religious faith and/or nurturing personal reflection and introspection.

In spite of the critical perspectives that exist, there is also a great deal of wider evidence to suggest that prison chaplains may do very valuable work in terms of providing supportive, trusting relationships and also facilitating new or revitalized religious faith that helps to strengthen a focus on generativity. Clearly, this could potentially represent a strong 'pull' factor for offenders in the liminal phase to begin to seriously consider leaving gang lifestyles and criminality behind, particularly if they have already begun to feel ready for change and began to reassess their lifestyles (Decker et al. 2014). It could potentially enable them to undertake preliminary 'agentic moves' that form the beginning of evolving self-narratives conducive to masculine identity reconstruction and desistance-related attitudes (Hallett and McCoy 2014, p. 12).

Insights into the Impact of Chaplaincy in Scottish and Danish Prisons

In this chapter I focus on describing the additional insights I gained from a smaller sub-group of the men I worked with more intensively in Scottish and Danish prisons. Each of these 13 men had—for one reason or another—sought out contact with prison chaplains while in prison and were willing to engage in further discussion with me about their experiences. During intermittent visits to the prisons, I interviewed them but also had wider, informal discussions with them during their participation in recreational activities and study groups. Table 7.1 provides details of the sub-section of males who participated in this phase of the research, listing their ages, countries of birth and residence and indicating whether they were already sentenced or being held on remand.

Table 7.1 The sub-group of research participants engaged with Prison Chaplaincy

Name	Age	Country of origin	Country of residence	Sentenced/remand
Fergus	20	Scotland	Scotland	Sentenced
Adam	20	Scotland	Scotland	Sentenced
Tarone	20	Jamaica	Scotland	Sentenced
Connor	19	Scotland	Scotland	Sentenced
Paul	19	Scotland	Scotland	Sentenced
Keith	21	Scotland	Scotland	Sentenced
Martyn	20	Scotland	Scotland	Sentenced
Stefan	24	Poland	Denmark	Remand
Umar	23	Denmark	Denmark	Remand
Yusuf	28	Turkey	Denmark	Sentenced
Ahmed	28	Kuwait	Denmark	Sentenced
Patric	40	Denmark	Denmark	Remand
Søren	37	Denmark	Denmark	Sentenced

To re-cap on these men's offending histories, in Scotland five of the participants had been involved in—and sentenced for—gang-related crime while two (Adam and Keith) had been convicted for sex offences. During my extended discussions with them, it came to light that two of the participants came from families where their parents had regularly taken part in religious practice. Connor, who was white and had been born in Edinburgh, and Tarone, who was black and had been born in Jamaica before moving to Scotland, had both been raised by Christian mothers and Muslim fathers. Three of the other men (Paul, Adam and Fergus) also talked about having had some exposure to Christianity during their childhoods, while the two remaining participants (Keith and Martyn) had no religious background and no prior interest in it at all.

In Denmark, three members of the sub-group of inmates I worked with had been convicted while a further three were on 'remand' awaiting their trials. Five had been involved in gang-related violence and crime. One other (Stefan, as referred to in Chapter 6) was awaiting his trial for suspected gang-related drug dealing, but claimed during my interviews with him that his offending had taken place *outwith* the context of gangs. Two of the participants (Umar and Ahmed) disclosed that they had grown up in Muslim homes where the family was dutiful in worship. One participant (Stefan) revealed that he had a Catholic mother, another (Patric) had grown up in a Christian home and the two remaining participants (Yusuf and Søren) described how they had been raised in non-religious homes.

In both the Danish and Scottish prisons, Christian chaplains (also known as priests and ministers) from different churches were working closely together with Muslim chaplains. They shared office space and non-institutionalised meeting rooms where they met with inmates, shared coffee and had informal discussions with them. In the Danish prisons I visited, one Christian chaplain had established a regular football training initiative that was inclusive of all religions and none, and in Scotland the chaplains had set up film clubs and opportunities for engaging in recreational activities such as pool and table tennis. Christian and Muslim chaplains also regularly collaborated on the organisation of shared study groups in both Scotland and Denmark.

In addition to the insights I gained from male inmates (in Table 7.1), I also conducted exploratory semi-structured interviews or had informal discussions with three Christian chaplains and one Muslim chaplain who worked in the YOI in Scotland, as well as two Christian chaplains and one Muslim chaplain who worked in the prisons I visited in Denmark. I also interviewed one additional Danish chaplain, Maddi, who had a Christian background but who had also studied Islam. Maddi regularly arranged inter-faith study groups for inmates drawing on her dual insights into Christian and Islamic doctrine.

In the following sections, I report on the insights gained from the male participants during interviews and informal discussions in relation to the nature and perceived impact of the chaplaincy services. I also provide some supplementary insights gleaned from interviews and/or discussions with a selection of the prison chaplains. Case studies are included that illustrate the turning points and evolving journeys experienced by one Scottish and one Danish inmate, as well as more generic insights from the other participants.

Social and Emotional Support and Reducing Pressure from the 'Prison Code'

In spite of their variable religious backgrounds (described briefly above), all of the men in both Scotland and Denmark described the way in which they had begun to feel a need for some type of support from the chaplaincy service while in prison. This sometimes came about as they began to search for wider meaning and purpose in life and as they became more motivated towards change (as with some of the offenders described at the end of Chapter 6). In other cases, it came about as they found themselves grappling with pain, emotional distress and trauma. In some cases, the men disclosed that they had suffered from mental health issues during their incarceration. In both Scotland and Denmark, they revealed that they did not talk to other inmates about the trauma of prison life because of their deeply-entrenched perceptions of hegemonic masculinity and the dominance of the 'prison code' (Johnson and Larson 2003, p. 28). This included a tendency to avoid public displays of behaviour that could be in any way associated with softness or femininity (see McFarlane 2013).

Furthermore, the men had a clear lack of trust in prison guards since they viewed their role as purely custodial and found them distrustful and disrespectful (Deuchar et al. 2016; Deuchar and Bhopal 2017). Against this backdrop, they felt that prison chaplains were the ones who made them feel like human beings again:

> They talk to us like normal human beings, know what I mean? ... They talk to you like a fuckin' pal, like a family member. (Fergus, Scotland)

> Everywhere else in jail, you know, you're in a jail and it feels like a jail. But in here, in here it feels as if you're not, kind of outside in a way, like a bit more relaxed. (Martyn, Scotland)

Adam was one of the small number of men in the Scottish sample who had not been convicted for gang offences but (in his case) for sex offences. As detailed in Chapter 6, he had grown up in a home where the male members of his family had difficulty communicating, and this had led him to struggle in social contexts. He explained that having the opportunity to have an open and trusting informal relationship with chaplains enabled him to begin to open up emotionally:

> It's only really this last few months that I've opened up emotionally ... I turn to the chaplains more for things that are on my mind for a given time. (Adam, Scotland)

In his work in Rio de Janeiro prisons, Johnson (2017) raises the observation that the support offered by the Christian church is especially valued by convicted sex offenders, given their vulnerable status. During wider discussions I had with the Christian prison chaplains, they indicated that it was common to find that those young men convicted of sex offences in Scotland (like Adam, above) would regularly attend their study groups and seek out pastoral support.

Chaplains felt that an important initial element of the 'humanizing' process was ensuring that inmates were exposed to opportunities for collaborating together in groups and gaining life skills. As touched on above, in both Scotland and Denmark Christian and Muslim chaplains often collaborated on the organisation of recreational activities and study groups. In study groups, they sometimes used texts from various religions including Christianity and Islam, and other times used secular texts or drew on current affairs or historical events as the basis for shared intellectual discussion. In Danish prisons, those who had been convicted (or remanded in custody) for specific gang-related offences often found that they could participate in these activities and groups only with those who were from their own street or biker gang due to prison segregation rules, while sex offenders in Scotland generally also only participated with other more isolated inmates. The segregation issues apart, in both countries initial informal contact between inmates and chaplains through recreational activities or study groups could often lead on to inmates seeking out confidential one-to-one supportive counselling sessions in response to personal and sensitive issues.

Against the backdrop of an otherwise 'painful' prison experience to add to the existing multiple 'strains' that the men had experienced as young adults, the emotional support that chaplains offered was seen as refreshing (Sundt et al. 2002). In Chapter 6, I made reference to Stefan's experiences of growing up in a family where his father was a member of a prominent biker gang and a convicted drug dealer. Although Stefan claimed that he had resisted becoming involved in biker gang membership, he described his transition to steroid dependency as a young adult and his eventual narcotics charge. Box 7.1 illustrates the positive emotional impact that chaplaincy began to have on Stefan following his experience of depression and suicidal tendencies in prison.

> **Box 7.1:** *Stefan's Transition from Depression, Suicidal Thoughts and Anxiety*
>
> Stefan was arrested on suspicion of drugs charges at the age of 24, and placed on remand in prison in Denmark. He was put in an isolation wing because it was suspected that he had been involved in gang-related dealing of large quantities of amphetamines, cocaine and marijuana. Prior to his arrest, he had been coming towards the end of his latest cycle of anabolic steroids connected to his ongoing bodybuilding regime. While in isolation, his initial feelings of aggression and anger gradually evolved into

anxiety, depression and suicidal thoughts. His first two months in prison were therefore very traumatic for him:

Everything was as black as it could be ... I remember when I was going to bed that I hoped I wouldn't wake up. And maybe my heart would stop ... I don't know how many times I was sitting with my belt ... I just couldn't do it, but I just wished so much I was dead.

During these early weeks in prison, Stefan was offered no medical help or personal support while he was suffering from the withdrawal effects from steroids. Eventually, a nurse came to visit him in his cell and asked him questions about his mental health. She saw that Stefan was in need of support and suggested that he could write a note to request to see one of the prison chaplains. Although Stefan's mother had been Catholic and he felt he had some belief in God, he was sceptical about some Biblical stories and themes. Nonetheless, he wrote a note and asked to meet with one of the Christian chaplains. Within a few days, Casper (the senior Christian chaplain) came to meet him; Stefan told him about all of his experiences, and shared his dark emotions with him:

I was telling him everything, you know? I was broken down. So he was like, 'be strong, you have to.' He was telling me stories about others, like everyone in the beginning thinks it's very bad ... but 'it gets brighter and brighter, just believe it.'

Casper continued to visit Stefan in isolation and once he was released back into the main part of the prison Stefan began to visit Casper in the chaplaincy office space, where he had informal discussions and enjoyed coffee and cookies. He felt a sense of liberation when he was in the chaplaincy office because he felt normal again. In contrast to his experiences with prison guards, who were mostly aggressive and unhelpful, he found it easy to open up to Casper because of his caring, open-minded approach. Casper later invited Stefan to participate in a mini-retreat within the prison, where he and another three male inmates spent four days together, engaging in silent meditation and contemplation alongside four Christian chaplains. Stefan found that participating in the retreat forced him to move away from the feeling he had to present himself in a way that would impress the other guys:

You actually don't stress yourself about what to say. You don't have to impress anyone at the table. You are just in the moment. Actually that was relieving in some ways, I think. I just had to sit there and actually don't think about anything ... I don't have to impress anyone ... being the cool guy ... there's just silence.

Through the continual support of Casper and the experience of engaging in the retreat, Stefan experienced a greater sense of peace and began to

> feel his depression lift. He also felt less inclined to feel angry and aggressive. At the same time, he began seeing a psychologist to talk about and get some support with his dependency issues related to steroids

Stefan's desire to address his 'deep-seated feeling of inadequacy' arising from his early childhood and family experiences and to attain a sense of status through hypermasculine displays of physical strength and muscularity led him to abuse Anabolic Androgenic Steroids (AASs) (Klein 1993, p. 280). It also led him to engage in suspected drug dealing. As discussed in Chapter 6, the long-term use of AASs among male bodybuilders can often lead to significant psychiatric symptoms including aggression, violence and even psychosis and suicidal tendencies (Trenton and Currier 2005). Stefan's traumatic experience of being placed in the isolation wing of the prison while suffering the psychotic effects of steroid withdrawal led him to seek solace in prison chaplaincy.

In a previous study of Catholic Prison Ministry in Australia, Webber (2014) illustrates that inmates found chaplains to be non-judgmental which helped to establish and maintain trust. Armstrong's (2014) work in England also illustrates that prison chaplains offer 'unearned proactive trust' to inmates and work hard to nurture positive communication, compassion and connection through vulnerability (pp. 306, 309). The insights from Stefan's experiences illustrate that the non-judgmental approach and unconditional positive regard that prison chaplaincy offers can enhance inmates' self esteem at times of crisis. Even although Stefan was not overtly religious and was sceptical about some Christian doctrine, the provision that Casper offered came in the form of social and emotional support that was mostly unconnected to religion, and largely unavailable from other sources (Whitehead 2013).

Beyond his experiences in isolation, informal discussions over coffee with Casper stimulated feelings of integration and normalcy. Stefan's participation in the mediation-based retreat helped to reverse the influence of the 'prison code' by removing the pressure to display acts of masculine 'bravado' (Johnson and Larson 2003, p. 28; Deuchar et al. 2016). His emerging feelings of calmness, peace and security were therefore largely related to his exposure to comforting, trusting and non-judgmental relationships with Casper and the other chaplains during periods of isolation, emotional trauma and psychological illness (Sundt and Cullen 2002).

Several other inmates I spoke to, particularly among the younger men in Scotland, described the way in which contact with chaplains helped them to deal more effectively with ongoing mental health issues including depression. For instance, Adam (who had been convicted for sex offences) described how he had been put on 'suicide watch' during the early part of his sentence because of previous mental health issues. As described earlier, his contact with the chaplains had led him to begin to open up emotionally, although he later admitted to me that he was 'still not very good at shedding a tear'. In addition, Tarone (who had been involved in gang-related offences) admitted that, the more he talked to chaplains, the more he found that he was able to 'refurbish his mental state'. Further insights into the way in which wider spiritual practices helped to address issues of depression and mental illness among Danish prisoners can be found in Chapter 8.

It was clearly evident that Stefan and some of the other male inmates I have referred to in this section gained most from the non-religious, confidential emotional support offered to them by prison chaplains. However, some of the men I interviewed had initial informal and largely secular discussions with chaplains but then later became more engaged in reading religious texts and engaging in worship and prayer. In turn, they began to apply the lessons and insights they gained from this to their own life circumstances. These particular insights are now explored in more detail.

'Times of Trouble', Religion, Prayer, Values and Identities

In Scotland, both Christian and Islamic chaplains highlighted that one of the most common reasons that the inmates requested a one-to-one meeting with them was because of unresolved bereavement issues from the past or because they were currently grieving a personal loss:

> Bereavement issues … are huge with this age-group. The number of kids in here who have come to get involved in drugs and alcohol often as a

result of a significant adult in their life disappearing, usually as a result of early death through cancer or drug abuse or whatever else … and being completely unresolved and undealt with. (Edward, Christian chaplain: Scotland)

Sometimes it'll be a request, someone wants to speak to me … I'll go down and speak to them, find out how they are … some people, they'll be going through bereavement. (Aafa, Muslim chaplain: Scotland)

On some occasions, the men in Scotland described the way in which their initial meetings with chaplains led on to a deeper engagement with religion. In the previous chapter, I outlined the challenges that Paul faced as a young man that led on to him engaging in increasingly severe forms of violence as a tool for masculine expression. He was ultimately charged with serious assault and permanent disfigurement when he attacked a rival gang member who disrespected his girlfriend on the street. Box 7.2 illustrates the additional insights I gained from Paul during his prison sentence. It documents the way in which informal engagement with one of the Christian chaplains led on to deeper levels of support against the backdrop of bereavement, and ultimately to a re-igniting of Paul's Christian faith.

> **Box 7.2:** *Paul's Experience of Personal Support, Faith, Prayer* **and** *Forgiveness*
>
> During the early part of his five-year prison sentence in Scotland's largest YOI, Paul often felt restless and angry and on occasions he was sent to the isolation unit for assaults on other prisoners and staff. Once back in the mainstream prison, he began to participate in a film club that was organised by one of the Christian prison chaplains. He found that Ryan, the young chaplain, talked informally to him and the other young men who were there and that they were able to have a laugh with him. When Paul found out that his girlfriend had lost the baby they were expecting, Ryan visited him in his cell a few times and supported him during this difficult time. Paul began to place great trust in Ryan, because he knew that anything he said to him would remain confidential.
>
> Paul's mother and father had been brought up as Roman Catholics, and when he was younger Paul had felt that he would have liked to have been baptised. However, after he was taken into care as a young boy this never took place, and Paul eventually lost interest in religion. After engaging

informally with Ryan in the film club and in his cell, Paul contacted Daniel, the Catholic Chaplain within the prison, and began to talk to him about Catholicism and the process of baptism. He also began to engage in study groups that Daniel ran where he explored stories and themes from the Bible. When Paul found out that his grandmother had died, Daniel came to his cell and prayed with him and also arranged a small mass for him. Paul's interest in Christianity began to deepen, and he was eventually baptised while he was in prison and was given his own Bible and rosary beads to use while praying in his cell. He slowly began to feel that praying enabled him to feel close to his late father, who he had lost when he was aged 12:

I get to pray to my dad. It feels as if he's alongside me if I dae that ... that's one of the main reasons I really started going to chaplaincy because I wanted to feel close to my dad.

Paul gradually began to ensure that he went to mass every Friday. He regarded the chaplains as solid role models. He felt that they treated him with respect; they took time to get to know him and had been there for him during his lowest points. Paul was convinced that, if it had not been for the support that the chaplains offered him, he would have been in a much worse place:

If it wasn't for Ryan and the support of Ryan and Father Daniel and Edward when my gran n'that died and when my girlfriend lost the baby, it wouldnae have been so easy. And I maybe would no' have got out of that bad place that I was in at the time.

As Paul was nearing the end of his sentence, he felt that the time he had spent in prayer and talking and engaging with the chaplains had helped him to change, and was beginning to feel that God had given him a second chance:

When I pray to God I always ask for forgiveness from making mistakes, and ... I feel in myself that God has forgiven me and has given me the second chance to push forward and look towards the future.

Paul's renewed faith and his sense of being forgiven for his violent crimes combined with the personal support that he had received from the chaplains had made him feel more secure, less inclined to be aggressive and violent and more ready and willing to support others. Instead of getting involved in fighting in the prison, he had begun to help other young inmates who were newly incarcerated, taking time to explain the daily routines to them and giving them small supplies of toothpaste and shower gel when they arrived in their cells at first. Paul was looking forward to being released, and had new ambitions to become a personal fitness trainer while also spending time looking after his disabled mother.

Vaswani (2014) draws attention to the high rates of traumatic and multiple deaths that young male offenders in Scotland have experienced, and the negative impact this has on their mental health while in custody. During the early part of his sentence, the combined experience of mourning the loss of his unborn child followed by grieving for his grandmother led Paul to seek out personal support from prison chaplains. Through forging caring and trusting relationships with Paul, the Christian chaplains supported him through these emotional experiences (Whitehead 2013). In time, Paul's newfound feeling of support rekindled his interest in developing a spiritual relationship with a higher power (Deuchar et al. 2016).

Maruna et al. (2006, p. 162) discuss how 'converts' in jail gain a strong sense of forgiveness that enables them to regain feelings of self-worth, and that their conversion narratives often provide a sense of hope for the future (see also Healy 2012). Paul's Catholic baptism in prison led him to believe that he had been given a 'second chance'. He developed a greater propensity to react compassionately towards other inmates, and a clear focus on his future possible self that was complemented by a new interpretation of the past (Maruna et al. 2006; Healy 2012). Most of all, the regular discipline of prayer evidently enabled Paul to feel closer to his deceased father. Combined with his solid, trusting relationship with the male chaplains, this was clearly bringing about a greater sense of peace, a reduced tendency to display hyper-masculinity through violence and a propensity towards generativity (Maruna 2001).

In Denmark, issues relating to personal loss, grief and bereavement were evidently not as much to the fore among inmates as I found they were in Scotland. However, Christian and Islamic chaplains there talked about the way in which some inmates also began to look towards a presence and source of power beyond themselves. Some turned towards religion to help them cope with the realisation that their criminal lifestyles had led to nothing but despair:

> They find out, when they're in prison … what they believed in themselves and what they worked for – it didn't work out. I mean, it was shit, it was no good. So when as a human, when the legs disappear from under you

7 Support in Times of Trouble: Chaplaincy in Scottish ...

and you fall down, you tend to reach out for something and somebody outside of yourself which can help you stand again. (Alec, Christian chaplain: Denmark)

They start seeking out the religion, because now they find themselves under stress, pressure and they see they've done something wrong. (Yaasir, Muslim chaplain: Denmark)

In similar ways to Paul, other men in both countries talked about seeking out chaplains during times of trouble, and slowly finding or rekindling a religious faith that was characterised by prayer and reflection. For example, among the Scottish sample Connor had a Muslim father and Christian mother. He had contacted the Muslim prison chaplain when he felt in need of personal support, who then invited him to participate in a Friday Muslim prayer meeting. He felt that this had helped to 'revive' his faith; he had regularly begun to read the Qur'an and to pray while in his cell, and found that this helped to give him 'peace of mind'. Similar stories emerged from some of the men I referred to at the end of Chapter 6, who had actively begun to reassess their lifestyles and felt ready for change. For instance, in Denmark Umar (a reforming gang member) had grown tired of his violent lifestyle and had begun to yearn for a more peaceful and 'normal' life when he was released. He had been raised as a Muslim, and after being introduced to the Muslim prison chaplain he began to rekindle his prayer time and became more committed to it:

Five times a day, I pray. I was raised [that way] when I was a little child, I always prayed. But, you know, the time I was older I was stepping down – I hadn't time ... but my prayer has got to be bigger, you know? (Umar, Denmark)

Others who had no prior religious backgrounds began to feel an emerging faith once they felt ready for lifestyle change and began meeting with chaplains. For instance, in Scotland Keith had been convicted for sex offences but had begun to realise he wanted to change his future life path and avoid further periods of incarceration (see Chapter 6). He began to pray when meeting privately with Christian chaplains, and felt that he now wanted to seek forgiveness for his previous humiliation of female victims:

> I tend to pray when I'm really struggling. I've sat down with Edward or Ryan, we've had a talk and then we've had a prayer … I seek forgiveness. One day I would love … to be able to sit down with my victims and say, 'look, I'm deeply, deeply sorry' … 'cause I know I've put fear into some women and that's wrong. (Keith, Scotland)

As I referred to in Chapter 6, Ahmed (who had come from a Muslim home) had convictions related to being a senior member of a large immigrant street gang, but had developed a strong yearning to leave his criminal lifestyle behind and to see his daughter get married. Through his contact with the Muslim chaplain, he had begun reading the Qu'ran and praying again and felt that he now sought to do good things to help and support others in need:

> I read the Qu'ran and I started praying … it has had an impact. When I see somebody who needs help, I want to help even here in the prison. (Ahmed, Denmark)

Those with mixed Muslim and Christian backgrounds like Tarone also felt that their contact with the chaplains had resurrected dormant religious beliefs and prayer times against the backdrop of challenging prison experiences:

> The only time I actually do focus on my religion is in times of trouble … sometimes I pray from the heart and I'll pray for wisdom, kind of some understanding. (Tarone, Scotland)

Similar to the description of Paul's journey in Box 7.2, one other interviewee in Scotland (Fergus, who came from a Christian family) and one in Denmark (Søren, who had been raised in a non-religious home) described the way in which they had been baptised while in prison. For others, although they did not choose to be baptised to Christianity or convert fully to Islam, they felt that engaging in study groups with chaplains had led them to regularly read religious texts (as with Ahmed, above). In turn, it appeared to me that some of these men had begun to assimilate the core themes in the Bible or Qur'an into their own self-narratives. For example, Søren drew upon the Biblical teachings of Jesus to effectively reject his previous criminal identity and conceptualise his former life as 'dirty', while Connor indicated that his reading of Islam had led him to become more humble and (like Ahmed, above) to seek to help and support others (Maruna et al. 2006):

> I have read the [New] Testament, I read the book … Jesus is good for me now … in this criminal life, I see everything … it's not a good life, it's a dirty life … the money is not clean … it's not good to sell drugs because somebody you sold the drugs to maybe's dying. (Søren: Denmark)

> [I'd] just like, you know, [to] try and be humble eh? And not judge people or whatever n'that. Just try and be a good person all round, and try and help people. (Connor, Scotland)

Those who began to engage more fully in the Christian or Islamic faith also indicated that they gained a deeper sense of support not only from chaplains but also other inmates who were interested in their religion. For instance, in Scotland Keith talked about his enjoyment of discussing Biblical texts in a group and enjoying hearing the viewpoints of others; in Denmark, Patric, who had begun to yearn for a 'normal life' away from violent crime, felt that engaging in Christian worship opened up opportunities to 'talk to other prisoners in a nice way'. Although he was segregated due to gang-related offences, Umar also felt he enjoyed talking to other gang members he met in study groups about 'life' as well as about the Qur'an.

Insights from informal discussions with some of the inmates in Scotland and Denmark suggested to me that they engaged with chaplaincy as a means of feeling 'normal' again. They enjoyed escaping from their cells, drinking coffee and engaging in recreational pastimes with chaplains. By their own admission, in some cases (like Tarone, above), they were also slightly hypocritical in terms of drawing on religion only when they were under stress and experiencing 'times of trouble'. These insights resonate with previous scholarship that has explored prison inmates' manipulation of religion or chaplaincy services for their personal benefits (see, for instance, Thomas and Zaitzow 2006).

However, it was also evident that some of the men were beginning to draw upon the emotional support they received from chaplains and the social bonds and capital that they gained from other inmates. The support and social bonds combined with their experiences of religion through readings and prayer appeared to be leading them to adopt pro-social values. They were beginning to embrace new 'possible selves' more wholeheartedly, and to project alternative narrative identities that replaced their previous focus on the type of hyper-masculinity that spawned gang-related and wider types of criminality (Healy 2012; Hallett and McCoy 2014).

Broadening Perspectives and Community Re-Entry Support

In Chapter 4, I discussed the way in which the men I met in Los Angeles were evidently embarking on early desistance journeys, but still regarded themselves as 'works in progress'. The sample of Scottish and Danish men I have referred to in this chapter were clearly more limited in their capability to test their initial inclinations to desist due to continued incarceration. However, the insights from my extended discussions with them suggested that they were adopting broader, more rational outlooks and perspectives on their future decision-making processes and potential role transitions as a result of their contact with prison chaplains (Decker et al. 2014). Two particular examples from Scotland illustrate this: Paul felt he had become more patient and would have a greater ability to think before acting when he was released, while Tarone had committed himself to moving to a rural location upon his release so as to avoid the negative influences that encouraged and affirmed gang-related lifestyles:

> They've taught me to be patient, they've taught me to be calm and relax … They've taught us like to always think aboot what you're goin' to dae and don't go away and dae it. Think about the positives and the negatives to it. (Paul, Scotland)

> Most of the people … think that my life is all right and it's nice even – 'cause I was selling drugs, I was making money and all the girls I've fucked … they go 'your life [is] nice' … but [chaplains] see through that … if I am going to behave … I need to abandon everybody and just like focus on me. (Tarone, Scotland)

In Denmark, broader perspectives were also clearly emerging that challenged the previous dominance of gang masculinity. For instance, Yusuf's exposure to the emotional support that chaplains offered and the spiritual and philosophical discussions in inter-faith study groups in prison had made him more determined to devote his time to family and employment as opposed to crime. And Ahmed's engagement with the Muslim chaplain and increased Islamic faith had made him even more focused than before on striving towards gang disengagement and supporting his daughter:

> I am a grown man, I will be 29 years old so it is time to move on. High time. I want a family and I want a good job I can work on and do something good for other people. (Yusuf, Denmark)

> I have a good relationship with him [chaplain] and he's helped me a lot … I'm one hundred per cent sure, I can't go back to [gangs] – I can't do it anymore. I have plans in my head now … I have a daughter now. (Ahmed, Denmark)

McNeill et al. (2012) argue that desistance is partly about discovering personal agency, while Giordano et al. (2002) highlights the relationship between individual agency and social structures. In order to ensure that the inmates' evolving desistance commitments and narratives turned into actions, it would be desirable for the chaplains to continue to work *with* offenders (but not *on* them) once they were released back into communities (McNeill et al. 2012). In Scotland, chaplains described the way in which they had been actively discouraged from keeping in contact with inmates once they had been released but did feel that the chaplaincy service was beginning to change its perspective on this and to focus more on supporting community re-entry.

Denmark's policy and practice appeared to be more advanced in this regard, and several initiatives existed that enabled chaplains to continue to support offenders and work with them once released. For instance, Maddi (an inter-faith chaplain) described the work of the Islamic-Christian Study Centre in Copenhagen, which she and a wider group of religious pastors had established to build positive relationships between citizens with Christian and Muslim backgrounds. Ex-prisoners (of Christian or Islamic faith or none) regularly visited the Centre and benefited from personal mentoring and support. Maddi felt that the Centre's ethos was particularly helpful for supporting ethnic minority men who were recently released from prison and came from Muslim backgrounds. Even although they may not always be overtly religious, she believed that their sense of marginalisation was reduced because of the Islamic and cultural material that was present in the Centre:

> We have books about their backgrounds, their religion. And when they see that there are Qur'ans there and books about Islam then they will also feel that this is the place for them. They feel secure in a way. (Maddi, Christian/Muslim chaplain: Denmark)

Previous projects focused on community-based chaplaincy have prioritised the need to help prisoners achieve successful re-entry, by offering them support and services once released (Whitehead 2011). Although under-developed in Scotland, there were initiatives emerging in Denmark that were culturally and religiously inclusive. These types of post-release services hold the capacity to build on the type of identity and behaviour change that was beginning to emerge among the male offenders I interviewed. They could potentially further sustain the emergence of 'pull' factors that could support the men's future gang disengagement and desistance efforts (Decker et al. 2014).

Concluding Discussion

In contrast to the insights I provide in other parts of the book against the backdrop of rehabilitation programmes in the community, in this chapter the focus has been on examining the support provided for male offenders in prisons—and thus reflects the premise that prisons can and should hold the capacity to become 'moral institutions' (Cullen et al. 2001, p. 268).

The men I talked to had often experienced tough and emotionally-devoid family lives. In the majority of cases, this was followed by their involvement in highly masculinized gang culture, hyper-masculine displays of physical strength and muscularity and the assertion of marginalised masculinities against other men (Connell 2005). However, in the case of the two sex offenders in Scotland a somewhat contrasting masculine code had evidently been adopted that focused on asserting marginalised masculinity via the abasement of women. Whatever the case, all of the men had become exposed to a prison environment that prioritised bravado and was characterised by a macho 'prison code' (Johnson and Larson 2003, p. 28). In addition, in Denmark convicted gang members I met were particularly stigmatised and demonized through the segregation policies they became exposed to, as were the two sex offenders I worked with in Scotland (see also Johnson 2017).

Hence, experiencing unconditional personal support from prison chaplains where they no longer felt compelled to 'regulate and suppress emotionality' clearly came as a welcome relief (Weaver 2016, p. 122). This was particularly the case with those whose vulnerability and stigmatism had led them to experience psychological distress including depression and suicidal tendencies while in prison—as was the case with Adam (a convicted sex offender in Scotland) and Stefan (a former steroid abuser and drug dealer in Denmark who experienced solitary confinement). In addition to offering caring, supportive relationships, Whitehead (2013, p. 8) identifies that chaplains also offer prisoners the 'commodity of time' that is not always available to them from statutory agencies. The time that the chaplains were able to spend with these men and others in Scotland and Denmark, combined with the confidentiality they were able to offer them, was seen as invaluable.

Beyond the humanist, secular methods of treatment and support that the chaplains offered, they also provided religious support to those with existing or emerging Christian or Islamic faith (whether gang members or not). The traumatic experience of bereavement in Scotland and the realisation of failed criminal enterprise in Denmark were common catalysts for this, as was the emerging feeling among some inmates that they were eager to change their future lifestyles and were seeking further support to do so. In such cases, the strong bonds to a higher spiritual power that emerged during the liminal phase often spurred on a further change in the inmates' values and attitudes. Weaver (2016) highlights that, for some offenders, engaging in religiously-informed practices can lead to the emergence of transformed personal and social identities that support their efforts to change. In some cases, the men's experience of religious conversion provided them with a 'language and framework for forgiveness', an increasing sense of control over their futures and the opportunity to begin to establish alternative non-offending identities (O'Connor and Duncan 2011, p. 592).

Although some clearly enjoyed the social benefits that came from visiting chaplains, through prayer and the reading of religious texts (whether the Bible or Qur'an) the men in my sample were also beginning to develop a renewed moral compass and a deeper awareness of generative commitments (Weaver 2016). The focus on inter-faith approaches in study groups, particularly evident in Denmark, enabled an inclusive approach to be upheld, avoided a situation where Christianity occupied a hegemonic position and ensured that Muslim inmates' needs were met (Spalek and Wilson 2001).

Accordingly, the effects of religion on these reforming but still incarcerated gang members and wider offenders could be viewed through the lens of both social control and differential association theory. Newfound or revitalized religious practice certainly provided a source of external control over their conduct. But in addition, although somewhat limited in some cases due to segregation policies (for gang members in Denmark and sex offenders in Scotland), the inmates gained pro-social contacts and bonds from chaplains and other religiously-oriented inmates that, if sustained following their release, could contribute to gang disengagement and desistance (Giordano et al. 2002).

Although it was difficult to predict whether the Scottish and Danish inmates I met would actually desist from violence and other types of gang-related or individualised offending after their release, their gradual redefinition of their own masculine identities was conducive to recovery (Flores 2014). Through both secular and religious support from chaplains, the men were gradually reasserting their commitment to humility, patience, avoidance of external corrupting influences and a focus on generativity. In turn, conventional culture was beginning to trump gang culture and criminal identities within their personal narratives (Maruna 2001; Flores 2014).

Reference to prison chaplaincy is often omitted in discussions about prison coping and criminal desistance (Sundt et al. 2002; Parkes and Bilby 2010). Although based on small-scale research, the positive impact that I have highlighted in this chapter suggests that it may be important to widen the provision and reach of chaplaincy services alongside other forms of care-giving support in northern European prisons. This could be relevant for gang-related offenders but also for those with other types of offences such as sex offenders and drug dealers and within the context of fostering 'virtuous', 'moral' prison environments (Cullen et al. 2001; Liebling 2014). As I have argued elsewhere (Deuchar et al. 2016), this extended provision should place an emphasis on personal and emotional support, but with opportunities for inclusive, inter-faith religious exploration if it is desired and sought.

As I alluded to in earlier chapters, in addition to pastoral and religious support, wider spiritual practices such as yoga and meditation can provide offenders with positive resources to draw upon while in the liminal phase and on the threshold of change (Healy 2012). The next chapter presents in-depth insights from another sub-group of men from my original Danish sample (referred to in Chapter 6) who had participated in these ascetic-spiritual practices. It explores the impact that the practices seemed to be having on supporting personal introspection, transition and growth.

References

Armstrong, R. (2014). Trusting the untrustworthy: The theology, practice and implications of faith-based volunteers' work with ex-prisoners. *Studies in Christian Ethics, 27*(3), 299–317.

Clear, T., & Sumter, M. (2002). Prisoners, prison, and religion. *Journal of Offender Rehabilitation, 35*(3/4), 125–156.

Connell, R. W. (2005). *Masculinities*. Cambridge: Polity Press.
Cullen, F. T., Sundt, J. L., & Wozniak, J. F. (2001). Virtuous prison: Toward a restorative rehabilitation. In H. N. Pontell & D. Schichor (Eds.), *Contemporary issues in crime and criminal justice: Essays in honor of Gilbert Geis* (pp. 193–102). New Jersey: Prentice Hall.
Decker, S. H., Pyrooz, D., & Moule, R. K., Jr. (2014). Disengagement from gangs as role transitions. *Journal of Research on Adolescence, 24*(2), 268–283.
Deuchar, R., & Bhopal, K. (2017). *Young people and social control: Problems and prospects from the margins*. Basingstoke: Palgrave Macmillan.
Deuchar, R., Morck, L., Matemba, Y. H., McLean, R., & Riaz, N. (2016). 'It's as if you're not in jail, as if you're not a prisoner': Young male offenders' experiences of incarceration, prison chaplaincy, religion and spirituality in Scotland and Denmark. *The Howard Journal of Crime and Justice, 55*(1–2), 131–150.
Flores, E. O. (2014). *God's gangs: Barrio ministry, masculinity and gang recovery*. New York: NYU Press.
Giordano, P. C., Cernkovich, S. A., & Rudolph, J. L. (2002). Gender, crime and desistance: Toward a theory of cognitive transformation. *American Journal of Sociology, 107*, 990–1064.
Hallett, M., & McCoy, J. S. (2014). Religiously motivated desistance: An exploratory study. *International Journal of Offender Therapy and Comparative Criminology, 59*(8), 855–872.
Healy, D. (2012). *The dynamics of desistance: Charting pathways through change*. New York: Routledge.
Johnson, A. (2017). *If I give my soul: Faith behind bars in Rio de Janeiro*. Oxford: Oxford University Press.
Johnson, B. R., & Larson, D. B. (2003). *The inner change freedom initiative: A preliminary evaluation of a faith-based prison program*. Waco, TX: Baylor University.
Klein, A. M. (1993). *Little big men: Bodybuilding subculture and gender construction*. Albany: State University of New York Press.
Liebling, A. (2014). Moral and philosophical problems of long-term imprisonment. *Studies in Christian Ethics, 27*(3), 258–273.
Maruna, S. (2001). *Making good: How ex-convicts reform and rebuild their lives*. Washington, DC: American Psychological Association.
Maruna, S., Wilson, L., & Curren, K. (2006). Why god is often found behind bars: Prison conversions and the crisis of self-narrative. *Research in Human Development, 3*(2–3), 161–184.

McFarlane, H. (2013). Masculinity and criminology: The social construction of criminal man. *Howard League of Criminal Justice, 52*(3), 321–335.
McNeill, F., Farrall, S., Lightowler, C., & Maruna, S. (2012). How and why people stop offending. In *Volume 15 of Insights*. Glasgow: IRISS.
O'Connor, T. P., & Duncan, J. B. (2011). The sociology of humanist, spiritual and religious practice in prison: Supporting responsivity and desistance from crime. *Religions, 2*, 590–610.
Parkes, R., & Bilby, C. (2010). The courage to create: The role of artistic and spiritual activities in prison. *Howard Journal, 49*, 97–110.
Spalek, B., & Wilson, D. (2001). Not just 'visitors' to prisons: The experiences of Imams who work inside the penal system. *The Howard Journal, 40*(1), 3–13.
Sundt, J. L., & Cullen, F. T. (2002). The correctional ideology of prison chaplains: A national survey. *Journal of Criminal Justice, 30*, 369–385.
Sundt, J. L., Dammer, H. R., & Cullen, F. T. (2002). The role of the prison chaplain in rehabilitation. *Journal of Offender Rehabilitation, 35*(3–4), 59–86.
Thomas, J., & Zaitzow, B. H. (2006). Conning or conversion? The role of religion in prison coping. *The Prison Journal, 86*(2), 242–259.
Tipton, L. (2011). *The role and contribution of a multi-faith prison chaplaincy to the contemporary prison service*. Cardiff: Cardiff Centre for Chaplaincy Studies.
Trenton, A. J., & Currier, G. W. (2005). Behavioural manifestations of anabolic steroid use. *CNS Drugs, 19*(7), 571–595.
Vaswani, N. (2014). The ripples of death: Exploring the bereavement experiences and mental health of young men in custody. *The Howard Journal of Crime and Justice, 53*(4), 341–359.
Weaver, B. (2016). *Offending and desistance: The importance of social relations*. Abingdon: Routledge.
Webber, R. (2014). *'I was in prison …' An exploration of Catholic prison ministry in Victoria*. Melbourne: Catholic Social Services.
Whitehead, P. L. (2011). *Evaluation report of research at six community chaplaincy projects in England and Wales*. Middlesbrough: Teesside University.
Whitehead, P. L. (2013). Touching the void: Community chaplaincy as an ethical-cultural agency in criminal justice re-formation in England and Wales. *Social and Public Policy Review, 7*(1), 40–54.

8

'Warriors' to 'Peacemakers': Yoga, Breathing and Meditation in Denmark

In this chapter I present insights from follow-up semi-structured interviews I conducted and wider informal discussions I had with a second sub-group of the Danish sample I referred to in Chapter 6. Some of these men were still incarcerated when I worked with them, but the majority had recently been released from prison. While most were former members of Danish street gangs and biker gangs, a minority had offending histories outwith gang structures. These men had regularly begun to participate in yoga exercises, dynamic breathing techniques and meditation practices, and in this chapter I combine their insights with some complementary ones from interviews I conducted with their coaches and instructors. I explore the way in which the men discussed and described the deeper cognitive and identity shifts they experienced through the practices, and the way in which they felt able to deal more effectively with negative and destructive emotions and the personal strains that had led them into gang violence and wider criminality. Additional, supplementary reflections on my own personal experiences of participating in the practices are also included in the form of field-notes from participant observation.

'Sudarshan Kriya Yoga', Its Psychological Impact and Rehabilitative Potential

In Chapter 3 I briefly examined the existing scholarly insights that suggest that engagement in holistic spiritual practices may play a role in the type of identity and behaviour change that stimulates progression towards desistance. I referred to the potential role of ascetic-spiritual practices such as yoga and meditation, and the emerging insights that suggest the way in which engaging with these practices may enhance positive psychological states. I also considered the evidence that suggests that these practices may enable offenders to manage the prolonged negative repercussions of criminal behaviour that often stimulate re-offending. In this chapter, I focus attention on Sudarshan Kriya Yoga (SKY), which has been described as a 'sequence of specific breathing techniques' (Brown and Gerberg 2005a, p. 189) and an example of 'indigenous Hindu spirituality' (Pandya 2016, p. 134). Its use is coordinated by the *Art of Living Foundation*, a nonprofit service organisation founded in 1982 by the spiritual Indian leader Sri Sri Ravi Shankar (Vedamurthachar et al. 2006).

SKY comprises four components, all conducted in a sitting posture: threestage slow Ujjayi pranayama, consisting of slowdeep breathing; Bhastrika pranayama, consisting of forced inhalation and exhalation twenty times; chanting of 'om'; and Sudarshan Kriya, a process consisting of slow, medium and fast cycles of breathing practiced for a total duration of around 30 minutes (Vedamurthachar et al. 2006). Variations of the techniques are used in many traditions including Raja yoga, Hatha yoga, Iyengar yoga and Zen, and can be combined with physical yoga stretches and meditation (Brown and Gerberg 2005a). Extensive demonstration and coaching by trained instructors is required in order to prevent any potential adverse effects such as dizziness or headaches (Brown and Gerberg 2005a, b).

Studies conducted in the 1990s by Satyanarayana et al. (1992) suggest that the practicing of Kriya within a yoga discipline can lead to increased calmness of mind and spiritual happiness (see also Pandya 2016). Indeed, as I alluded to in Chapter 3, some evidence has also implied that positive relationships between these types of ascetic-spiritual practices and mental health may be more robust in males than in females (Pandya 2015).

In clinical trials in India, Murthy et al. (1998) found that symptoms of depression among male participants improved significantly following participation in SKY over a three month period. Vedamurthachar et al. (2006) subsequently tested the effects of SKY therapy on mood symptoms and hormone levels in male participants (age 18–55 years) with alcohol dependence immediately following an acute detoxification period. All participants completed the Beck's Depression Inventory at the end of the first week after admission and two weeks later. The results illustrated that participation in SKY reduced the depressive symptoms in the alcohol dependent subjects, thus suggesting that SKY can be a 'potential yet safe antidepressant therapy' (Vedamurthachar et al. 2006, p. 251).

Further, in randomized controlled trials conducted on a sample of major depressive disorder patients in India, Janakiramaiah et al. (2000) also found a high remission state within four weeks. Wider clinical studies have also illustrated that programmes that include Ujjayi pranayama, yoga postures and meditation can lead to reductions in anxiety and stress (Brown and Gerbarg 2005b). Some have also suggested that the intense nature of the practices can lead on to a greater sense of eudemonic wellbeing (Pandya 2016).

Qualitative research interviews conducted with staff and officials in maximum security prisons in India suggested that regular practice of SKY significantly reduced violent behaviour among inmates (Brown and Gerbarg 2005b). Further, a pilot study of juvenile offenders and gang members convicted of violent crimes with deadly weapons in Los Angeles County found that those given SKY training for one week followed by 30 minutes of guided meditation and pranayama three nights per week showed 'significant overall reduction' in anxiety, anger, reactive behaviour and fighting (Brown and Gerbarg 2005b, p. 714). These reported results suggest that SKY could play an important rehabilitative role, particularly with male offenders who struggle with the pressure to enact the commonly recognised forms of hegemonic and hyper-masculinity in western society such as aggression and violence.

Breathe Smart and *Prison Smart* Programmes in Denmark

The *Breathe Smart* programme was established in Denmark in 2002, with the specific goal of teaching and coaching participants to use SKY as a means of potentially supporting them to deal with challenging life circumstances (*Breathe Smart* 2016). Its partner programme, *Prison Smart*, is focused specifically on supporting prison inmates to address the same issues (*Breathe Smart* 2016). Both programmes draw upon a traditional model of SKY that combines the use of Ujjayi pranayama, Bhastrika pranayama and Sudarshan Kriya as per the teachings of Sri Sri Ravi Shankar and promoted globally by the *Art of Living Foundation* (Brown and Gerberg 2005a; Vedamurthachar et al. 2006; Pandya 2016).

In the *Prison Smart* programme, teachers primarily engage in one-to-one coaching with predominantly male inmates. They introduce them to physical yoga exercises and the SKY breathing and meditation techniques across an intensive five day programme, and then following this up with top-up sessions while also encouraging inmates to practice on their own. The *Breathe Smart* programme, which is delivered in the community, tends to involve group participation and the fostering of fellowship with others (Ahlmark 2015). Although the two programmes were first established in Denmark in 2002 by Jakob Lund under the umbrella of the *Breathe Smart* organisation, the *Prison Smart* programme was actually founded as early as 1992 in the United States. It has developed into a globally recognised programme implemented in over 50 countries and has benefited more than 250,000 prisoners and staff. The *Breathe Smart* programme is also implemented in several other parts of the world, including the UK.

The Impact of SKY on Danish Gang Members and Offenders

The remainder of this chapter focuses on insights I gained from a second sub-group of the men from the wider Danish sample discussed and referred to in Chapter 6 (see Table 6.1). Just as those described in the previous chapter had turned towards prison chaplains for support, the men I discuss in this chapter had chosen instead to engage with *Prison Smart* and (in some cases) later progressed to participate in the *Breathe Smart* programme following their release from prison.

In total, I conducted follow-up semi-structured interviews and engaged in wider, informal discussions with nine of the Danish men. To re-cap on their ethnic backgrounds, while five (Jesper, Hans, Lasse, Lucas and Damon) were white ethnic Danes the remaining four were first generation immigrants. Specifically, Abbad and his family had transitioned to Denmark from Saudi Arabia when he was age seven; Ivan had moved to Denmark from Macedonia (after a short period of living in Africa) with his family when he was a teenager; Cumar's family had brought him from Somalia to Denmark as a baby; and Jamaal had been born in Uganda and moved to Denmark with his parents when he was age twelve. Table 8.1 provides a list of the sub-group of male participants, their ages, countries of origin and geographical locations. It also indicates whether or not each participant was still in closed or open prisons or had been released by the time the fieldwork took place.

Table 8.1 The sub-group of research participants engaged with 'Prison Smart'/'Breathe Smart'

Name	Age	Country of origin	Country of residence	Prison/released
Abbad	37	Saudi Arabia	Denmark	Released
Jesper	42	Denmark	Denmark	Released
Ivan	47	Macedonia	Denmark	Open prison
Hans	49	Denmark	Denmark	Released
Lasse	37	Denmark	Denmark	Released
Lucas	43	Denmark	Denmark	Released
Damon	34	Denmark	Denmark	Closed prison
Cumar	23	Somalia	Denmark	Open prison
Jamaal	32	Uganda	Denmark	Released

As I described in Chapter 6, the men had mostly been involved in gang-related violence or crime at some point during their periods of offending, but in two cases in this sub-group the men had been imprisoned for criminal acts that were not directly related to gang structures. While Ivan had been convicted for individualised drug dealing, Lasse had conducted armed robberies outwith a specific gang context. As Table 8.1 illustrates, while three of the participants (Ivan, Damon and Cumar) were still inmates in closed or open prisons at the time that the interviews were conducted, the remainder had been released (albeit in some cases very recently). However, most of the participants had begun to engage with the SKY practices while inmates via the *Prison Smart* programme and, in the case of those who had now been released, had continued to practice on their own or in a group context out in the community. Interviews and informal discussions were therefore conducted either in prisons or within the premises of the Danish *Breathe Smart* organisation, depending on the personal circumstances of individual participants at the time.

Additional semi-structured interviews were also conducted with three SKY teachers and coaches, including the Director of the *Breathe Smart* organisation. In addition to the interviews, drawing upon the 'participant as observer role' (Gold 1958) I actively engaged with the introductory five-day *Breathe Smart* programme on a one-to-one basis with one of the lead coaches in the Danish programme. As in Los Angeles, I routinely recorded 'jottings' of my observations, 'impressions and feelings' (Emerson et al. 1995, pp. 31–32) and later drew upon these jottings to create full fieldnotes. The purpose of this element of the research was mainly to gain firsthand experience of the breathing and meditative practices and to reflect more closely on their potential psychological, emotional and physical impact.

In the following sections, I report on the insights gained from the nine men during interviews and informal discussions, supplemented with the personal reflections I gained from participant observation and some brief additional insights from coaches. Similarly to Dr Robert Weide and Father Greg Boyle (referred to in previous chapters), Jakob Lund (Director of *Breathe Smart* and lead coach within the programmes) consented to his real name being used during data reporting. Otherwise, pseudonyms are used as before.

Anger Management, Emotional Release, Empathy and Spiritual Engagement

As mentioned above, all of the men had initially become introduced to the SKY practices within the context of the *Prison Smart* programme while incarcerated, and some had subsequently engaged with the *Breathe Smart* programme post-release. Their initial motivations for engaging with the programme varied. As I alluded to in Chapter 6, several of the men had reached a stage where they had begun to reassess themselves while in prison, to gain an increased desire to give back to others and to live non-violent lifestyles (Giordano et al. 2002; Paternoster and Bushway 2009). For instance, Ivan had become motivated to stay away from crime because of his son, while Damon had simply begun to feel tired of the gang lifestyle and yearned for a 'normal', peaceful life (Healy 2012). As with those who turned towards the support of prison chaplains, some had experienced psychological difficulties due to previous participation in violence combined with prolonged drug abuse and (in cases such as Abbad and Ivan) had also experienced early trauma in the countries where they were born and/or raised. Regardless of the reasons, some originally self-referred to the *Prison Smart* programme because they had heard about it from other prison inmates while others were referred to it by social workers who felt that the programme may be beneficial for them.

The men talked about their initial reactions to the yoga movements, forced inhalation and cycled breathing techniques that they experienced on the initial five-day programme, and the progressive impact they felt from practicing the techniques on their own afterwards. Some described an initial frustration with the presence of the Sudarshan Kriya mantra that was played on a tape while they practiced, or admitted that they found the physical yoga exercises tough. However, they also made reference to feelings of psychological release that in some cases led to a clarity of mind or even intense emotional responses:

> The first time I did this I was so angry that I wanted to like to go up and go out of the room or even smash the ghetto blaster where this guy was saying 'so ... om' ... but I was like, something else tell me 'no, you've got

to stay, you've got to see what this is because you're scared, there's something you're scared about.' Afterwards, I could feel some release in my brain actually. (Ivan)

The first day I took the course … it was OK. And the second day it was Ok, and then the day came we had to do the Sudarshan Kriya for the first time, the breathing … and when I get home and I get inside the door, you know, I sat in my kitchen for a while and I [was] then just crying … it was really looking into myself for the first time in my life, and see all the fucked-up things I've been doing. (Lucas)

Through personal experience of participating in the Kriya, I realised the way in which it could initially feel strange or frustrating, but in a short time led to feelings of intense psychological and physical release:

> Haggi switches on the tape, and I am completely unprepared for what comes next. As I listen, sitting in the chair with my hands on my lap, I am guided by a high pitched, Hindu voice which repeats a mantra over the loud speaker. At first the mantra is slow and the corresponding breaths by nature are deep and relaxed, but after several minutes the pace quickens and the breaths then also speed up – until they are shallow and guided with some urgency. Following this, the mantra slows again and the quick intakes of breathe slow down in pace. I don't feel in my comfort zone, but I decide to stick with it … After what feels like about 20 minutes I am completely carried away with the pace and form of the breathing and the mantra until I feel my head becoming light and the knot in my stomach subsiding. (Researcher's fieldnotes)

In Chapter 6, I described the way in which Jesper had been a member of a prominent motorcycle gang in Denmark. He had served 16 years in prison for a gang-related murder, and admitted that he had been completely driven by his own ego and his admiration for and celebration of toughness and hyper-masculinity. He had continually attempted to reassert his gender insecurity through accumulating physical capital (through bodybuilding and steroid use) and violence capital (through gang membership). Box 8.1 illustrates the additional insights I gained from Jesper during my extended discussions with him post-release. It documents the way in which he had found that engaging in SKY gradually supported him in gaining a less self-centred and less aggressive, destructive view of the world.

> **Box 8.1:** *Jesper's Gradual Progression from 'Warrior' to 'Peacemaker'*
>
> When he reached the age of 39 and was still in prison, Jesper began to reflect a little more about his past and future. When his mother and father visited him periodically, he could see that his mother had become ill and that the worry about Jesper had begun to destroy her. Jesper slowly began to soul-search, but felt that it would be difficult for him to change his lifestyle because he did not want to lose the violent reputation he had worked so hard to establish. His ego was still driving him, and he wanted to ensure that people were still afraid of him when he was released back into the community.
>
> During the last year of his sentence, Jesper was told that he could be transferred to an open prison and to go out and work for part of the week, but first the prison authorities wanted him to engage with some type of rehabilitation programme in order to deal with his remaining anger issues. His social worker suggested that he try to engage with the *Prison Smart* programme, and Jesper had an initial meeting with Jakob Lund (Director of the Danish programme) and told him he would try it. When he first began to do the breathing and meditation practices, he found them challenging and was sceptical about their benefit, but as he persevered with them he gradually began to feel more peaceful and relaxed. As his engagement with the SKY practices progressed, he found that the combination of the breathing exercises and the personal reflection and introspection that Jakob helped him to engage in supported him in gaining a less self-centred and destructive view of the world:
>
> *I was living in a world that everything was around me, my ego ... Jakob, when we do the exercises we also do some talking ... he was asking me questions ... he ask me, 'what ... when you are driving around and this guy comes, how did it make you feel? What does it make you think? And what does it do inside you? How do you feel when the anger comes? Where is it in your stomach?'... he begin to do some exercises along with that and ... I begin to make my mind and my body in another balance, and begin to see the world different. I begin to understand the guy in the car is just trying to get home, he's not driving around the town just to fuck with me ... I begin to [see] the world is not me.*
>
> As Jesper transitioned to the open prison arrangements and began to spend more time back in the community, he continued to visit the *Breathe Smart* studio once or twice a week to engage in SKY practices while also practicing in his own time. He gradually found that his previous tendency to scan for danger as he entered into a public place began to submerge. Instead, he began to acquire and project a more passive attitude, to look

> for the good in other people and to adopt a less confrontational and aggressive mindset:
>
> *I can tell you, when I go into a room before I'm scanning the room, I watch everybody ... I could tell you when I come into the bar, 'those two guys over there' ... I could look into their eyes and tell their attitude ... I could stand in the room and see who's who in five seconds ... I have this animal instinct ... [now] my way of going into a room is totally different, even I'm the same eyes ... when I go into a room I expect this room to be peaceful, I don't expect to come into any trouble.*
>
> Following his final release from prison, Jesper continued to engage in SKY during private sessions with Jakob and also on his own at home. Although he still participated in weightlifting, he had become less obsessed by his own body image and physical size and no longer took steroids. He had a full-time job in the business sector but admitted that he sometimes still had a 'warrior' mentality within him that meant that he struggled with taking instructions from his boss. He admitted that he was still afraid he might eventually go back to his 'old self' and become violent again, particularly since he was constantly aware that he still had enemies around that could seek retaliation. However, he also felt that the SKY practices had enabled him to adopt a new mindset where he generally felt more peaceful and at ease with himself.

As with so many of the other men I interviewed in other contexts, Jesper began to experience *pull* factors that made him feel ready for change while in the liminal carceral space (Decker et al. 2014). Reaching a mature age and becoming more aware of the impact of his offending lifestyle on his mother's health acted as initial 'hooks for change' (Giordano et al. 2002). However, he continued to be reluctant to let go of the status, reputation, sense of honour and prestige that emerged from his position as a leading member of a biker gang and that fuelled his masculine ego. This initially prevented him from committing towards criminal desistance (Harding 2014). The turning point for Jesper came when he realised his potential transition to an open prison was dependent upon him engaging in rehabilitation. Drawing on Decker et al. (2014, p. 2), his initial, emerging doubts about continuing with the gang lifestyle led on to him beginning to weigh up the 'costs and benefits of a transition'. Agents of social control helped to initiate his more profound introspection, and he came to engage in the *Prison Smart* programme as a means of trying to secure his partial release back into the community.

Although initially sceptical and uncertain about the SKY practices, Jesper's participation in them gradually began to have a profound effect. He clearly viewed himself as still being a 'work in progress' with a potential 'warrior' mentality still threatening to re-emerge due to gang embodiment issues and 'stigmata' (Densely 2013; Flores 2014). However, Jesper's reduced reliance on physicality and violence capital as a source of gaining status and respect combined with his increasing feelings of calmness, wellbeing and reduced confrontational mindset were conducive to enabling greater 'progression towards desistance' (Carlsson 2012, p. 14).

Other men in the sample also talked about the way in which the yoga, breathing and meditation exercises provided them with a tool that enabled them to manage their aggression and anger and deal with potentially destructive thoughts, feelings and stressful situations more productively. Some also talked about the intense feelings of happiness and joy that they began to experience after practicing the SKY techniques for some time:

> Some people cry but I get gladness in me, you know, it's a good feeling. So when I get out of there I'm positive, you know, I'm on like drugs but in a good way and I'm pumped up … I get this, you know, strong energy, yeah a lot of energy. (Jamaal)
>
> There's happiness, but it's a peaceful thing and… when you have done this thing, everything else feels and looks different, you know? (Lasse)

Indeed, my own personal experience of the practices quickly led me to experience the type of energy, joy and peace that the men described during interviews:

> When the Kriya practice has concluded, I realise that I cannot stop smiling – I feel a great joy, a peaceful presence that surpasses anything I have experienced before either in meditation or in real-time. Slowly, I am beginning to understand why the transformations that the offenders I have been talking to have been happening. If my stress and anxiety can be relieved through this, it is highly likely that their anger and aggression will also be impacted positively by it. (Researcher's fieldnotes)

In a minority of cases, the men felt that participating in SKY had enriched their religious engagement. For example, Abbad and Cumar had both been brought up as Muslims. They described the way in which the breathing and meditation practices had helped to enable them to become more disciplined and calm enough to pray and had also made their daily prayers feel more profound. Damon also believed that the breathing and meditation practices enabled him to 'get more in contact with his soul' which in turn led to calmness and a greater ability to manage stress. However, as I described in Chapter 3, the concept of spirituality goes beyond religion. Spiritual engagement is often defined in terms of gaining a 'heightened awareness of oneself and others' (Nurden 2010, p. 122) or as a subjective experience that results in 'greater knowledge and love' (Hall et al. 2011, p. 207). It was this form of spirituality that the men I interviewed most commonly cited as being integral to the SKY practices they engaged with. They felt that the deep breathing and mediation enabled them to get more in touch with innate, softer feelings associated with love and kindness for self and others, and an increased focus on empathy:

> Something happens when you meditate – it's like you're coming home … you get in touch with some part of yourself which is maybe [from when you are] three, four, five years old and when you are three, four, five year old then you don't harm anybody so by practicing every day you become a better person … you start to be more kind to people. (Hans)
>
> When you can feel yourself you can start to feel other people, and you can start to feel other people's feelings (Lasse)
>
> I had a problem with one person, and then he wrote something very bad to me. And normally I would just go out and I would just totally destroy him. But for the first time I could see how the other one feels, so I wrote it as a message. It was more like 'what's wrong with you? You must feel bad or something, you know?' I start to be able to sit in another person's place. (Abbad)

Four possible spiritual journeys have been identified by Lee (1999), namely *inward* journeys (self), *outward* journeys (others), *downward* journeys (social and cultural environment) and *upward* journeys (God) (see also Deuchar 2013). It was evident that engaging with the practices had taken the men on *inward* and *outward* journeys: they regarded the yoga, breathing and meditation practices as having had a profound impact on their ability to become more aware of and react differently to their own thoughts and feelings, and to become more sensitive to other people's perspectives. Some believed that the practices had strengthened their ability to go on *upward* journeys that deepened their awareness and contact with a higher religious presence through prayer. However, one of the biggest impacts to emerge from the programme was the way in which participants were taken on *downward* journeys, where the wider social and cultural influence of hegemonic forms of hyper-masculinity slowly became deconstructed, problematized and re-defined (Connell 2005; Deuchar et al. 2016).

Masculinizing SKY, Confronting Emotions and Re-conceptualising Morality

Insights gathered during interviews with the men suggested that, in contrast to some other forms of yoga and meditation that may be seen as 'soft' or 'gentle', they viewed the intensely challenging physical exercises and breathing techniques associated with SKY as 'masculine'. They therefore found it acceptable to engage with the programme. For example, in a similar way to Jesper (above), Jamaal had also become obsessed with bodybuilding and steroid abuse during the years when he was offending, and viewed it as a means of reasserting his sense of masculine self-worth (Gillett and White 1992). As he became more adept at practicing the challenging yoga and breathing techniques, his obsession with bodybuilding diminished since he felt he no longer needed it to make him feel more masculine:

> I trained a lot before … [in prison] I was in a bad mood because I couldn't do weights … you feel you're falling apart … my masculinity was mainly the training, when you are bigger you feel more masculine but now I find something in this that I feel masculine … in the beginning I missed the weight training … [but now] my mind is not so much in the weight training. (Jamaal)

In addition, Damon had recognised that the feminised nature of yoga and meditation portrayed in the media was inaccurate; he had begun to masculinize the inherent challenges involved in practicing the physical techniques of energetic stretching and breathing:

> Of course I don't wanna be like the 'weak' guy, but I don't feel like weak … you only see [meditation] in the *Sex in the City* movie … then it's suddenly just feminine, but actually it's really tough. (Damon)

Certainly, my own personal experience of engaging in the yogic exercises brought it home to me the extent of the intense levels of physical exertion involved in the *Breathe Smart* programme:

> As Haggi gives the instruction, I lie on my front, with my hands in a tight clench tucked in against my waist. Then I slowly try and lift both of my legs at the same time, but feel that it is almost impossible to do. 'It can be done!' Haggi encourages me, and I push again with an almighty effort and slowly lift my legs behind me, while keeping my back straight and my stomach pinned to the floor as I continue to breathe deeply. Now I realise why the guys I have spoken to enjoy this programme – not only are the meditations challenging for the mind, but the yoga techniques and the breathing exercises are physically challenging too. (Researcher's fieldnotes)

However, engaging with SKY also involved the men having to face up to their own emotions and confronting their dominant feelings. The programme was mostly delivered to them on a one-to-one basis by coaches in prisons, and the men were encouraged to open up and express inner feelings and emotional difficulties after they had completed the yoga, breathing and meditation practices. As lead coaches within the programme, Jakob Lund and his team recognised that this involved the men getting in touch with what they described as their 'feminine' sides; they had to confront deeply held views and attitudes and be brave enough to admit that they needed a 'toolbox' to assist them with life's challenges. This could be difficult for those who had become entrenched in the hyper-masculine world of gang culture and violence:

A thing which I see in many of the gang members ... is the rigidity of seeing the world as black and white ... and they have all the dangerous tattoos, and they maybe also have a big dog and then they maybe have a weapon ... there must be something extremely fearful inside, some kind of impotence in their masculinity, and needing to prove all the time. When they start to trust you a little bit ... they start to be able to regulate themselves more. (Jakob Lund, *Breathe Smart* Director)

[The hardest issue is] their own emotion, their own opinions about what a man's gotta do and is not gotta do ... they have learned that the feminine side is the stronger side ... it's feminine strength, and it's stronger. (Haggi, *Breathe Smart* coach)

It's admitting that you need a toolbox – that's actually the feminine side, I think ... you have to be disciplined but [also] have to be soft. (Christoffer, *Breathe Smart* coach)

In a similar way to those men who gained secular and religious support from prison chaplains, the men who participated in SKY during the liminal phase were beginning to experience more profound personal shifts in identity. In Chapter 6, I discussed the strong sense of morality that frequently guided the wider sample of men's participation in gangs and criminality, and the way in which their offending behaviour patterns were often a result of rational choices based on 'anticipated costs and benefits'. (Cornish and Clarke 2014, p. xviii). The men who participated in the *Prison Smart/Breathe Smart* programmes had evidently begun to re-position themselves as 'reformed' or 'reforming' offenders, and to re-direct their moral and ethical precepts in positive, non-criminal directions (White 2013). For instance, Damon was still in a closed prison but had been practicing SKY regularly on a one-to-one basis with Jakob Lund for several months; Cumar had been transferred to an open prison, was able to go home every three weeks and practiced SKY both on his own and in the *Breathe S*mart studio with trained coaches; and Hans had been fully released and now practiced on his own every day. In all three cases, these men (and others I interviewed) had gradually begun to focus more on generative actions and to re-discover and express innate forms of compassion and love to others:

I'm starting to think, 'oh, okay I'm not gonna have these parents forever. So I have to use the time perfectly and tell them that I love them and show them that I appreciate that they have been a good parent to me. (Damon)

I want to … be a good man for my wife and a good son for my parents and a good brother for my brothers and sisters, and good friend and … just do the right thing. (Cumar)

You are not born a tough guy … you are not born with status as a criminal or money-maker. I was born like a creature who was open and full of love and creativity … and when you start to really feel your meditation then you get some small bits of being that way come back. (Hans)

With repeated exposure to the practices both in a coaching situation and on their own, it appeared that the men experienced what could be described as *downward* spiritual journeys (Lee 1999) where they confronted and problematized deeply engrained socially and culturally-influenced attitudes and values. Like those I had met in other parts of the world, they appeared to become more willing to perform broader versions of masculinity and able to enact morality in non-criminal contexts (Deuchar et al. 2016). However, over and above the cognitive and identity changes that the men were beginning to experience, they also revealed to me that the practices had also had an impact on addressing some of the remaining 'stigmata' that could potentially hinder their later progression from *primary* to *secondary* desistance (Maruna and Farrall 2004; Densley 2013).

Addiction, Drugs, Depression and Progressive Desistance Journeys

In Denmark (as in many other geographical contexts), it has been found that a significant proportion of gang members and violent offenders report high levels of drug use (Pederson 2014). Just as I found in Los Angeles, these addiction issues had sometimes created 'stigmata' in the lives of the men I interviewed in Denmark and had frustrated their desistance efforts in the past. However, during my more prolonged discussions with them several of the men talked about the way in which the practicing of SKY had literally replaced their tendency to use drugs to deal with their problems. For instance, some described the way in which they had stopped smoking cannabis, taking cocaine or—as with Jesper and Jamaal—using anabolic steroids as part of bodybuilding regimes. Some even described the way in which they now felt 'addicted' to the SKY practices instead; for instance, Abbad described the way in which his body 'craved' the practices if he missed engaging with them for more than a day.

Jakob Lund described the way in which many of the men he worked with had tended to use drugs as a means of dealing with difficult and anxious thoughts, and the way in which meditation could provide an alternative release from this:

> Sometimes if they have so many thoughts … when you come up there [with drugs] it's like you are released – you are out of control and that's what they're seeking, but the same way when you meditate also you can come out of the more thinking brain … so the more they learn these things the less they need for destructive ways of doing. (Jakob Lund, *Breathe Smart* Director)

For some, the gains and benefits that emerged as a result of the breathing and meditation practices also enabled them to come off of prescribed medication for mental health conditions related to issues from their past. For example, Damon was serving a long prison sentence for a gang-related double murder and had often suffered from unsettling flashbacks to the violence he had been involved in. The following extract from an interview with Damon illustrates the way in which he was prescribed anti-depressants for symptoms of anxiety and trauma while in prison, but he eventually managed to replace this with the daily breathing and meditation practices, which led to increased feelings of happiness and wellbeing:

> I don't think killing people or making violence makes anybody happy … I got these anxiety pills … it helped me a little bit, I didn't get all the thoughts … then I told the doctor, you know, 'I'm never happy'. So he

said, 'Ok, I do this' … in Denmark we call it happy pills, but these pills don't bring you any happiness, they just make you a walking zombie. So I used that for half a year and then I said to my doctor, 'I don't wanna do this anymore … I got [therapy] from healing myself … It's like putting on new glasses … you see the world differently. Before I was aggressive of course, but I've been a pretty calm guy. (Damon)

As I referred to in Chapter 6, Abbad had experienced early childhood trauma when his father had become violent after being tortured in Palestine. Following his prolonged involvement in biker gangs where he became addicted to cocaine and often acted as the 'muscle' to collect financial debts from drug sales, Abbad later suffered from distressing flashbacks to the violence he had been involved in. He also suffered further psychological distress as a consequence of prolonged illicit drug use and the fact that he his wife had left him and taken their son with her while he was still in prison. Like Damon, Abbad described the way in which he had been prescribed anti-depressants, and had taken them for six years. Also like Damon, he subsequently stopped taking the pills when he started the *Prison Smart* programme and felt like he had a new lease of life:

It was like a miracle … it's like I was dead but I became alive again … I stopped taking depressive medicine after six years … I was so much influenced by the drugs that I was just going round like a zombie … when I started the course, I stopped during the programme. (Abbad)

Hans also described the way in which engaging with the SKY practices gave him renewed feelings of energy that helped him to deal with depression:

When you are breathing in those levels you do in Sudarshan Kriya then you fill up your body and the [blood] cells with energy. And when you do that every day and slowly, slowly the body is like an engine. It gets more and more fuel. And that's, that can be a way to work with depression. (Hans)

The men felt that the renewed sense of calmness and peace they felt, combined with their widening views about masculinity and their ability to manage the 'stigmata' that offending lifestyles had left them with, had given them a stronger determination to desist. Regardless of whether they were still in prison or back in the community during the time of the interviews, their comments often indicated that the SKY practices had helped them to feel a sense of remorse but also self-forgiveness and a commitment towards non-criminal lifestyles:

> It was really good to look into myself for the first time in my life, you know? And see all the fucked up things I've done ... I talked about it a lot because it was so deep ... remorse and ... inner peace, and I could forgive myself ... for the life I've lived and the violence I do to people and all that kind of shit. (Lucas)

> I've felt bad for the people I've hurt by violence ... I'm not proud of it [but] it's a part of me and I accept it, I cannot change it but I can learn from it ... I think I have dealt with all these things ... I will just charge forwards on getting this company up and try getting a lot of work and just use the time with the friends that are not doing crime. (Damon)

As with the insights I gained from other men in Denmark, Scotland and the USA who were exposed to different forms of religious or spiritual engagement, I found that engaging in the yoga and mediation practices was helping these Danish participants to embrace pro-social values. They were increasingly discarding their 'old selves' and finding new 'possible selves' (Paternoster and Bushway 2009, p. 1113) through a gradual contemplative process of 'rebiographing' (Johnson and Larson 2003: 27).

Concluding Discussion

Against the backdrop of feeling ready for change while in the liminal phase (Healy 2012), the nine Danish men I have focused on in this chapter had sought out the support of yoga and meditation instructors. This was often as a result of various *push* and *pull* factors, psychological difficulties and/or because they had heard about the benefits of SKY from other prison inmates (Decker et al. 2014). Most of the men had been gang members, while two had evidently been involved in criminal activity outwith the context of gangs. However, the crimes that the latter had been involved in (such as drug dealing and armed robbery) were similar to those associated with gang environments and still driven by a sense of marginalised masculinity (Flores 2014). Exposure to the SKY practices evidently enabled all of the men to continue to embrace and express hegemonic masculine ideals focused on physicality, while also encouraging them to begin to problematize deeply engrained attitudes and values, perform broader versions of masculinity and open up to and discuss their emotions and feelings (Deuchar et al. 2016). They experienced a range of personal journeys and turning points. These were sometimes punctuated and characterised by a deeper awareness and engagement with a higher religious presence, or (more commonly) a subtle focus on spirituality whereby they gained a heightened awareness of their own personal emotions and a greater commitment to take account of other people's feelings.

The insights I gained from the men verify previous evidence from clinical trials that suggests that SKY can be a potential yet safe antidepressant therapy, and can help to improve emotional processing, help participants manage stress and anxiety and lead to increased feelings of calmness and eudemonic wellbeing (Janakiramaiah et al. 2000; Brown and Gerbarg 2005a, b; Vedamurthachar et al. 2006; Pandya 2016). The participants' self-confessed ability to move away from both prescription and illegal drugs and to use the practices as a means of managing the 'stigmata' (Densley 2013, p. 132) that participation in gangs and violence often brings about (including stress, anxiety and depression) have significant implications for offender rehabilitation.

In similar ways to those who drew upon emotional support from prison chaplains and to assimilate themes from religious texts into their self-narratives (see Chapter 7), the men who engaged in yoga, dynamic breathing and mediation practices were literally beginning to discard 'old selves' and to adopt new masculine identities. In many ways, this was enabling them to re-direct their innate proclivities towards moral and ethical precepts in positive, non-criminal directions. Thus, within their personal narratives they were beginning to focus on values such as commitment and loyalty through earning an honest living, being a good parent and family man and—most importantly—desisting from crime (Maruna 2001; Johnston and Larson 2003).

As Bilderbeck et al. (2013, p. 1443) has highlighted, research and policy surrounding mental health interventions in prisons has thus far largely focused on 'psychological and psychosocial treatments'. However, these are costly, and often found to be 'inaccessible, stigmatising and undesirable because of their time-consuming and emotionally demanding nature' (ibid). The use of behavioural- oriented, ascetic-spiritual interventions like SKY may offer a more 'socially acceptable' alternative. This is particularly salient given the evidence in this chapter that suggests that participating in the practices (a) upheld the male participants' sense of physicality and prevented them from feeling emasculated; and (b) led them to problematize the use of aggression and violence, to engage in open emotional expression and to express more empathy.

Given the high rates of psychological problems, social pressures and reduced wellbeing experienced by prisoners and reforming offenders and the holistic nature of factors that have been found to contribute to the desistance process, it is possible that the positive illustrations outlined in this chapter could hold significance in future policy related decisions in wider Europe. The wider use of ascetic-spiritual interventions like SKY could be an important means of nurturing deeper shifts in cognitions, identities and social circumstances of male gang members and wider groups of violent and drug-dealing offenders within the context of prison and post-prison offender support and rehabilitation (Giordano et al. 2002).

However, as in other parts of the book I am cautious about over-generalising the insights from this part of my research, given its small-scale focus on the experiences of just nine offenders. As with earlier studies (Bilderbeck et al. 2013; Ahlmark 2015), one particular limitation of my research was its inability to identify the specific elements of the SKY practices (such as yoga postures, rhythmic breathing techniques or meditation) that gave rise to the most salient benefits described by the participants. In addition, there was a lack of scope to explore the extent to which wider groups of men may have begun to engage in SKY and then later dropped out of the *Prison Smart/Breathe Smart* programmes. Finally, it was also unclear whether the social support and complementary use of reflective dialogue and 'talking therapy' during sessions and/or the social effects of practicing SKY as part of a group post-release may also have contributed towards the described impacts in terms of enhanced mood states and cognitive identity reconstructions (see also Bilderbeck et al. 2013). Clearly, additional research with wider samples of participants that involve a fine-grain analysis of these individual factors during interviews and participant observation is required as a means of further enhancing the applicability of the evidence-base.

In the next part of the book, I focus attention on one final geographic location—Asia, with a specific spotlight placed on Hong Kong. In Chapter 9, I present key insights emerging from life history interviews with a small group of reforming male triad gang members. I then draw on wider evidence from fieldnotes and interviews in Chapter 10 to illustrate the way in which participation in a Christian-based religious intervention enabled these men to challenge and realign their entrenched beliefs about masculinity and crime.

References

Ahlmark, N. (2015). *Forandring gennem andedraet: Breathe smart Som en vej ud af Kriminalitet og Misbrug*. Copenhagen: Syddansk Universitet.

Bilderdeck, A. C., Farias, M., Brazil, I. A., Jakobowitz, S., & Wikholm, C. (2013). Participation in a 1-week course of yoga improves behavioural control and decreased psychological distress in a prison population. *Journal of Psychiatric Research, 47*, 1438–1445.

Breathe Smart. (2016). Available at: http://www.breathesmart.co.uk/. Accessed 4 September 2017.

Brown, R. P., & Gerbarg, P. L. (2005a). Sudarshan Kriya yogic breathing in the treatment of stress, anxiety, and depression: Part I neurophysiologic model. *The Journal of Alternative and Complementary Medicine, 11*(1), 189–201.

Brown, R. P., & Gerbarg, P. L. (2005b). Sudarshan Kriya yogic breathing in the treatment of stress, anxiety, and depression: Part II—Clinical applications and guidelines. *The Journal of Alternative and Complementary Medicine, 11*(4), 711–717.

Carlsson, C. (2012). Using 'turning points' to understand processes of change in offending. *British Journal of Criminology, 52*, 1–16.

Connell, R. W. (2005). *Masculinities*. Cambridge: Polity Press.

Cornish, D. B., & Clarke, R. V. (Eds.). (2014). *The reasoning criminal: Rational choice perspectives on offending*. New Brunswick, NJ: Transaction.

Decker, S. H., Pyrooz, D., & Moule, R. K. Jr. (2014). Disengagement from gangs as role transitions. *Journal of Research on Adolescence, 24*(2), 268–283.

Densley, J. (2013). *How gangs work: An ethnography of youth violence*. London: Palgrave Macmillan.

Deuchar, R. (2013). *Policing youth violence: Transatlantic connections*. London: Trentham Books/IOE Press.

Deuchar, R., Søgaard, T. F., Kolind, T., Thylstrup, B., & Wells, L. (2016). 'When you're boxing you don't think so much': Pugilism, transitional masculinities and criminal desistance among young Danish gang members. *Journal of Youth Studies, 19*(6), 725–742.

Emerson, R. M., Fretz, R., & Shaw, L. (1995). *Writing ethnographic fieldnotes*. Chicago: University of Chicago Press.

Flores, E. O. (2014). *God's gangs: Barrio ministry, masculinity and gang recovery*. New York: New York University Press.

Gillett, J., & White, P. G. (1992). Male bodybuilding and the reassertion of hegemonic masculinity: A critical feminist perspective. *Play and Culture, 5*(4), 358–369.

Giordano, P. C., Cernkovich, S. A., & Rudolph, J. L. (2002). Gender, crime and desistance: Toward a theory of cognitive transformation. *American Journal of Sociology, 107*, 990–1064.

Gold, R. (1958). Roles in sociological field observation. *Social Forces, 36*, 217–223.

Hall, R. E., Livingston, J. N., Brown, C. J., & Mohabir, J. A. (2011). Islam and Asia Pacific Muslims: The implications of spirituality for social work practice. *Journal of Social Work Practice, 25*(2), 205–215.

Harding, S. (2014). *The street casino: Survival in violent street gangs*. Bristol: Policy Press.

Healy, D. (2012). *The dynamics of desistance: Charting pathways through change*. New York: Routledge.

Janakiramaiah, N., Gangadhar, B. N., Murthy, P. J. N. V., Harish, M. G., Subbakrishna, D. K., & Vedamurthachar, A. (2000). Antidepressant efficacy of Sudarshan Kriya Yoga (SKY) in melancholia: A randomised comparison with electroconvulsive therapy (ECT) and imipramine. *Journal of Affective Disorders, 57*, 255–259.

Johnson, B. R., & Larson, D. B. (2003). *The inner change freedom initiative: A preliminary evaluation of a faith-based prison program*. Waco, TX: Baylor University.

Lee, J. (1999). *Spiritual development*. London: United Reform Church.
Maruna, S. (2001). *Making good: How ex-convicts reform and rebuild their lives*. Washington, DC: American Psychological Association.
Maruna, S., & Farrall, S. (2004). Desistance from crime: A theoretical reformulation. *Kolner Zeitschrift fur Soziologie und Sozialpsychologie, 43*, 171–194.
Murthy, P. J. N. V., Janakiramaiah, N., Gangadhar, B. N., & Subbakrishna, D. K. (1998). P300 amplitude and antidepressant response to Sudarshan Kriya Yoga (SKY). *Journal of Affective Disorders, 50*, 45–48.
Nurden, H. (2010). Working with faith. In T. Jeffs & M. K. Smith (Eds.), *Youth work practice* (pp. 121–132). Hampshire: Palgrave Macmillan.
Pandya, A. P. (2016). Sudarshan Kriya of the art of living foundation: Applications to social work practice. *Practice: Social Work in Action, 28*(2), 133–154.
Pandya, S. P. (2015). Adolescents, well-being and spirituality: Insights from a spiritual program. *International Journal of Children's Spirituality, 20*(1), 29–49.
Paternoster, R., & Bushway, S. (2009). Desistance and the feared self: Towards an identity theory of criminal desistance. *Journal of Criminal Law and Criminology, 99*(4), 1103–1156.
Pedersen, M. L. (2014). Gang joining in Denmark: Prevalence and correlates of street gang membership. *Journal of Scandinavian Studies in Criminology and Crime Prevention, 15*(1), 55–72.
Satyanarayana, M., Rajeswari, K. R., Jhansi Rani, N., Krishna, Ch. Sri, & Krishna Rao, P. V. (1992). Effects of Santhi Kriya on certain psychophysiological parameters: A preliminary study. *Indian Physiological Pharmacology, 36*(2), 88–92.
Vedamurthachar, A., Janakiramaiah, N., Hegde, J. M., Shetty, T. K., Subbakrishna, D. K., Sureshbabu, S. V., & Gangadhar, B. N. (2006). Antidepressant efficacy and hormonal effects of Sudarshana Kriya Yoga (SKY) in alcohol dependent individuals. *Journal of Affective Disorders, 94*, 249–253.
White, R. (2013). *Youth gangs, violence and social respect: Exploring the nature of provocations and punch-ups*. Basingstoke, UK: Palgrave Macmillan.

Part V

Hong Kong: From Triad-Affiliated Gangsters to Christian Brothers

9

Foot Soldiers, Gangsters and Drug Addicts in Hong Kong

This part of the book brings the focus to a third and final Continent of interest—Asia, with a specific spotlight placed on Hong Kong. The suggested connections between youth gangs and triad societies are examined, and I draw attention to the particular ways that male youth gang members can become 'triadized' and immersed in organised criminality. I then move on to explore and examine the potential impact of a Christian-based religious intervention in terms of supporting male offenders to begin to move away from triad-related crime.

In this chapter, I begin by sharing insights from life history interviews conducted with a small sample of men of various ages in Hong Kong who had become members of street gangs and slowly transitioned to become part of triad-affiliated crime groups. Through drawing on the most salient themes from interviews, I explore the underlying social and cultural influences that led the men to engage with and (in some cases) progress through triad hierarchies, and the links with masculinity. I also examine the range of factors that triggered a readiness for change among these men.

Contextual Background for Youth Gangs and Organised Crime in Hong Kong

Compared to other international provinces, over the years Hong Kong has earned the reputation of having low crime rates and very little concern with juvenile delinquency (Wong 2000; Adorjan and Chui 2012; Harding 2016). With a population of just over seven million, there were fewer than 20 homicides there in 2011 (Fraser 2017). By comparison, Glasgow (a city over ten times less populated) had around the same number, while Los Angeles (with a metropolitan city population that is approximately double that of Hong Kong) had 15 times more homicides in the same year. However, some reports suggest that there has been an increase in juvenile crime in Hong Kong in recent years. This has emerged against the contextual backdrop of rapid economic transformation and increased pressure on families and young people to compete within a rapidly growing capitalist society (Harding 2016).

While street gang culture is at a relatively early stage of development, Hong Kong has a long history of organised criminal gangs related to triad society (Harding 2016; Fraser 2017). Triad is a branch of one of the formal secret societies that originated in mainland China (Wang 2017). Secret societies emerged in earnest in China in the eighteenth century with a strong 'patriotic doctrine' (Lo 2012, p. 556), thriving and prospering on corruption and involvement in a range of 'legal and illegal businesses' (Lintner 2004, p. 84). However, Lo (2010, p. 851) traces the founding of the Chinese triad society to the seventeenth century with a focus on overthrowing the Ch'ing Dynasty and restoring the Ming Dynasty (see also Lo 2012). The core values associated with triad society were (and continue to be) 'loyalty, righteousness, secrecy and brotherhood' and a key focus on *guanxi* (Lo 2010). *Guanxi* is a cultural characteristic that has 'strong implications for interpersonal and inter-organisational behaviours in Chinese society', and is characterised by 'interpersonal connections' and 'reciprocal exchange' (Jiang et al. 2012, p. 207, and see Chapter 10 for further discussion).

Evidence suggests that triad leaders exert rigid control over the behaviour of members who are ultimately expected to regard each other as 'blood brothers', to be fiercely loyal to one another and even to sacrifice themselves for their group (Lo and Kwok 2014, p. 5336). Prominent criminal activity has traditionally revolved around gambling, vice and money laundering as well as drug dealing and prostitution and it is apparent that gangsters have, in the past, often operated 'under the "protective umbrella" of government departments and judiciary departments' (Harding 2016, p. 309; see also Fraser 2017). Accordingly, in many ways triad members have frequently been compared to the Sicilian mafia (Broadhurst and Wa 2010), with a strong ability to sustain their criminal endeavor through forming partnerships with prominent Chinese political leaders and business organisations (Lo 2012).

In spite of the evidence that suggests that there may be strong links between triad society, organised crime and juvenile street gangs, research in this area to date has been under-developed due to the lack of availability of or access to relevant data (Lo 2010, 2012). In one of the few accounts available, Lo (2012, p. 556) demonstrates how young people of teenage years are socialised into street gangs and eventually experience submission into triad subcultures and values: a process he refers to as 'triadization'. He argues that young men tend to initially join gangs as a means of seeking wider socialization networks, to gain a sense of protection and fun. Wider research evidence by Wong (2001) has also suggested that some youths may drift into delinquency as a result of relative social deprivation, low attachment to parents, poor relationships with teachers and low academic performance (see also Pyrooz and Decker 2013). In addition, it has been suggested that those living in the more disadvantaged neighbourhoods of Hong Kong may feel that they cannot engage safely and securely in recreational activities on the street or in game or leisure centres unless they have a 'Big brother' figure from gang subcultures to protect them, for fear of bullying (Wong 2001, p. 99; Lo 2012). Thus, in some cases becoming involved in street gangs may act as a device for 'saving face', a value that is very important in Chinese culture (Wong 2001).

Lo's (2012) research has suggested that youth gangs tend to be scattered around Hong Kong, but 'localised in certain neighbourhoods' where the chances of teenagers befriending triad-affiliated gangsters are greater (p. 559). Over time, these youth members of street gangs become hired by triad 'snakeheads' or enforcers to provide the lowest tier of triad society, acting as 'foot soldiers' in order to collect drug dues, transport large quantities of money to and from triad leaders and engage in violence where required (Lintner 2004, p. 87). Following formal initiation services where incense is burned and oaths are taken to swear lifelong allegiance to triad society, juveniles become disciplined by triad gangsters. They may be given material goods such as designer suits, mobile phones and expensive sunglasses as a further means of cementing their sense of masculine status and belonging (ibid).

As their associations with triads evolve into adulthood, some men progress from being associate members within the context of youth gangs to professional gangsters who have closer connections with, or may even help to coordinate and lead, triad societies (Lo 2012). Initially recruited in the role of affiliated member (often referred to as 'Hanging the Blue Lantern'), through the process of triadization they may progress to be a '49 boy' (formal member) to one of the officer bearers and eventually to liaison officer, fighter, mastermind, deputy boss and then ultimately to triad boss (Lo 2012, p. 566). Although their increasing involvement in serious organised crime clearly means they become dangerous, these men are also victims of exploitation and evidence also suggests that they often become drug addicts (Lo 2012).

Although still prominent in Hong Kong society, some evidence suggests that triad associations have become 'more diffuse and fragmented' in recent years due to various government-initiated crackdowns and social interventions (Fraser 2017). Further, a reform of the police corruption that may at one time have helped to protect triad societies via the Independent Commission Against Corruption (ICAC) has helped to diminish their stronghold (Fraser 2017). For those who begin as street gang members and become influenced by triad norms, outreach social work provides a preventative means of re-engaging young men before they become further immersed in triad subcultures (Wong 2000; Lo 2012). Outreach workers provide them with the type of 'social support' that may motivate initial desistance journeys (Adorjan and Chui 2012, p. 581). Due to the continued importance placed on religion in Hong Kong, some evidence also suggests that engagement in Christian-based interventions may be a powerful tool for motivating the 'hooks for change' needed by those who may have risen further up the ranks within triad hierarchies (Stewart et al. 1999; Adorjan and Chui 2012).

Research into the Experiences of Male Gang Members in Hong Kong

The empirical focus in this chapter and the next emerges from small-scale ethnographic research I conducted in Hong Kong in the winter of 2015. Lo (2012) has previously highlighted the extreme challenges associated with trying to access gang members who may have (or previously had) triad associations and are therefore reluctant to share information. I was therefore particularly conscious of the need to engage informally with those who may be in the process of transitioning away from triad lifestyle associations in a confined environment as a means of building trust before engaging in any formal interviews or observations.

The site for my data collection was a renowned non-government religious organisation based in Hong Kong, which (due to particular issues relating to confidentiality) I refer to under the fictitious name of the *Hong Kong Christian Society (HKCS)*. *HKCS* is focused on supporting male offenders and gang members to try to reform, and with a particular emphasis on treating the drug addiction issues that are often a major factor in their prolonged involvement in criminality (further details on *HKCS* can be found in Chapter 10). Through the use of gatekeepers who were involved in coordinating the programmes within *HKCS*, I was initially able to visit the organisation during times when support sessions were being implemented and engage informally with the male participants during dinner breaks and recreational activities.

Since most of the men had limited English proficiency, rapport-building was challenging but benefited from the presence of volunteers within the programme who were on occasions able to act as interpreters and translate informal conversations amongst us. Once trust had been established, I sought the men's willingness to engage in life history and follow-up interviews, to be observed while engaging in religious-oriented workshops and study groups and to continue to

Table 9.1 The research participants in Hong Kong

Name	Age	Role within *HKCS*
Ling	60	Programme participant
Peng	62	Programme participant
Choi	50	Programme participant
Lee	31	Programme participant
Chan	30	Programme participant
Simon	27	Programme participant
Chase	27	Programme participant
Cedric	30	Volunteer/mentor

engage in informal discussion with me during these support sessions. In this chapter, I report on the insights from life history interviews, before drawing on wider data emerging from participant observation, follow-up interviews and informal discussions in the next.

In total, I conducted life history interviews with eight men who (as with my other data collection sites) could be described as 'reforming' gang members on the threshold of change (Healy 2012). Table 9.1 provides an overview of the participants, specifying their names (pseudonyms), ages and whether (during the time of research fieldwork) they were engaging in *HKCS* as participants or (in one case) had already completed the various support sessions within it and now engaged in voluntary mentorship to support other men. As Table 9.1 illustrates, the age-ranges of the men spanned between late twenties and sixty at the time that the interviews took place. All had been born and raised in socially disadvantaged housing estates in a variety of geographical areas of Hong Kong, and all were Chinese.

Unlike in other geographical areas where I worked (including Denmark), for the most part the interviewees in Hong Kong were somewhat limited in their proficiency in the English language, and did not therefore feel confident to converse with me in English. Accordingly, through arrangements put in place by the Christian Pastor who had founded and coordinated *HKCS* (see further details in the next chapter) and with the consent of the male participants, on most occasions interviews were conducted with the assistance of interpreters. All of the interpreters were volunteer mentors within *HKCS* and therefore known to and trusted by the interviewees. In most cases, the voluntary interpreters sat in on interviews, translated my questions into Chinese for the participants and then subsequently translated the interviewees' responses back into English for me. The English translation was later transcribed from audio recordings. Interpreters were made aware of the confidential nature of the interviews and the importance of not sharing or discussing the content with anyone (Murray and Wynne 2001).

Although this was seen as a reasonably efficient means of gaining insights from participants, I also recognised the challenges associated with conducting cross-language interviews using interpreters (Wallin and Ahlström 2006; Squires 2009; Williamson et al. 2011). In particular, I was conscious that some subtle elements of the participants' described experiences and insights may have been skewed by the different interpreters' elucidations, and some meanings may have been lost. However, wherever possible I ensured that two interpreters were present during interviews so that insights passed on by one were verified by the other, thus increasing the relative trustworthiness of emerging data. Even during the occasions when this was not practically possible, since the full interviews were tape recorded (including the translations made by interpreters) it was still possible to get a second interpreter to verify the accuracy of the first interpreter's translations at a later stage (Murray and Wynne 2001). Overall, I believe that the strategies I used enabled the authenticity of emerging data to be maintained. In the sections that follow, the themes emerging from life history interviews are presented and salient quotations from participants highlighted.

Family Strains, Relative Disadvantage, Cultural Values and Masculinity

In previous chapters I documented the recurring emphasis that American, Scottish and Danish participants placed on the difficult family circumstances they experienced while growing up, and how this often stimulated their offending. This was frequently characterised by missing father-figures, lack of wider positive male role models, alcohol, drug abuse and criminality. In contrast to this, the men I interviewed in Hong Kong did not allude specifically to absent fathers, nor to any form of substance dependency/abuse or criminality within their family environments as an initial stimulus for their gang involvement. However, they did talk about experiencing a general lack of parental attention and monitoring due to pressures of work and low communication skills (Wong 2001). They also referred to being exposed to angry outbursts by fathers and to experiences of living in relative deprivation compared to wider Hong Kong society:

> I always felt neglected by my own parents when they were always busy with making money. During my childhood I suffered from low parental attachment. (Cedric)
>
> My family was running a business – something like a labour business, and they were very busy and they [parents] have no time to take care of me … when I was seven years old, I didn't stay home already – I would just sleep overnight at other places. (Simon)
>
> I had many complicated events happen in my life. I was living in the poorest area … my parents had low education and they have very brief words. So the family affects a lot in my life … so my father work, and didn't [give] any attention to his children. When he has any trouble outside he … shifted those angers to his children. (Ling)
>
> I saw some people who had a richer family, so I felt some pressure. (Peng)

In contrast to any other findings I had gained from my wider international research, one of the Hong Kong participants, Lee, described the way in which he felt that his parents had given him too much love and attention and not enough discipline during his formative years because of his experiences with childhood illness. He believed that this had contributed towards his subsequent tendency towards delinquency:

> When I was younger I had blood cancer so my family members loved me very much. So even up to High School and throughout my years in school I was very loved by my family. But too much love and so I had a lot of freedom to go do things, bad things with friends. (Lee)

Chen and Starosta (1997, p. 7) draw attention to the central focus on *mientze* within Chinese culture. *Mientze* refers to the 'projected image of ourselves in a relationship network' and the central focus on 'saving one's face' as a means of heightening one's self-esteem. In addition to feeling as if he had been overwhelmed with attention and had experienced a lack of social boundaries at home following his childhood illness, Lee's experiences of being bullied by other teenagers led him to seek creative ways of 'saving face' through the protection that street gangs offered him:

> Growing up I had a very innocent face and I was bullied a lot so there's this group, and the gang were like, 'hey, join us'. So I wanted to join so I would be protected. So just being in a gang, you know it's a lot of people, it's fun and it's also just – I guess having that protection helps. (Lee)

In addition to Lee, Peng also indicated that he sought security from having strong gang-affiliated males around him to deal with problems of bullying:

> In the surrounding area I just got bullied and I felt that it's better to find someone more strong, more people afraid of, to follow … in order for me to get enough protection. (Peng)

In other cases, hegemonic masculine values that dominated the social landscape in the more rural parts of Hong Kong combined with boredom played a part in encouraging the interviewees to participate in street violence as teenage boys, as Chan described:

> Up in [name of community] they have villages … they have a very special culture in the village, you know? The man is always powerful. Always the power to do everything … male dominated culture … if you are the male, you have the privilege, you know? … so I was brought up in that kind of culture … in the village, we had nothing to do – so what we do is fight with each other for fun … we fight with each other to show our macho-ness. (Chan)

A number of the men admitted that their initial involvement in street gangs and violence had become sustained through the influence of other young boys with similar home backgrounds to their own. For example, Ling and Simon described the way in which they offended with other boys who also suffered from parental neglect (also see the next section for further details), while Cedric evidently viewed the gang as a surrogate family:

> At 12, I got along with groups of people 12–13 years old ... from similar backgrounds because most of the families were quite complicated ... when it started we went to steal together, to steal food. When we grow up a bit more we start to rob with a knife. (Ling)
>
> When I was young I stayed with guys with the same background, similar backgrounds ... some of them were in the same situation – no one takes care of them. So it was a group of people that's abandoned, I would say that. (Simon)
>
> Members of the same gang call each other 'brother' ... they provide each other with unconditional support on the basis of solidarity and companionship. One of the main attractive factors of gangs is their sense of familial closeness. (Cedric)

Accordingly, it appeared that a complex array of factors first led the men I worked with in Hong Kong to gravitate towards gang culture, delinquency and violence. In similar ways to the USA, as a strongly capitalist society Hong Kong places a huge emphasis on economic success and those who are disadvantaged experience a disjunction between what the culture extols and what the social structure makes possible (Lilly et al. 2015, drawing on Merton 1968). This clearly induced a somewhat Mertonian-like pressure for deviance among some. However, more commonly the insights from interviews reflected the wider, holistic views of Agnew (1992), suggesting that strain emerged in the lives of the men during their childhood years as a result of a myriad of factors. The feeling of being excluded by or rejected by parents (as with Cedric and Simon) combined (as in the case of Ling) with the presence of stressful emotions within the family or even (in Lee's case) the experience of overly lenient parenting styles led to low social control and reduced attachment to the family home (Lilly et al. 2015). For both Lee and Peng, seeking protection from bullying through gang membership was also essential as a means of upholding a sense of status and 'saving face' among their peer groups, while for Chan street violence was a means of simple masculine expression.

The multifaceted factors that appeared to lead the men into Hong Kong youth gangs therefore reflected earlier empirical insights focused on issues of low self-control, household strains, low parental monitoring, perceptions about masculinity and wider peer delinquency within communities (Wong 2001; Lo 2012; Pyrooz and Decker 2013). And as the next section illustrates, the men's initial involvement in street gangs ultimately led to 'triadization', drug dependency and wider criminality (Lo 2012, p. 556).

'Triadization', Drugs and Organised Crime

For the men I interviewed, their initial involvement in street gangs, petty crime and violence as a means of finding protection and social support from older male peers or expressing their masculinity gradually evolved to wider forms of criminality. As Lo (2012) has described in his earlier research, the process of 'triadization' is usually characterised by gradual submission to triad subcultures and values and by increasing levels of control being exerted upon marginalised young men in local communities. Boxes 9.1 and 9.2 illustrate the way in which early experience of social disadvantage and lack of parental support led Simon and Ling to hang out with other young boys on the streets. They also document how their emerging dependency on, and eventual addiction to, drugs opened them up to being influenced and recruited by triad leaders.

> **Box 9.1:** *Simon's Story*
>
> Being raised in a disadvantaged neighbourhood in Hong Kong and having parents who had to work all the time to try and make a living led to Simon feeling neglected and unhappy during his childhood. He began to hang around with older boys in the street with similar family situations from a young age. At the age of 12, Simon had joined a local street gang and began selling pirate DVDs to make some extra money. During the next few years, he continued to become influenced by the older boys in the gang and began using drugs, including ketamine. As time went on, these gang leaders continued to influence him and encouraged him

to engage in more and more criminal acts. This eventually led Simon to become violent, and at the age of 16 he became involved in a fight with another young man in a local games arcade and was then charged for violent offending and given a short-term prison sentence. When he was released, Simon continued to be influenced by the local gang leaders; he began to realise that they had triad connections and slowly became conscious that his criminal record enabled him to gain the credentials for full access to triad membership:

There was some older guy, maybe the leader in the gang – they just keep telling me that 'it's easy, it's normal [to commit crime]'. So, yeah, you have to keep doing this to show your identity. If you wanna show up, you have to do more and more ... and when they get you into like doing crime things it's still, 'it's part of it.' And then when you get into prison and you come out to be part of the triad – it's normal to have crime records.

Simon's mother warned him about using ketamine and tried to get him to stop, but Simon was again influenced by the triad elders who told him not to be 'weak' and to keep on using it to prove he was a 'man'. As Simon continued to use the drug, he began to feel more and more powerful and happy but increasingly also realised that the cost of the drug meant that he had to earn more money.

At this point, Simon began to sell drugs to try and make enough cash to feed his addiction. Since he had to submit some of the profits to the triad leaders, he realised that he often did not have enough money for his own consumption and so he began to sell larger volumes of drugs. At one point he was caught by the police and went to prison for six months, but disclosed nothing to the police about the operations of the triad networks. As his reputation for drug dealing, street violence and loyalty to the triads spread, he was introduced to wider criminal networks and he eventually went into business with another young triad member. Together, Simon and his partner began engaging in drug trafficking for the triad leaders, who trusted that neither of the men would disclose any details of the triad networks to the police because they had 'proved' their loyalty to the 'brotherhood' in the past.

By the time he reached his early twenties, Simon became conscious that his addiction to ketamine had got out of control. He was stealing money from his parents to pay for his habit, and he was losing weight and feeling that his health was deteriorating. He began to lose confidence and felt weary from the lifestyle he had as a 'foot soldier' for the triads:

I had stolen my parents' money, I cannot look people in the eye, I lost my confidence, no motivation, I wasn't feeling young anymore.

At the age of 25, his diminishing confidence led Simon to become more careless in his criminal acts. He was eventually caught by the police and sent to prison for a long-term sentence for drug dealing and trafficking charges, forcing him to reconsider his future lifestyle.

Box 9.2: *Ling's Story*

Ling's early exposure to social disadvantage and lack of attention from his parents led to him engaging in petty theft and knife carrying as a young boy. Having been influenced by other disadvantaged young men, Ling eventually began using drugs at the age of 13, including ketamine. The older boys in the local gang he joined, who were influenced by the triad leaders, encouraged Ling to begin selling drugs for them in order to make more money. Ling subsequently spent his teenage years dealing drugs and engaging in street violence, and by his early 20s he increasingly realised that he was becoming more and more valued by the senior triads because he was seen as someone who was able to bring in money from drug deals and also intimidate others:

When we find money to serve to the elder, like big 'brothers', you get more 'valuable', more important in the triads ... so I got more important in the triads and people fear me.

As he progressed into his 30s, Ling found that he got promoted and rose up to the senior ranks in the triads. He realised that the triad leaders respected him due to the large volumes of money he had been able to earn from drug dealing, and because of his loyalty to the triad 'brotherhood':

The one who earns the most money becomes the highest guy ... all I wanted to do was protect my family, protect my brothers and this is how I got promoted to the highest [level], like people respect me.

Although Ling continued to be promoted and gained status within the senior triad echelons as one of the leaders who was giving orders to affiliated members, he also found that his dependency on ketamine and later on cocaine and cannabis intensified. He also developed a personal addiction to gambling, and this drove him to try and earn more and more money. Because of the unwritten protection agreements between the triad society and the police at the time, Ling was always able to avoid lengthy prison sentences and so his coordination of criminal activity continued until he was in his 50s.

However, a turning point came for Ling when the Independent Commission Against Corruption (ICAC) began to become more stringent in its investigations and the police protection that had thus far existed began to disappear. Ling began to feel more paranoid about potential retaliation from enemies, and to struggle more and more with ill health from his drug addiction. The combination of these factors eventually forced Ling to a point where he resigned from his position within the triads.

As discussed earlier in the chapter, it has been found that secret and corrupt triad societies are endemic in many parts of Asia, and particularly in Hong Kong (Lintner 2004). 'Snakeheads' from various triad societies are known to recruit young men as 'foot soldiers', and those who have become distanced from their parents, have developed drug addiction issues and/or feel in need of protection from older peers are often most susceptible to exploitation (Lintner 2004; Wong 2001; Lo 2012). Lo (2012) refers to a typology of gangs in Hong Kong: first, deviant youth groups mainly socialise together on street corners or games centres and engage in recreational activities together; second, youth gangs are actively involved in occasional violent and deviant activities and have associations with criminal gangs run by triad societies; and third, triad criminal gangs are professional criminals with close connection to senior triad leaders, are cohesive and concerned mainly with money-oriented criminal activity and tend to suppress violence in order to avoid police attention. Through the delegated influence of existing youth gang members, triad leaders tend to recruit secondary school-aged young men in public housing estates who are already involved in deviant groups. They slowly become manipulated and used as 'criminal tools' (ibid., p. 559).

The case studies outlined in Boxes 9.1 and 9.2 illustrate clearly that both Simon and Ling were subjected to this 'triadization' process, albeit with slightly different longer-term outcomes (ibid., p. 556). In both cases, as teenage boys these men were vulnerable to triad influence because of their exposure to household strains, low parental monitoring and wider peer delinquency within their neighourhoods (Wong 2001; Lo 2012; Pyrooz and Decker 2013). Their involvement with deviant youth groups and petty crime led on to a subtle initiation into drug dependency and street violence. It has been found that illicit drug use in Hong Kong has become a grave concern over the past two decades and that there is a growing belief among young people that psychotropic substance abuse is non-addictive and a 'valid choice of life' (Shek 2007, p. 2021). In particular, it has been found that ketamine abuse among adolescents is somewhat unique to Hong Kong and that the light sentences associated with its use makes it attractive (ibid). Simon and Ling's early use of ketamine to prove their sense of masculinity to delinquent peers led on to increased susceptibility to becoming more influenced by these older 'brothers' in their neighbourhoods who were triad members. Their transition into drug dealing 'foot soldiers' was evidently the result of gradual 'triadization' (Lo 2012, p. 556).

As I referred to in Chapter 2, Harding (2014) discusses how gang members are constantly attempting to acquire 'street capital' by building personal reputations and branding. Accumulating masculine status on the streets allows significant others to rank their position within the gang hierarchy (for further discussion, see Chapter 11). Both Simon and Ling were able to form criminal rackets linked to triad subcultures as a result of proving their 'manhood' through gaining 'street capital', which was contingent on displaying their commitment to strong patriotic values such as loyalty, secrecy and brotherhood (Lo 2012; Harding 2014, 2016). Criminal credentials were further enhanced (in the case of Simon) through serving a prison sentence, while for the older Ling his ability to *avoid* arrest during a time when there was enhanced police protection for triads made him valuable to leaders. Neither of the men disclosed any details of a formal initiation ceremony during my interviews with them. However, their commitment to protecting triad leaders through intense loyalty to their subcultures suggested that they may have taken oaths at some point to swear unreserved allegiance and patriotism to the triad brotherhood through a focus on *guanxi* (Lintner 2004; Lo 2012).

However, in both cases their personal addictions became obstacles to continued criminal entrepreneurship, and brought them into a liminal phase (Lintner 2004; Healy 2012). Ling appeared to rise up the triad ladder further than Simon and had taken on leadership roles that continued into his 50s. However, the increasing crackdowns against triad society via ICAC combined with his drug-related health problems, gambling issues and concern about retaliation eventually created 'push' factors that made Ling feel ready for change (Pyrooz and Decker 2011; Decker et al. 2014; Carson and Esbensen 2016). For Simon, continuing addiction-related health issues also had an adverse effect at a much younger age than with Ling; his spiralling confidence led to prolonged incarceration and a diminishing of his commitment to the triad lifestyle.

Among the other men I interviewed, there were also examples of early exploitation by triad leaders. Like Simon and Ling (above), some described the way in which—as vulnerable teenagers—they had only been distantly aware that the street gangs they joined were under the influence of triads. They gradually became conscious of the intense pressure that triad leaders exerted on younger members to become more involved in serious criminal activities in order to prove their credentials and rise up the ranks. Several of the men like Peng described in detail their experiences of being slowly influenced by the triads over time:

> In triads they have stiff orders – there are certain things you cannot do … my friends, when they get along with the triads they seem to have protection so then [I thought] 'ok then, just follow' … [but] the triads, they pushed us to illegal stuff. (Peng)

Conversely, men like Chan described how, having had experience of street violence, he had actively set out to become involved in serious organised crime. The movies had evidently romanticized Mafia culture in his mind and influenced his desire to embrace the gangster persona as a means of expressing exaggerated forms of masculinity through joining the triads (Rawlinson 1998; Larke 2013):

> One movie changed my life. It's a Hong Kong-style movie. It's about gangsters, about the Mafia … I see the people in the movie, they are so awesome. They are so tough and they attract me … like the hero thing. So I started thinking, 'it's the role model I want to become' … I had the same background as the movie people, I grew up in a small village. The guys in the movie, same situation. So I start to think, 'I can be that guy too. They are so famous, they are like hero, everyone like them. Maybe I can fight and then I get famous … I become a gangster, and I can be famous and get more attention … I can be like him, so handsome and macho' … after I saw the movie I want to become Mafia too. And then I ask my friend to bring me in … into the Mafia, become the gangster, become part of … the triads. (Chan)

Boxes 9.1 and 9.2 illustrate the reasons that two of the men reached a point where they were ready for change. Others also described wider 'push' and 'pull' factors that brought them to a liminal phase (Healy 2012), as the next section documents.

'Push' and 'Pull' Factors and Initial Transitions

Like Simon and Ling (above), the other men I interviewed also talked about the way in which becoming involved in youth gangs coincided with slowly becoming dependent on drugs. Also like Simon and Ling, some described the way they had risen up the triad ranks into the world of organised crime, but that drug-related health issues eventually stimulated their formal departure from triads. For instance, Peng described the way in which prolonged use of cocktails of drugs had created a feeling of 'madness' within him and had a detrimental effect on his family:

> I really wanted to get away from drugs ... because drugs give many problems to my family and to my life, all kinds of drugs - I tried all of them so there was like a kind of madness in my body. (Peng)

By the time he reached his 50s, the negative impact of his drug use had led Peng's behaviour to become impulsive, whereby violence became out of control. Lo (2012, p. 558) describes the way in which triad criminal gangs are highly 'cohesive and organised' and members follow triad subculture and norms closely, which increasingly includes the need to 'minimize violence in order to avoid police attention' in the post-ICAC period. Having entered a world inhabited by professional gangsters, it was evident that Peng's erratic behaviour was no longer going to be tolerated by the leaders within his triad organisation. Hence, he was eventually sold to another triad 'clan' before eventually he decided to try and quit the lifestyle:

> Because I was too mad ... all kinds of stuff I tried and many people hate me, and they said the only thing that I hadn't tried is to kill ... [an] enemy in the triad in the same group ... [so] the whole triad sold me ... so I left the triads. I wanted to become a good guy and a normal guy again. (Peng)

In another interview, Chase also made reference to the mental health repercussions he experienced from prolonged drug use and exposure to violence. As a much younger man than Peng or Ling, he had not yet developed the credentials to become involved in organised criminal networks. He was still involved in violence and drug dealing both to provide him with the 'street capital' needed to satisfy triad leaders but also to fund his own drug habit (Harding 2014). Difficult emotions rose to the surface combined with paranoid illusions and suicidal thoughts that finally made Chase begin to reject his 'feared self' (Paternoster and Bushway 2009, p. 1103):

> When I hurt people, I feel a lot of guilt every time … I got illusions after taking drugs, very serious illusions. I felt alone and I felt … not safe, insecure, paranoid and because of that I want to commit suicide … I got scared … that sense of guilt … and the delusion … I think no one wants to be that guy … I strongly felt that 'I don't want to be that person.' (Chase)

Choi, who in his 40s had been promoted by triad leaders and had begun to commit organised criminal acts on their behalf, had (like Simon and Ling) become deeply engulfed in ketamine and cocaine use. He began to gain an increased motivation to change his habits, fueled by his disillusionment with the professional gangsters who were controlling the triad organisation:

> I saw that the people inside the gang were very fake and very selfish … I just saw that I didn't want to be involved in that with those people. (Choi)

Finally, two of the other younger men in the sample described the way in which they arrived at the threshold of change as a result of the concern they had about the impact of their offending lifestyles on their mothers' health (Healy 2012). While Chan could see the way his offending lifestyle and drug addiction was impacting negatively on his mother's emotional wellbeing, Cedric indicated that his mother's physical health scare had influenced him to begin to reflect on his behaviour:

> I saw my mum worry so much and then I start to change, start to think to change, because of the power of my mum's love … I saw the pressure

on my mum, that it is affecting her health and her emotion, her psychological emotion. (Chan)

My mum got breast cancer, and then it made me take stock of my life, what I did in the past. (Cedric)

Pyrooz and Decker (2011) argue that 'push' factors for first attempting to leave gang-related offending lifestyles often include specific events that drive a wedge between gang members and their peers and/or leaders. It was evident that some of the older, more criminally-oriented participants in Hong Kong had experienced such 'push' factors. In such cases, the negative impact of prolonged drug use had led them to be viewed as liabilities within the context of the triad brotherhood. For other, younger men who were aspiring towards but had not yet reached the senior echelons of triad organised crime, a range of 'push' and 'pull' factors led to 'first doubts' about their continued involvement in triad-controlled youth gangs (Decker et al. 2014, p. 2). These included personal mental health issues from drug use, negative emotions and disillusionment with the lifestyle and the people (Carson and Esbensen 2016), as well as concern for significant others within family networks.

Concluding Discussion

Building on and extending previous empirical research (Lo 2010, 2012), this chapter has drawn upon insights gleaned from in-depth life history interviews with a small sample of men of various ages in Hong Kong. Each of these men had embraced locally-defined gang identities, participated in violence and criminality and (to varying degrees) had slowly became immersed in triad societies. Early marginalisation and peer pressure combined with low parental monitoring and social control led to street gang membership during the participants' teenage years. They subsequently became susceptible to being subsumed within the 'spider web' structure of local triad-affiliated crime groups as a means of masculine expression (Fraser 2017, p. 189). In most cases, drug addiction played a prominent role in deepening their vulnerability to being influenced and exploited by the triad 'brotherhood' and to transition to membership of what was effectively a 'reserve army' of triad societies, ready and able to provide muscle for the collection of dues within the context of drug dealing (Lo 2012, p. 573). For some, a prolonged recognised ability to display loyalty to the subcultural norms and values within triad associations led on to promotion into the larger triad structure and participation in wider criminal activity, while for others their contribution to the triad subculture reached its limits earlier.

In earlier sections of the book, I described the cross-neighbourhood 'gangbanging' focused on firearms use and the enhanced gang masculinity emerging from prison gang membership in Los Angeles; the knife-carrying, largely territorial and recreational violence as a means of masculine reassertion in Scotland; and the accumulation of masculine respect through projecting hyper-masculine body images, through male solidarity in street gangs and (for some) through motorcycle gang membership and more organised criminality in Denmark. In Hong Kong, the clear links between men's involvement in youth gangs and their susceptibility towards exploitation by Mafia-style criminal networks was somewhat different from anything I had seen in other geographical locations. The underlying cultural influences associated with *mientze* ('saving face') and *guanxi* ('reciprocal obligation') that acted as both triggers for initial triadization and for continued involvement with and progression through triad hierarchies was unique to this context (Chen and Starosta 1997; Lo 2010). However, in many ways the men's continual attempts to express and prove their sense of masculinity through gang activity was the same in Hong Kong as in other parts of the world.

Whether the men progressed only as far as being socialised into triad-influenced youth gangs or were subsumed more deeply into triad criminal gangs (Lo 2012), their own personal drug dependency and addiction issues often represented the initial obstacles that acted as preliminary turning points. Alongside this, a range of other 'push' and 'pull' factors led to a readiness for change among the men and stimulated an initial 'separation phase' where their thinking patterns and attitudes began to change (Healy 2012, p. 35). This included personal health issues and concern about the health of significant others, personal dips in confidence or disillusionment with the lifestyle. In some cases, the increased social control that had emerged against the backcloth of reduced police corruption and removal of triad protection also exerted an influence (Harding 2016; Fraser 2017).

It was, of course, evident that—as my insights from other global geographical areas had illustrated—the men's attempts to move towards desistance could potentially be threatened by a range of continuing 'gang embodiment' issues and 'stigmata' (Densley 2013, p. 139; Flores 2014, p. 176). As in other parts of the world where I worked, I found that the interviewees had all begun to seek out additional support to nurture their transitions and deal with their continued challenges. For the men in Hong Kong, engagement with the Christian religion further motivated their desistance journeys while in a liminal phase (Healy 2012). In the next chapter, I draw on additional insights from follow-up interviews and discussions with the same men I have referred to in this chapter, as well as from fieldnotes constructed during participant observation and from interviews with pastors and volunteers. I explore and examine the nature of the Christian support sessions the men engaged in and their apparent impact in terms of challenging and realigning their entrenched beliefs about masculinity and crime.

References

Adorjan, M., & Chui, W. C. (2012). Making sense of going straight: Personal accounts of male ex-prisoners in Hong Kong. *British Journal of Criminology, 52*, 577–590.

Agnew, R. (1992). Foundation for a general strain theory of crime and delinquency. *Criminology, 30*, 47–87.

Broadhurst, R., & Wa, L. K. (2010). The transformation of triad 'dark societies' in Hong Kong: The impact of law enforcement, socio-economic and political change. *Security Challenges, 5*(4), 1–38.

Carson, D. C., & Esbensen, F.-A. (2016). Motivations for leaving gangs in the USA: A qualitative comparison of leaving processes across gang definitions. In C. L. Maxson & F.-A. Esbensen (Eds.), *Gang transitions and transformations in an international context* (pp. 139–155). Switzerland: Springer.

Chen, G.-M., & Starosta, W. J. (1997). Chinese conflict management and resolution: Overview and implications. *Intercultural Communication Studies, 7*(1), 1–13.

Decker, S. H., Pyrooz, D., & Moule, R. K., Jr. (2014). Disengagement from gangs as role transitions. *Journal of Research on Adolescence, 24*(2), 268–283.

Densley, J. (2013). *How gangs work: An ethnography of youth violence*. London: Palgrave Macmillan.

Flores, E. O. (2014). *God's gangs: Barrio ministry, masculinity and gang recovery*. New York: New York University Press.

Fraser, A. (2017). *Gangs and crime: Critical alternatives*. London: Sage.

Harding, A. (2014). *The street casino: Survival in violent street gangs*. Bristol: Policy Press.

Harding, S. (2016). From 'little flowers of Motherland' into 'carnivorous plants': The changing face of youth gang crime in contemporary China. In S. Harding & M. Palasinski (Eds.), *Global perspectives on youth gang behavior, violence and weapons use* (pp. 301–331). Hershey, PA: Information Science Reference.

Healy, D. (2012). *The dynamics of desistance: Charting pathways through change*. New York: Routledge.

Jiang, G., Lo, T. W., & Garris. F. P. (2012). Formation and trend of Guanxi practice and Guanxi phenomenon. *International Journal of Criminology and Sociology, 1*, 207–220.

Larke, G. S. (2013). Organized crime: Mafia myths in film and television. In P. Mason (Ed.), *Criminal visions: Media representations of crime and justice* (pp. 116–132). New York: Routledge.

Lilly, J. R., Cullen, F. T., & Ball, R. A. (2015). *Criminological theory: Context and consequences* (6th ed.). Thousands Oaks, CA: Sage.

Lintner, B. (2004). Chinese organized crime. *Global Crime, 6*(1), 84–96.

Lo, T. W. (2010). Beyond social capital: Triad organized crime in Hong Kong and China. *British Journal of Criminology, 50*(5), 851–872.

Lo, T. W. (2012). Triadization of youth gangs in Hong Kong. *British Journal of Criminology, 52*, 556–576.

Lo, T. W., & Kwok, S. I. (2014). Triads and tongs. In G. Bruinsma & D. Weisburd (Eds.), *Encyclopedia of criminology and criminal justice* (pp. 5332–5343). New York: Springer.

Merton, R. (1968). *Social theory and social structure*. New York: Free Press.

Murray, C. D., & Wynne, J. (2001). Using an interpreter to research community, work and family. *Community, Work and Family, 4*(2), 157–170.

Paternoster, R., & Bushway, S. (2009). Desistance and the feared self: Toward an identity theory of criminal desistance. *Journal of Criminal Law and Criminology, 99*(4), 1103–1156.

Pyrooz, D. C., & Decker, S. H. (2011). Motives and methods for leaving the gang: Understanding the process of gang desistance. *Journal of Criminal Justice, 39*, 417–425.

Pyrooz, D. C., & Decker, S. H. (2013). Delinquent behavior, violence, and gang involvement in China. *Journal of Quantitative Criminology, 29*(2), 251–272.

Rawlinson, P. (1998). Mafia, media and myth: Representations of Russian organized crime. *The Howard Journal of Crime and Justice, 37*(4), 346–358.

Shek, D. T. L. (2007). Tackling adolescent substance abuse in Hong Kong: Where we should and should not go. *The Scientific World Journal, 7*, 2021–2030.

Squires, A. (2009). Methodological challenges in cross-language qualitative research: A research review. *International Journal of Nursing Studies, 46*(2), 277–287.

Stewart, S. M., Betson, C. L., Chung, S. P., & Chung, T. C. F. (1999). The correlates of depressed mood in adolescents in Hong Kong. *Journal of Adolescent Health, 25*, 27–34.

Wallin, A.-M., & Ahlström, G. (2006). Cross-cultural interview studies using interpreters: Systematic literature review. *Journal of Advanced Nursing, 55*(6), 723–735.

Wang, P. (2017). *The Chinese mafia: Organized crime, corruption, and extra-legal protection*. Oxford: Oxford University Press.

Williamson, D. L., Choi, J., Charchuk, M., Rempel, G. R., Pitre, N., Breitkreuz, R., & Kushner, K. E. (2011). Interpreter-facilitated cross-language interviews: A research note. *Qualitative Research, 11*(4), 381–194.

Wong, D. S. W. (2000). Juvenile crime and responses to delinquency in Hong Kong. *International Journal of Offender Therapy and Comparative Criminology, 44*(3), 279–292.

Wong, D. S. W. (2001). Pathways to delinquency in Hong Kong and Guangzhou (South China). *International Journal of Adolescence and Youth, 10*(1–2), 91–115.

10

From Criminal Gangsters to Men of God

In this chapter, I draw on additional insights from follow-up interviews and discussions with the same men I referred to in Chapter 9, as well as from fieldnotes constructed during participant observation and from interviews with staff and volunteers within *HKCS*. I explore and examine the nature of the Christian support sessions the men engaged in and their apparent impact in terms of supporting them with addiction issues, and enabling them to challenge their entrenched beliefs regarding criminal lifestyles. The insights are used to make inferences about the extent to and ways in which Christian-based interventions can potentially play a valuable role in supporting and enabling Hong Kong gang members to re-direct their entrenched beliefs about loyalty and obligation to brotherhood in non-criminal directions.

Religion, Evangelical Christianity and Identity Change

In Chapter 3, I considered the way in which religious engagement can act as a 'turning point' for some offenders, through enhancing their personal moral codes and generating social bonds and capital (Clear and Sumter 2002). Some authors have argued that social ties formed through worship and wider religious activities provide 'emotional and tangible support' for those in need (Schroeder and Frana 2009, p. 722). Additionally, it has been claimed that the spiritual elements of religion can provide offenders with renewed resilience and a 'critical resource' to draw upon to alleviate personal problems in a 'non criminal manner' (ibid; see also Haculak and McLennan 2010).

In particular, some have argued that Christianity provides a strong foundation for forgiveness, since the Bible is so full of narratives of individuals who 'went beyond the point where society can forgive' but were spiritually healed (Maruna et al. 2006, p. 177). Flores (2014, p. 202) highlights the way in which evangelical approaches to Christian worship can enable gang members to redirect their energies from violence towards social cohesion and 'brotherly love'. At the same time, it has been claimed that those offenders who suffer from continuing hard embodiment issues relating to gang membership such as drug addiction can begin to view their dependency issues as a 'disease of the spirit' that can be cured through connection to a 'higher power' (Bakken et al. 2014, p. 1324; see also Flores 2014). Brenneman (2012, p. 186) also highlights the way in which evangelical congregations can provide personal support to assist offenders in overcoming addiction through 'social policing', as well as through helping them find temporary work by providing personal recommendations to prospective employers.

For those who have committed serious criminal acts and have faced the realisation that they have become involved in behaviour that they never thought themselves capable of, Maruna et al. (2006) argue that conversion narratives become highly pertinent. Declaring and disclosing their religious conversion to others can enable such offenders to gain a strong sense of having been saved and 'washed clean', and to develop a 'hope and a vision for the future' (ibid., p. 177). By focusing their thoughts on, and directing their energy towards, a newfound relationship with God and religious identity as a Christian, some evidence suggests that offenders can begin to avoid reacting to the negative emotionality that often stimulates criminal activity and experience renewed feelings of strength, peace and harmony (Haculak and McLennan 2010).

As I argued in Chapter 3, some scholars have remained sceptical about the potential of religion to inhibit offending (Clear and Sumter 2002; Giordano et al. 2008). They have questioned the legitimacy of the conversion narrative and the extent to which religious participation can really provide authentic attraction for hyper-masculine gang members (Brenneman 2012). However, Brenneman (2012, p. 237) refers to Max Weber's famous claim that religious ideas can be the 'track switchers' that set the stage for a change in course that may not have occurred otherwise. In engaging with some forms of Christian worship and study, it has been argued that male gang members can distance themselves from world views and gang behaviours. Some may begin to re-frame their sense of masculinity from violent offender to 'man of God', increasingly sharing this newfound identity and having it reflected back on them by others within the context of 'brotherly love' (Flores 2014, pp. 201–202).

Background to and Focus of *Hong Kong Christian Society (HKCS)*

As I indicated in the last chapter, *HKCS* (as I refer to it) is a renowned non-government Christian organisation based in Hong Kong focused on supporting male offenders and gang members to try to reform through residential rehabilitation programmes. In particular, it places an emphasis on treating the drug addiction issues that are often a major factor in offenders' prolonged involvement in criminality in Hong Kong. The organisation was established in 2001 and is coordinated by its founder and head mentor (referred to under the pseudonym 'Pastor Lau' throughout this chapter). Pastor Lau is a former drug addict turned Christian minister; with his team of mentors and volunteers, he works intensively with male offenders and gang members offering them religious support and guidance through study groups, workshops and worship sessions. He also refers the men to opportunities for both paid and voluntary work via the wide range of external agencies *HKCS* collaborates with, including placements in local restaurants, manual labour industries and schools.

HKCS receives no State funding, but relies on donations from Christian churches across Hong Kong. The mentors employed in the organisation and those who volunteer in it have mostly had previous involvement in gang-related offending and/or drug addiction and have in certain cases transitioned through the *HKCS* programme themselves in the past. Pastor Lau and the wider team recognise that many of the men they work with in *HKCS* first drift into street-oriented youth gangs because of a lack of parental support, a drive towards making 'fast' money combined with peer pressure and the influence of hyper-masculine gangster images in the media. As outlined in the previous chapter, many have become addicted to narcotics, have become 'triadized' and in some cases have transitioned to leadership roles within triad gangs. Against this backdrop, *HKCS* places an emphasis on supporting offenders to move away from drug dependency and criminality through exposing them to work routines, supportive personal mentoring, life coaching and Biblical-driven forms of Christian engagement and worship within the *HKCS* centre.

Participant Observation and Follow-Up Interviews in *HKCS*

In addition to seeking volunteers for life history interviews (as described in the previous chapter), I sought the consent of wider groups of men who were engaged in the support sessions offered by *HKCS* to be research participants. While I participated actively in Bible study groups and Christian worship sessions, I also observed the men and their Pastors and mentors and recorded insights from their discussions, conversations and interactions with each other. In a small number of cases, I also observed the implementation of outreach work and the men's involvement in external work placements. As was the case with life history interviews, my observations were conducted with the assistance of *HKCS* volunteers acting as interpreters, who worked alongside me during participant observation sessions and translated dialogue for me that was then recorded in fieldnotes. As before, wherever possible I ensured that two interpreters were with me so that insights passed on by one were verified by the other either during or immediately following each observation, thus increasing the relative trustworthiness of emerging data.

Building on the findings from life history interviews outlined in the previous chapter, in this chapter I report on the additional insights I gained from the sample of eight reforming Hong Kong gang members (see Table 9.1). Through follow-up interviews and further informal discussions I had with them (again with the assistance of interpreters), I was able to explore the potential impact that the men's exposure to the *HKCS* support sessions and interventions was having on them. During my extended discussions with them, it transpired that two of the men (Choi and Cedric) had been raised in Christian homes during their formative years and had later begun to re-engage in their earlier faith during the period when they first began to become disillusioned with their criminal and drug-dependent lifestyles. In particular, Choi described the way in which volunteers from his former church visited him in hospital after he had experienced an infection in his heart as a result of drug misuse, and from that moment on he began to become more engaged again in Christian worship. One other man, Simon, had been a practicing Buddhist earlier in his life but began to embrace a Christian faith when he became involved in *HKCS*. In the remaining five cases, the men had become involved in *HKCS* first (often as a result of outreach work or through hearing about the organisation from others who had experienced it) and slowly began to transition towards practicing Christianity while there. Some had already been baptised by the time my fieldwork took place.

The additional interviews and informal dialogue with the men as well as participant observation during interventions and support sessions was combined with semi-structured interviews with a small sample of three paid and voluntary mentors from *HKCS*, as well as with Pastor Lau. Since all of the latter spoke fluent English, these interviews were conducted without the support of interpreters. In the sections that follow I present the emerging themes from fieldnotes, follow-up interviews and informal dialogue. Pseudonyms are used as per the previous chapter, and new ones added for mentors and volunteers, including Pastor Lau.

Outreach Work, Religious Engagement and Employability

As I outlined in Chapter 9, the criminal activity that gang members in Hong Kong become involved in often coincides with becoming drug addicts (Lo 2012). To that end, the staff within *HKCS* were clear about the need to provide drug counseling as a prominent part of the support they offered for moving away from criminality. During an interview, Pastor Lau described his own background as a drug addict and what brought him into the work. He also discussed the way in which he believed in the need for a holistic approach that combined the nurturing of religious faith with pastoral care and counseling, and a focus on enhancing employability skills. In addition, Jun (one of the voluntary mentors within *HKCS*) also emphasised the combined focus on religious support and on empowering the men to become ready for work and earn money in order to avoid relapsing:

> I was a drug addict before … and I believe that faith changed my life, and I … know this is the only way that can help … to introduce this to [others] … I'm a drug addict before, and also a Pastor and I'm a counselor, so I try to [integrate] these three elements … we encourage them to get some skill … they can reintegrate into society, they can get a job. (Pastor Lau, *HKCS* founder and coordinator)

> We'll help them get off drugs and to know Christ … will try to empower them or equip them with skills [so as] when they go back to society

at least they have some kind of work skill to help them get a job ... [because] they're desperate - no jobs - so they need to find money ... [otherwise] they go back to the old way of getting money and just get on drugs again and end up back in jail. (Jun, *HKCS* voluntary mentor)

Recruitment to *HKCS* came partly via 'word of mouth', whereby gang members who had benefited from the support sessions and rehabilitation interventions there passed on their experiences to others and encouraged them to come and find out more. However, there was also a proactive focus on outreach work, which I observed firsthand during my visit to one of the most socially deprived neighbourhoods in Hong Kong. As Box 10.1 illustrates, a focus on building a 'church without walls' at times enabled those who were in despair to become recruited to *HKCS*.

> **Box 10.1:** *Christian Outreach Work* **and Building a 'Church Without Walls'**
>
> As I look around me I am stunned to see the sight in front of me. All along the narrow road, shaded by the nearby trees, are makeshift 'homes' consisting of old mattresses, chairs, poles with old curtains and bed covers draped across them and old couches to sit on. I notice that several people are sitting around on the chairs or lying down on the mattresses, and in some cases they are surrounded by all their worldly possessions—namely, old pots and pans, cups, plates, towels and pieces of laundry. Pastor Lau introduces me to his best friend, Reverend Eddie, who is wearing a dog collar. He explains to me that he is the minister in a local church which is 18 years old. He spends a lot of his time down here, trying to bring some light to these people's lives.
>
> As we reach a gap in the various living sites, I see in front of me a small circles of chairs. In the middle of the chairs, on the ground, are some lit candles forming the shape of a cross. A number of people begin to gather and sit on the chairs. 'Most of the people here are from the churches, coming as volunteers.' Pastor Lau explains, 'so you see the idea is that it is a church without walls – if you asked these people living here to go to church, they wouldn't – but they might come and join us here.' As I sit down alongside the small group, four local men join us and after a few minutes there are around 15 of us sitting in the circle. After another few minutes has passed, I notice that all of the volunteers have opened their mobile phones and are sharing these with the locals, so that they can see the words of the hymn we are going to sing.

> All of a sudden the group bursts into song, and in the heart of this poverty-stricken area of Hong Kong voices are lifted skyward. 'Some people down here have been baptised,' Pastor Lau explains to me, 'these two guys over on the opposite side have both been converted, and the one in the white shirt was recruited to come to my programme.' I now realise that this Pastor's work extends far beyond the confines of the *HKCS* centre I have visited over the past few evenings; his work reaches into the communities, and focuses on strong collaborations with other Pastors and volunteers in order to reach the most marginalised. (Researcher's fieldnotes)

Flores (2014) refers to the way in which some Christian organisations tend to facilitate recovery from gang-related lifestyles and the embodiment issues that can emerge within them (such as drug addiction and homelessness) through proselytism. In doing so, evidence suggests that some view religious participation as a means of generating social cohesion through fostering shared norms and values (Clear and Sumter 2002). In particular, Kerley (2014, p. 10) highlights the way in which Pastors are often driven by the fundamental belief that religious involvement creates social networks and emotional support that may 'constrain criminal behaviour'.

The fieldnotes in Box 10.1 illustrate the way in which Pastor Lau drew upon his wider Christian pastoral networks to reach out to those who had become marginalised as a result of gang activity, drug addiction and poverty and actively tried to encourage them towards Christian conversion and/or enrolment in the *HKCS* initiative. As Pastor Lau and Jun (above) described, once there it was important for the men to be given employment opportunities in order to ensure that they were not tempted to go back to their old lifestyles (Brenneman 2012). My own observations enabled me to see firsthand how some of the men were active in external work placements while involved in *HKCS*:

> As we walk along the corridors of the old warehouse, I can see several younger and middle- aged men carrying crates and lifting boxes in and out of side rooms. 'Here we have many guys who are employed … washing dishes for the local restaurants,' Jun, one of the volunteers in *HKCS*, explains. As we walk into the first room we come to I can see a whole stack of dirty dishes lying in water in various plastic boxes around the

floor. I look up and see that the dishes are placed into one end of a huge dish washer, and then come out of the other end clean where they are transported on a conveyor belt into a hole in the wall. We walk into the adjacent room where I can see what happens next. Here, three guys – one middle-aged and two slightly younger – are working hard to stack all of the dishes as they arrive at the other end of the conveyor belt. Each of them are bare-chested, and are clearly sweating with the heat and the hard work they are involved in. But, by the looks on their faces they are also dedicated, determined to be able to earn a living and to change their lives. (Researcher's fieldnotes)

Accordingly, the Christian outreach work associated with *HKCS* combined with its growing reputation in the field provided a means for Pastor Lau's team to reach out to the most marginalised (Hallett and McCoy 2014). Similar to what I had uncovered in *Homeboy Industries* in Los Angeles, *HKCS* simultaneously offered gang members paid employment but also access to a 'therapeutic community' (Boyle 2010, p. 9). However, as the next section illustrates, in contrast to the focus on eclectic spirituality evident in *Homeboy Industries*, *HKCS*'s focus on holistic forms of Christian religious worship and Biblical engagement was seen as a 'critical resource' to draw upon within the context of the community-centred focus in evidence (Schroeder and Frana 2009, p. 722).

Community-Building and Holistic Forms of Christian Worship, Study and Prayer

In most cases, the men spent half their week in the *HKCS* centre engaging in collective Bible study classes and Christian worship and the rest of their time engaging in external work placements (as described above). Against this backdrop, it was evident that a focus on wrapping a supportive, therapeutic community around the men (to replace the gang 'community') was of fundamental importance:

> The community is very important. Even the gang community ... is very important [to them], they influence each other but they're just a negative

influence ... now, they get into another community. (Pastor Lau, *HKCS* founder and coordinator)

In the world, you meet a lot of good people and bad people and maybe in your past experience you met a lot of betrayal ... so basically here they have a community of people that support and accept them and encourage them to build them up. (Jun, *HKCS* voluntary mentor)

The men I interviewed talked a great deal about the way in which they experienced a strong sense of community within the *HKCS* centre. In contrast to the sense of distrust they had had when they were involved in gangs, they began to feel a somewhat surprising sense of unconditional positive regard from staff and other 'brothers' on the programme and to experience a profoundly loving ethos:

> In the gang ... [we were] very suspicious about everything; we don't trust anything ... here I feel that I am being taken care of ... I think 'whoa, what happened? You want something from me?' I think it's for some reason ... I was suspicious about [their] intentions. But after a period of time I find that they have no reason, there's no intention, they just really want to help you. (Simon)
>
> In here, the relationship between the 'brothers' is one of the most important things ... when you're in need, they will offer their help without asking back. (Peng)
>
> I felt some kind of unconditional acceptance from others ... I strongly felt that when I came here. (Cedric)
>
> I feel [an] unconditional love, without reason I was being loved ... This centre has reminded me of my mother's love. (Chan)

In addition to the pastoral support, acceptance, personal encouragement and affection from staff mentors, volunteers and other male participants, Christian-based study, worship and prayer were very important elements of the *HKCS* support programme. Pastor Lau described the way in which the *HKCS* mentors attempted to stimulate an interest in religiosity (in some) or to reignite dormant religious beliefs (in others). They encouraged them to recognise that welcoming

Jesus into their lives as their saviour meant that they literally become new creations, with more favourable identities and renewed hope for the future (Giordano et al. 2008):

> [Some of them], they believe in Jesus but they left it behind ... they left behind religion ... we have a key statement ... if anyone is in Christ, the new creation has come, the old has gone and the new is here ... [people] always stay in the past, so we talk to them – 'the old has gone, the new has come in', so they have a future. (Pastor Lau, *HKCS* founder and coordinator)

Within this faith-based, nurturing environment, Box 10.2 illustrates my observations of worship sessions and Biblically-oriented discussion-based workshops that were prominent within *HKCS*.

Box 10.2: *Practicing Religion Through Worship, Prayer* **and Bible Recitations**

As I gaze around the large room on Monday evening, I realise that a group of around twenty men of all age-groups has gathered. In one corner I notice two guitars, a drum set and some speakers plus a screen linked to a computer system. Around the rest of the room are chairs, and a small keyboard in one of the other corners. Pastor Lau takes his place at the front of the room and opens the time of worship. Two of the male volunteers begin to play the guitars while another plays drums and one other operates the powerpoint containing the Chinese words of a Christian hymn. We all begin to sing aloud and I notice that most of the men around the room are joining in enthusiastically—some are even doing actions to the music.

One of the male volunteers, who is a large Chinese man who looks around 40, then leads the group in prayer. As we all bow our heads, he says 'Dearest Father, we seek things that do not satisfy us – help us instead to seek you. Amen.' The members of the group then repeat 'Amen'. The volunteer Pastor then proceeds to read from Matthew 6—focusing on the Lord's Prayer. 'You know, sometimes people pray any way they want to – but Jesus here teaches us how to pray ... when you have a son or daughter they ask "I want this or that". Well, when we pray to God He wants things from us as well – because it is a relationship ... but we shouldn't have to be afraid to ask our Father for anything – He will want to give ... we can openly share our hearts with our Father.' The man then continues to explain other aspects of the Lord's Prayer to the large audience. 'Hallowed be thy name – we need to respect and glorify God's name,' he

> comments. He asks the men in the room how we can respect God. 'You know, if we pray only for a new car or a motorcycle that's not good,' one of the middle-aged men responds. 'Yes, that's true,' the volunteer goes on, 'we need to pray for what is in line with God's will – if it is in line with His will, he will answer us.'
> Pastor Lau then comes to the front and begins to facilitate a further discussion. 'If you have a problem would you pray to God?' Pastor Lau asks. One of the men, who looks about 40, raises his hand, 'sometimes ... I might gamble and pray for the team I want to win!' he jokes and everyone in the room laughs at this. 'That's not always good to pray for some things because they might not be good for you!' Pastor Lau laughs, and I realise that this session is one where the men can have lots of camaraderie and fun together as well as reflecting on more serious issues. As the group comes to a close, we finish by singing another Chinese hymn, following the words on the computer screen at the front of the room. The guys in the band play the music on their guitars, and more and more of the men clap enthusiastically and do actions to accompany the music.
> On Tuesday evening, I notice around eight men arriving in the same worship room as before, and Pastor Lau greets each one as they enter. All of the men lift a Bible from the table at the side of the room, and then sit down. One of the young male mentors, Jinhai, plays a few strings of the electric guitar as people arrive and all the men then recite a passage from the Bible together in Chinese. As I look around the room, I can see their faces focusing very intently on the words. I gather that the words are focused on Jesus' story of men working in the vineyards for various lengths of time and receiving the same pay, and Jesus' disclosing of the resurrection to his disciples. As I listen, Shen (one of the other young mentors) explains to me that they very much emphasise the reading of the Bible here, and the sharing of spiritual thoughts and reflections from the readings. Pastor Lau is now talking to the group. 'When we read the Bible – at first nothing special happens, but then God's power will work and when challenges come along the spirit will work through you ...' The men then sing a slow hymn in Chinese, and at once there is a real sense of peace all around the room. The group finishes by reciting a Christian prayer together. (Researcher's fieldnotes)

Kerley and Copes (2008, p. 228) draw attention to the way in which religious participation can provide offenders with a means of 'connecting with positive others in formal and informal settings', enabling them to gain inspiration and encouragement for pro-social behaviour. Some have also highlighted the way in which participation in group music therapy can be beneficial for reducing anxiety and building self-esteem among offenders (Chen et al. 2014). In *HKCS*, the collective singing of Christian hymns and sharing of upbeat Christian rock music as well as slower melodic hymns (Flores 2014) was evidently an important means of building a sense of community and enhancing emotional relaxation and engagement within a Pentecostal-influenced context (Schroeder and Frana 2009; Lin et al. 2010).

Flores (2014, p. 197) highlights that collective prayer can be used to enable recovering gang members to experience 'social cohesion' with each other and to 'consolidate' new social bonds and ties. In *HKCS*, lighthearted discussion about prayer and what should and should not be the focus of personal prayer-time was combined with serious messages about the need for the men to follow the 'will' of God, to form intimate relationships with Him, to respect and glorify God and allow His spirit to guide them (Flores 2014). As I discussed in Chapter 3 and above, some earlier evidence has suggested that religion can act as a 'social bond' and that spiritual capital can emerge through the discipline of daily prayer that in turn can stimulate feelings of wellbeing, support and fulfillment (Bakken et al. 2014, p. 1323). Bakken et al. (2014, p. 1334) also argue that becoming focused on faith-based principles can enable offenders to gain the clarity needed to choose to forgive their 'prior transgressions', to 'hope for a better future through the use of religious guidance' and to fill the void left by substance use with a 'higher power'. As Box 10.2 illustrates, in *HKCS* there was a strong emphasis on encouraging the men to become committed to practicing the Christian religion through worship, prayer and Bible recitations. In interviews with the men, it appeared that the strong belief system they were acquiring and the sense of love and support they were gaining through closeness to God and through Bible readings and prayer was viewed as a powerful influence and increasing source of happiness and peace:

> In here you can see that it's God working through the programme because without this kind of love, you cannot go on … I realise that God is more powerful than humankind and I know from the Bible that when I put all my load to this almighty God, I can be happy. (Peng)

> I was suffering from withdrawal [when I came here] … and then I start to pray. But I didn't know how to pray. And the Pastor said, 'just say a few

words.' And when I felt pain, I start to pray. And the first time, no difference – still pain, can't fall asleep. And then the second time, still nothing happen. And the third time, it's a miracle has happened. I can fall asleep very deeply for seven hour, eight hour … I can like sleep peacefully. And then that makes me, it's like … there's really a God. (Chan)

As Chan's words indicate, for those who were suffering from drug addiction, prayer was seen as the key to supporting them through the process of withdrawal. This supports earlier insights by Bakken et al. (2014, p. 1324) that suggest that Christian interventions may involve encouraging offenders to view addiction as a 'disease of the spirit'. The men's narratives suggested that they were beginning to believe that drawing upon worship and prayer enabled them to gain a sense of intimacy with God and to live the life they now believed that He wanted for them. In particular, Bible readings were seen to be influential; during interviews, several of the men made direct references to Bible passages and the values underpinning them that they saw as important and relevant to their personal journeys. They drew upon these in a way that helped them to focus on becoming less influenced by crime, less inclined to use drugs and more able to avoid what they now viewed as 'sinful' behaviour:

'Create in me a clean heart' – I always remember that. Because it reminded me … in the past I have a lot of opposite behaviour, and I hope God can clean me and renew myself to be a righteous person. (Chase)

What I took out of the Bible is it helps me to re-set my personal values, life values … in the past I think that freedom is whatever I want I can do. But today freedom is that I can choose to not do what I want to do. For example, in the past if there were drugs here then I would have to [take] it but today if there's drugs here I can choose not to [take] it … God's guiding me … I learned how … [to] communicate with other people … to socialise with people and discipline myself. Very importantly, there's Jesus in my heart leading me. (Choi)

It will be a coincidence that I will be going through a hard time or maybe faced with some hard problem and that day the Bible verse … will speak to me and help me. So, for example there's 'I put your words in my heart so that I will not sin against you.' A lot of times these Bible verses would just come in my head. (Lee)

In Chapter 9, I outlined the way in which Ling had had a difficult upbringing followed by experience of exploitation by triad leaders. I described the way in which he eventually progressed to be one of the triad's most valued drug dealers, before succumbing to drug addiction and experiencing declining health issues. During follow-up discussions with him, he shared with me the way in which key phrases and messages in the Bible had begun to help him to change his life. He also felt that forming an intimate relationship with Jesus had brought him to experience a deep sense of calm and peace and a feeling that a higher power was in control of his destiny:

> The Bible has changed me a lot because I realised that you don't have to memorise the whole Bible to become more spiritual, but maybe one sentence is already enough for me to change my whole life ... I've learned how to be more peaceful ... I used to always say 'I'm worried about money, about life', many worries in my life but since I've met Jesus, peacefulness and happiness come from me. I do not have to worry about my future because Jesus has already planned it and protected me. (Ling)

As I also described in the last chapter, Chase had previously acted as a 'street soldier' for the triads; he had become heavily involved in violence and drug dealing until paranoid illusions and suicidal thoughts emerging from his own prolonged drug addiction made him retreat from the lifestyle. In *HKCS*, he had gained the opportunity to do voluntary work involving the delivery of anti-drug education programmes to young people in schools. As part of this, he was able to share his own 'redemption script', and felt empowered by drawing on his past experiences to help others (Maruna 2001, p. 87):

> In here they give me a lot of opportunity to share my story to others in school during the day ... it really empowers me. So I feel ... I have the ability to do something good by my past experience. So this

empowerment really helped me to construct some power to face some challenges. (Chase)

Additionally, in Chapter 9 I made reference to the fact that Cedric had completed the *HKCS* programme by the time my fieldwork took place but had returned as a voluntary mentor. He worked intensively with other men to encourage them to move away from drugs and desist from crime. Although previously committed to the Christian faith, Cedric explained how his experiences of seeing other men fail and repeatedly turn back to crime had begun to make him question the impact of religion:

> I chose to stay, so I've been here for about two years now... I've been coming here to speak to the other brothers that come in, to support them ... for the first few times I will feel really passionate to help that brother, to counsel him. But after a few times, this guy comes in and out a lot of time ... I was passionate to help you, to counsel you but so many times ... [I think] 'are you really serious?' I start to question ... I think I was a strong believer when I was here ... I used to pray a lot. And, now through this experience I became not so strong because ... I tried to help people and people just ... [come back] a second time, third time ... so I start to think, 'is religion really helping the people?' (Cedric)

In sum, the experience of finding or re-visiting religion and establishing an intimacy with Jesus through Bible readings and prayer represented a salient turning point for many of the men. It appeared to be helping them to transition from being angry, anxious, addicted and/or depressed to being calm, peaceful and generally experiencing a greater sense of wellbeing and a commitment to generativity (Maruna 2001; Thomas and Zaitzow 2006; Giordano et al. 2008; Schroeder and Frana 2009). In some cases (as with Cedric), failed attempts to reach out and nurture serious desistance attempts in others had the capacity to damage personal commitment to religion. However, for others—as the next section outlines further—an intense focus on holistic Christian engagement was beginning to play an important role in nurturing the type of identity and behaviour change that stimulates progression towards desistance.

Transforming Journeys and Re-framing Masculinity

As the earlier interview extracts suggest, the majority of the men talked at length about the way in which their newfound or renewed relationship with God was gradually helping them to realign their personal values and priorities in life. This was clearly reinforced by personal mentors within *HKCS*; for instance, Yang (a former gang member turned mentor) talked about his own fundamental view about the importance of 'belief and faith in Jesus' in the recovery and desistance path. As I discussed in the last chapter, Choi had had addiction issues with ketamine and cocaine and had begun to be immersed in triad-directed organised crime until he became disillusioned with the lifestyle. He described to me the way in which he had begun to repent for previous transgressions and to develop a personal commitment towards moving away permanently from the addictions that had often been the source of his offending behavior. At the same time, Lee also felt that the faith he had developed was reducing his craving for the drugs he had taken while part of the triad-controlled street gangs:

> In other places it's very forced, you're forced [to come] off drugs so it's very restrictive, but I come here by my own will so it's my own choice. And also because I have the heart to repent and come to believe in God. (Choi)
>
> I have great faith, because I have faith ... I don't want to take drugs. (Lee)

In *HKCS*, the men were encouraged to see a difference between 'worldly' views and 'Biblical' views of masculinity, as Shan (a voluntary mentor within the organisation) described:

> I think there is a difference between the world's view of masculinity and the Biblical view on it. I mean, you only need to look at Jesus himself – the only time he really got aggressive was when he was in the Temple and for good cause. (Shan, *HKCS* voluntary mentor)

For Peng, whose addiction issues had driven him to become impulsive and erratic and had eventually led to the triad leaders dismissing him from their ranks, there were still some negative influences in his life. In particular, he made reference to gang members who tried to tempt him back to the lifestyle now that his addictions were under control. However, he felt that engaging with *HKCS* had enabled him to reject the priorities of the gang lifestyle such as violence and loyalty to triad brotherhood, and to focus more on softer ideals of manhood that the Bible projected:

> In here I can learn about humbleness, about gentleness which I haven't ever [thought] in my life before. In here, I see the Bible and words of God can give me the right way and the right teaching … the people around me say 'are you the same guy?' (Peng)

Peng's newfound Christian faith provided him with a strong redemption script and an opportunity to project an alternative, non-criminal, religious identity that was framed around being a 'believer'. This offered Peng an opportunity to draw upon his previous conversion experiences as a positive guide for others (Maruna 2001; Healy 2012):

> I found that when I protect my heart from the world I can eventually get more close to God and live a life that God would like me to have … I'm not going back to crimes and not going back to previous lifestyle … I met some old friends who said 'come and do these kinds of things' with them. But I say, 'no, I'm now in this programme, I'm Christian.' If I stay along with this programme and church I can stay away from drugs. [I say] 'I'm a believer'… I've found Jesus' … these guys are sort of curious. (Peng)

Although Cedric had become sceptical about the power of religion alone to support other men's desistance journeys, he also described experiencing attitudinal-change from engaging in the programme. He had become more focused on issues of morality and embraced a greater sense of patience and respect for others:

> My way of thinking has changed, and my attitude. I'm starting to know what's right and what's wrong, what's responsibility. Yeah, and be patient with people … and respect each other. (Cedric)

As with programmes and interventions I had observed in other parts of the world, it seemed that the men's exposure to a safe, supportive and unconditional loving community enabled them to embrace a 'counter-cultural frame of masculinity as an important identity marker' (Johnson 2017, p. 112). But in *HKCS* there was also a holistic focus on evangelical-Pentecostal worship, combined with a somewhat fundamentalist focus on literal interpretation and acceptance of the Bible's doctrine and of Christ as personal Lord and saviour. This holistic Christian ethos appeared to be an important channel for nurturing cognitive and identity change among the men while they inhabited a liminal space (Healy 2012; Hallett and McCoy 2014). They were gradually replacing the triad-oriented emphasis on violence, pride and reciprocal obligation to brotherhood with 'peace-seeking, humility, self-restraint' as well as a collective orientation towards upholding their faith and committing to the church and to Christ (Johnson 2017, p. 111):

> Before, if you look at me I will fight you. But now I'm like more calm. (Chan)
>
> I see hope in the future ... and what I wish for is that more people come to know Christ. (Lee)
>
> I've got little confidence to stay in a normal life, but I know that if I get along with this group and get along to the church I could grab Jesus ... and stay away [from crime] for sure. (Ling)

As Ling alluded to (above), and as I found in other areas of the world, there was also a recognition among some of the men that they were at an early stage of a desistance journey and still regarded themselves as 'works in progress'. However, they clearly felt that their Christian faith and identity provided them with a renewed sense of hope and growing determination to continue to desist against difficult odds.

Concluding Discussion

In this chapter I have placed the spotlight on a Christian rehabilitation and support programme in Hong Kong. I have explored *HKCS*'s dual focus on providing those gang members who have entered a liminal phase with opportunities for paid and voluntary work placements while also immersing them in pastoral and community support. The pastoral work was clearly focused around a holistic blend of evangelical-Pentecostal worship and a fundamentalist Christian focus on literal interpretation and acceptance of the Bible's doctrine.

Against the backdrop of the triad criminal subcultures they had immersed themselves in and the gang embodiment issues they had experienced in the form of drug dependency and addiction, the men enrolled in *HKCS* who participated in interviews viewed their religious engagement as empowering and influential. In addition to the earlier 'push' and 'pull' factors that had first led them to begin disengaging with gangs, they eventually viewed Christianity as a profound 'track switcher' while in the liminal phase (Brenneman 2012, p. 237).

I noted stark contrasts to the inclusive, spiritual focus I had seen in *Homeboy Industries* in Los Angeles that ultimately led the men there to develop a strong desire to 'give back' to the community and to associate masculinity with household, family and caring roles. In *HKCS*, I found that the holistic Christian focus on Bible study, prayer and worship ultimately led the majority of the former Hong Kong triad gang members I worked with to become focused on becoming 'men of God' (Flores 2014, p. 204). In particular, there was a strong perception that the closeness to a higher spiritual power and strong belief system that emerged through a consistent focus on Bible readings, worship and prayer was enabling the men to deal more effectively with their substance abuse issues. It was also enabling them to develop a focus and determination to live the life that they now felt God had intended for them, and to go where He called (Flores 2014).

As in *Homeboy Industries*, it appeared that the ethos of support within *HKCS* was focused on building a therapeutic community based on unconditional love and acceptance. However, as previously observed by Flores (2014), I found that *Homeboy Industries* placed an emphasis on inclusivity and integrating men into the broader local community. In contrast, although *HKCS* provided work placements outwith its central base, the organisation was more akin to what Flores (2014, p. 196) observed in *Victory Outreach* in Los Angeles. Fundamentally, it placed an emphasis on encouraging men to 'shelter from the broader community' through evangelical worship and fundamentalist-oriented approaches to Bible study and prayer. While it was apparent that failed attempts to reach out and nurture serious desistance attempts in others through peer mentoring had the capacity to damage personal commitment to religion among some, it was also evident that most men felt that their religious faith and the support they received in *HKCS* was helping them to build upon their initial feelings of being ready for change. Most articulated a strong sense of hope that, where difficulties arose in the future, their fellowship with other Christians and with Jesus and commitment to the Bible would continue to enable them to live 'moral and meaningful lives' (Johnson 2017, p. 184) as 'men of God' (Flores 2014, p. 2014).

In Chapter 9, I referred to the Chinese cultural characteristic of *guanxi*, defined as 'the embodiment of an institutionalised behavioural pattern on interpersonal relationships involved with human affective components and human obligations' (Jiang 2012, p. 207). Specifically, it is characterised by *reciprocity* as a means of saving face; *utilitarianism* emerging through a process of bonding people together; *transferability* through having third parties vouch for one's reliability; and *intangibility* emerging through invisible and unwritten codes of reciprocity among members (Jiang 2012, p. 210). It is rooted in Chinese Confucian culture, which places emphasis on the need for social harmony (*ibid*). In many ways, the triad ideology of 'loyalty to the gang, eye for an eye, secrecy and sworn brotherhood' and the expectation for members to regard each other as 'blood brothers' and to 'sacrifice themselves for their group' draws upon the notion of *guanxi* (Lo and Kwok 2014, p. 5336; see also Lo and Kwok 2012).

As in earlier parts of the book, I am cautious about generalising the insights gleaned from the small-scale research outlined in this chapter. As with *Homeboy Industries*, I recognise that Pastor Lau's organisation relies on the availability of funding for its continued operationalisation, and in *HKCS's* case it is dependent on charitable donations from Christian churches. This can potentially make the organisation vulnerable to budget shortfalls, and may inevitably restrict the number of rehabilitation places that can be offered at any one time. However, the largely positive insights emerging from my observations and interviews suggest that faith-based interventions like *HKCS* that focus on a holistic approach to Christian observance may potentially play a valuable role in supporting and enabling some Hong Kong triad-affiliated gang members to re-direct their entrenched beliefs about loyalty and obligation to brotherhood in peaceful directions.

In many ways, my observation of support sessions in *HKCS* suggested that the men were gaining opportunities for Christian fellowship characterised by reciprocity and utilitarian support. They were also gaining opportunities to spread a message about the sense of hope and redemption they were experiencing within *HKCS* (transferability) and to uphold intangible forms of bonding through belief in Biblical messages and Christian doctrine. Accordingly, participation in holistically-oriented Christian support and rehabilitation programmes may provide triad members with alternative means of expressing and projecting *guanxi* in non-criminal contexts.

As I alluded to within my earlier discussion on prison chaplaincy in northern Europe, I do of course acknowledge that wider, secular forms of outreach social work and support interventions may provide equally positive forms of support to triad members in Hong Kong. I also recognise that not all triad gang members will necessarily respond to, or sustain their involvement in, Christian religious interventions and it was beyond the scope of my research to explore and examine the experiences of those men who may have dropped out of the *HKCS* programme before completion. However, the potential for religious organisations to uphold and embed the type of moral beliefs and ethical cultural values into their programmes and interventions that male gang members have grown committed to relating to within triad contexts makes them worthy of further exploration and potential State funding.

Having reached the end of the empirical sections of the book, in the concluding chapter I look back across the evidence I have gathered across three Continents of the world. I draw upon Bourdieusian social field analysis combined with theoretical perspectives on hegemonic masculinity to provide a deeper analysis of the global insights I have outlined, and draw final implications for future policy, practice and research.

References

Bakken, N. W., DeCamp, W., & Visher, C. A. (2014). Spirituality and desistance from substance use among reentering offenders. *International Journal of Offender Therapy and Comparative Criminology, 58*(11), 1321–1339.
Boyle, G. (2010). *Tattoos on the heart: The power of boundless compassion.* New York: Free Press.
Brenneman, R. (2012). *Homies and hermanos: God and gangs in Central America.* Oxford: Oxford University Press.
Chen, X. J., Hannibal, N., Xu, K., & Gold, C. (2014). Group music therapy for prisoners: Protocol for a randomised controlled trial. *Nordic Journal of Music Therapy, 23*(3), 224–241.
Clear, T., & Sumter, M. (2002). Prisoners, prison, and religion. *Journal of Offender Rehabilitation, 35*(3/4), 125–156.
Flores, E. O. (2014). *God's gangs: Barrio ministry, masculinity and gang recovery.* New York: New York University Press.
Giordano, P. C., Longmore, M., Schroeder, R., & Seffrin, P. (2008). A lifecourse perspective on spirituality and desistance from crime. *Criminology, 46*(1), 99–132.
Haculak, S., & McLennan, J. D. (2010). 'The Lord is my Shepherd': Examining spirituality as a protection against mental health problems in youth exposed to violence in Brazil. *Mental Health, Religion and Culture, 13*(5), 467–484.
Hallett, M., & McCoy, J. S. (2014). Religiously motivated desistance: An exploratory study. *International Journal of Offender Therapy and Comparative Criminology, 59*(8), 855–872.
Healy, D. (2012). *The dynamics of desistance: Charting pathways through change.* New York: Routledge.
Jiang, G., Lo, T. W., & Garris, F. P. (2012). Formation and trend of Guanxi practice and Guanxi phenomenon. *International Journal of Criminology and Sociology, 1*, 207–220.
Johnson, A. (2017). *If I give my soul: Faith behind bars in Rio de Janeiro.* Oxford: Oxford University Press.
Kerley, K. R. (2014). *Religious faith in correctional settings.* Boulder, CO: First Forum Press.
Kerley, K. R., & Copes, H. (2008). 'Keepin' my mind right': Identity maintenance and religious social support in the prison context. *International Journal of Offender Therapy and Comparative Criminology, 53*(2), 228–244.

Lin, Y., Chu, H., Yang, C.-Y., Chen, C.-H., Chen, S.-G., Chang, H.-J., et al. (2010). Effectiveness of group music intervention against agitated behavior in elderly persons with dementia. *International Journal of Geriatric Psychiatry, 26*(7), 670–8.

Lo, T. W. (2012). Triadization of youth gangs in Hong Kong. *British Journal of Criminology, 52,* 556–576.

Lo, T. W., & Kwok, S. I. (2012). Traditional organized crime in the modern world: How triad societies respond to socioeconomic change. In D. Siegel & H. van de Bunt (Eds.), *Traditional organized crime in the modern world* (pp. 67–89). New York: Springer.

Lo, T. W., & Kwok, S. I. (2014). Triads and tongs. In G. Bruinsma & D. Weisburd (Eds.), *Encyclopedia of criminology and criminal justice* (pp. 5332–5343). New York: Springer.

Maruna, S. (2001). *Making good: How ex-convicts reform and rebuild their lives.* Washington, DC: American Psychological Association.

Maruna, S., Wilson, L., & Curran, K. (2006). Why god is often found behind bars: Prison conversions and the crisis of self-narrative. *Research in Human Development, 3*(2–3), 161–184.

Schroeder, R. D., & Frana, J. F. (2009). Spirituality and religion, emotional coping, and criminal desistance: A qualitative study of men undergoing change. *Sociological Spectrum, 29,* 718–741.

Thomas, J., & Zaitzow, B. H. (2006). Conning or conversion? The role of religion in prison coping. *The Prison Journal, 86*(2), 242–259.

Part VI

Conclusion

11

From Masculine Criminal Distinction to Masculine Spiritual Distinction

In this final chapter I draw upon Bourdieusian social field analysis combined with theoretical perspectives on hegemonic masculinity to provide a more granular analysis of the global insights outlined in the empirical chapters of the book. In doing so, I provide a deeper theoretical perspective on what provided the pathways into and out of gang membership, violence and criminality for the majority of the men I interviewed and the role of religion and spirituality in the latter. Towards the end of the chapter, final implications are made for future policy, practice and research.

Global Pathways into Gang Membership and Criminality

Across the pages of this book, I have attempted to explore the relationship between masculinity, gang membership, violence and crime. In the early chapters, I argued that, for almost a Century, recurring evidence has suggested that disadvantaged young men often turn towards gang membership as a means of creating a plausible male identity and against the backdrop of multiple forms of marginality (see, for instance, Thrasher 1927; Cohen 1955; Yablonski 1967; Klein 1971; Patrick 1973; Pitts 2008; Deuchar 2009; Densley 2013; Harding 2014). Building on this, against the backdrop of three different Continents of the world, the insights outlined in the empirical sections of the book shed light on the collective reasons the men I worked with joined gangs and/or participated in violence and crime during their formative and (in some cases) adult years. They also illustrate the ways in which the men experienced masculine ascendency against a structurally marginalised backdrop as a result (Connell and Masserschmidt 2005). In this section I will elaborate on this through drawing upon Bourdieusian social field analysis combined with theoretical perspectives on hegemonic masculinity, before then going on to summarise the journeys that the men were experiencing as a result of their exposure to spiritual interventions.

Harding (2014) draws upon Bourdieu's (1969, 1984, 1991) theories to argue that the goal of actors within a social field is to 'overcome their unequal allocations of skills and resources to achieve advantage that will lead them ultimately to success' (p. 5). As it has been argued, Bourdieu's theories are particularly helpful since they cross the structure/agency divide inferring that individuals are neither completely free to choose their own destinies nor forced to behave according to rules or norms imposed upon them (Coles 2009; Harding 2014). Within Bourdieu's theoretical framework, habitus forms the 'crux in the nexus between structure and agency' (Coles 2009, p. 34). It can be defined as a system of dispositions (Bourdieu 1984, 1990); an 'internalised cognitive framework' (Harding 2014, p. 5); or a set of 'habits, traits, and quirks of behaviour' that allows individuals to negotiate and re-negotiate situations they encounter (Fraser 2013, p. 973) through practices that are coordinated with others' actions (Coles 2009). Habitus is thus largely acquired through contact with agents of socialisation (Bourdieu 1984). As Coles (2009, p. 35) highlights, 'fields' can be viewed as metaphors for domains of social life and shape the 'structure of the social setting in which habitus develops' and are thus central to how habitus is operationalised.

In addition, Bourdieu's concept of capital is an essential one to consider in relation to fields and habitus since accumulating forms of capital can impact upon the dispositions that emerge within any given field. Bourdieu argued that several types of capital tend to exist: economic capital (in terms of financial resources); social capital (referring to social networks); cultural capital (cultural tastes, preferences and qualifications); and symbolic capital (honour, prestige and recognition) (Bourdieu 1984; Swartz 1997; Coles 2009). As I referred to briefly in earlier chapters, Harding (2014, p. 6) argues that the premium capital to be acquired in the gang 'field' is 'street capital', which can be viewed as an 'amalgam' of highly valuable resources acquired out on the street. This includes street knowledge and street skills (cultural capital); internalised behaviours and ways of being and thinking (habitus); local history, family connections and networks (social capital); and relationships, recognition, honour and prestige (symbolic capital). Clearly, in some contexts gang members also gain access to valuable forms of economic capital that can further enhance their overall street capital (through, for example, drug dealing).

It has been argued that combining Bourdieu's concepts of habitus, capital and field with those associated with hegemonic masculinity produces a 'theoretical model that ably describes how men negotiate masculinities' within a range of social contexts (Coles 2009, p. 33). Within the overarching *field of masculinity* (Coles 2009, p. 39), there are positions of dominance and subordination (ibid., p. 42), and as in other social fields the various forms of capital listed above become contested. In addition, the male body also becomes central to producing physical capital that is also contested (ibid., and see also White 2013).

Accordingly, drawing upon Harding's concept of street capital (which applies Bourdieu's theoretical concepts to a gang context) with those of hegemonic masculinity enables a more granular analysis of the global insights I have outlined in the empirical chapters of this book in relation to the pathways *into* gang membership, violence and criminality experienced by the majority of the men I interviewed. I have adapted Coles' (2009, p. 40) illustrative analysis of the subfields in the overarching *field of masculinity* in Fig. 11.1. Perhaps with the exception of the minority of instances where I found that the men had become involved in crimes completely outwith and unrelated to gang structures, this provides a diagrammatical summary of my collective insights. In the following discussion I elaborate further on this.

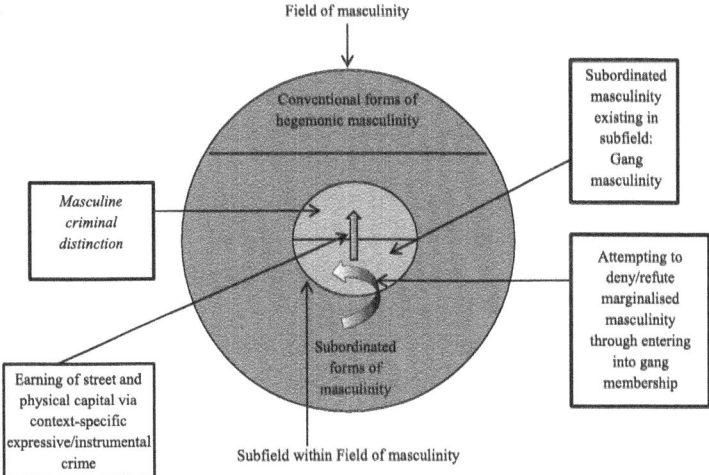

Fig. 11.1 Subfields in the *field of masculinity* and the transition to gang membership and *'masculine criminal distinction'* (Adapted from Coles 2009, p. 40)

During my fieldwork, it was very evident to me that the men I interviewed had become disadvantaged during their formative years in such a way that conventional means of expressing hegemonic masculinity were frustrated. In each of the geographical settings where I worked, I found that there were common causes of this: context-specific forms of economic deprivation combined with lack of social support and attachment at home and/or early exposure to traumatic events, peer pressure and—most commonly—a sense of marginalised, subordinated masculinity (Connell 2005; Coles 2009; Flores 2014). A small number of the men (in Scotland) had evidently become involved in sex offending and some (in Denmark) had begun dealing drugs or committing robberies in non-gang-related contexts. However, as Fig. 11.1 indicates, I found that the majority of the men had attempted to 'deny or refute their position as subordinated or marginalised' (or, more specifically, to reassert a sense of masculinity) via the status afforded them through gang membership and gang-related offending (Coles 2009, p. 39).

As they entered this masculine subfield, characterised by a focus on alternative forms of hegemony where extra-strength versions of *machismo* came to the surface (Williams 1977; Johnson 2017), they had often struggled over and contested street capital. Partially reflecting Harding's (2014) earlier insights from his qualitative gangs research in South London, I found that those who had acquired the right type of street and physical capital became more skilful in this subfield. Although very much still marginalised in relation to many other men in wider, mainstream society, they had ultimately earned more status and progressed towards alternative, compensatory forms of distinction (Baird 2012; Harding 2014).

In the locations where I gathered data, I found that the men had ultimately cemented this status and earned what I characterise as *masculine criminal distinction*. The exact nature of this was guided and shaped by the geographical, historical and cultural specificities that provided the backdrop to their offending behaviour (Fraser 2015). Prior to their incarceration, the majority of the young men I interviewed in Scotland had evidently earned it through their involvement in expressive forms of criminal activity characterised by participating in largely territorial and recreational violence out on the streets against other young men. They had often reasserted their masculinity by carrying knives, demonstrating physical prowess and defending turf, with a small minority progressing beyond this and beginning to engage in more business-oriented criminality (predominantly drug dealing) (McLean et al. 2017). Although a small minority had sidestepped gang membership and instead become involved in sex offending, it could be argued that they too had evidently reasserted their sense of marginalised masculinity through using sex as a weapon against women (Johnson 2007). In Denmark, the incarcerated and recently released men I interviewed reflected on the way in which they had accumulated masculine respect through projecting hyper-masculine body images and enacting male solidarity in street gangs. But for many, the mobility that motorcycle gang membership offered had lent itself to more instrumental, organised forms of criminality and further distinction (Mclean et al. 2017).

In Los Angeles, the men I met had evidently earned masculine distinction through participating in cross-neighbourhood 'gang-banging' focused on firearms use. In addition, the enhanced credibility that often emerged as a result of prison gang membership had further cemented their criminal distinction. And in Hong Kong, the underlying cultural influences associated with *mientze* and *guanxi* combined with drug addiction issues had acted as both triggers for initial triadization and for continued masculine reassertion for the men I interviewed. This had been projected through their ability to progress through triad hierarchies and become entrepreneurial in their engagement in the illegal economy and serious organised crime (McLean et al. 2017).

In sum, Fig. 11.1 illustrates my ultimate interpretation of the way in which the men in my sample experienced subordinated, marginalised masculinity but attempted to overcome this through (in the majority of cases) transitioning to gang membership. Although still located within a subordinated sub-field, they ultimately gained *masculine criminal distinction* through earning street and physical capital via context-specific forms of expressive or instrumental criminality. However, although their dominant focus was on violence and criminality, in many cases ethical and moral values often guided their behaviour within the gang masculinity subfield, with a particular focus on the upholding of loyalty, brotherhood and respect (Yablonsky 2000; White 2013).

In my research, I took cognisance of the evidence that draws attention to the plurality of masculinities and the way in which they can become subject to change (Connell 2005; Connell and Messerschmidt 2005; Messerschmidt 2005). Accordingly, just as the majority of men I interviewed had developed an ability to experience forms of masculine ascendency against the overarching backdrop of marginality through gang-related offending, their arrival at a liminal phase enabled further transitions to become possible.

Global Pathways Out of Gang Membership and Criminality

Throughout my research, I was interested in exploring the extent to and ways in which hegemonic masculine identities that have become toxic can ultimately become contested. I focused on examining how views about the most culturally honoured ways of being a man within gang contexts might become 'displaced by new ones' and how less oppressive and destructive conceptualisations of manhood might 'become hegemonic' (Connell and Messerschmidt 2005, p. 833). As such, during my fieldwork in diverse global locations I explored the cognitive and identity shifts that were occurring in the lives of the men I encountered, who could all be described as liminal beings when I worked with them—'betwixt and between' criminality and desistance (Healy 2012, p. 35). Reflecting Healy's (2012) insights, I found that the liminal phase—whether emerging while the men were entering rehabilitation programmes in the community or while beginning to interact with support structures in prison—did, indeed, become characterised as a time of 'fruitful darkness'. Personal transformation, growth and identity reconstruction gradually took root, but at the same time challenges and obstacles continued to form a backcloth (ibid.).

As I discussed in the empirical chapters, each of the men I interviewed had been influenced by initial 'hooks for change' (Giordano et al. 2002, p. 1000). These had formed the 'first doubts' in their minds about staying in gangs and criminality, and stimulated a gradual 'weighing' up of current and alternative lifestyles and the emergence of 'turning points' that reinforced their initial determination to change (Decker et al. 2014, p. 269). However, transitioning away from *masculine criminal distinction*, as I have called it, and fully emasculating gang life and offending lifestyles was often hampered by lasting gang embodiment issues and stigmata (Densley 2013; Flores 2014). The subfield that they had worked so hard to progress to was a difficult one to exit, given the street capital they had acquired, physical capital they had developed and habitus they had formed as well as the social and structural barriers they faced. This, of course, meant that potent and destructive forms of hegemonic masculinity often continued to define them.

Throughout the book, my empirical insights have illustrated the important role that religious and spiritual interventions played in supporting the men I worked with to gradually re-focus their masculine orientations. In different ways, exposure to these interventions helped to enhance the influence of the social phenomena working to push and pull the men out of gangs and the criminal and violent lifestyles that had enabled the accumulation of *masculine criminal distinction* within the subordinated subfield (Coles 2009; Decker et al. 2014).

As I have argued, spirituality is associated with personal, experiential and transcendal experiences that are connected to inner-awareness, a growing concern with personal integration and with relationships to others (Lindsay 2002; Guest 2007; Hall et al. 2011). This contrasts with religion which is associated more with transcendal beliefs and systems of worship that manifest within institutional settings (Schroeder and Frana 2009; Guest 2007; Whitehead 2013). Again, linking Harding's concept of street capital (which applies Bourdieu's theoretical concepts to a gang context) with those of hegemonic masculinity but also including a focus on spirituality and religion enables a more granular analysis of the global insights I have outlined in the empirical chapters of this book in relation to the pathways *out of* gang membership, violence and criminality experienced by the men I interviewed. In each of the geographical settings where I worked, I found that engagement with and participation in religious or spiritual interventions was gradually enabling the men to reject the dominant views of masculinity that had characterised their ascendency to *masculine criminal distinction*. In many ways, it was also enabling them to deal with the remaining embodiment issues that held them back.

Bourdieu's (1991) views on religion contrasted with his more dynamic views of lifestyle practices within the wider context of social field analysis (Dillon 2001). He viewed religion as having its own relatively autonomous field, and had a 'categorical view of the production of religious capital'—regarding the process in dichotomous terms where 'religious specialists' were the exclusive holders of knowledge, and the consumers or 'laity' could merely 'demand' but not 'supply' religious meanings and habitus (Dillon 2001, p. 414). It has been argued that this view left little room for the idea of viewing lay-people as social actors capable of nurturing the emergence of religious identities on their own behalf (Verter 2003), and was inattentive to religion's interpretive pluralism and the diversity of meanings people inject into religious 'discourses, experiences and participation' (Dillon 2001, p. 426). Verter (2003, p. 151) argues that Bourdieu's view of religious capital was too rigid to account for the 'fluidities of today's spiritual marketplace', and conversely regards religious capital as positional and relational. He also posits that 'spiritual capital' is a form of cultural capital and a product of social relations, and that spiritual knowledge, competencies and preferences can be regarded as valuable assets in the 'economy of symbolic goods' (ibid.).

In the empirical chapters of this book, I have illustrated the diverse range of experiences that the men in my international sample had depending on the context-specific nuances of how religion and spirituality was defined and enacted within the programmes and interventions they engaged with. In Hong Kong, the holistic blend of Pentecostal worship and fundamentalist-oriented Bible study within *HKCS* provided triad members with alternative means of expressing and projecting *guanxi* in non-criminal contexts. Specifically, the form of Christian religious engagement was positional and relational, rather than monolithic and dichotomous (Dillon 2001; Verter 2003). The men experienced a sense of emerging fellowship with other Christians and with Jesus combined with deep, personal reflection on Biblical insights and principles and a form of reciprocity and bonding with other reforming and religiously-influenced gang members. Collectively, this generated the type of religious capital that enabled them to deal with substance abuse issues, to uphold the cultural, ethical precepts they valued and to effectively become 'men of God'.

In Scotland and Denmark, the focus on unconditional social support from prison chaplains meant that the men no longer felt compelled to suppress their emotionality. For some, the religious support the chaplains offered—which was again seen as strongly positional and relational—provided them with a language and framework for change and an increased sense of confidence and control over their future life trajectories (Dillon 2001; Verter 2003). Importantly, this social and religious support reached beyond those with gang-related criminality to impact on others (such as sex offenders and drug dealers).

For some men in Denmark, exposure to yoga, dynamic breathing and meditative practices simultaneously enabled them to apply physical capital in non-criminal contexts while also gaining deeper awareness of their own personal emotions, a greater empathetic nature and ability to deal with 'stigmata' without the use of drugs. In such cases, the men (both gang members and non-gang members) were quite literally drawing on the spiritual capital they acquired from renewed competencies and practices to become 'men of peace'.

Finally, in Los Angeles it seemed that *Homeboy Industries* could be seen as an electic mix of all of the above. The men engaged in group therapy, mindfulness, the building of therapeutic alliances and the embracing of unconditional love and kinship through engaging in story-sharing at the podium (Flores 2014). This led to a holistic type of spiritual capital that was very much a product of social relationships and ultimately enabled gang members to becoming more focused on being 'family men' beyond the context of the programme. Again I have adapted Coles' (2009) illustrative analysis of masculine subfields in Fig. 11.2 to provide a summary of my insights.

Collectively, the type of religious and spiritual capital that emerged among the men represented the fluidity of the spiritual marketplace in the twenty-first century. As Fig. 11.2 attempts to represent diagrammatically, the men's initial hooks for change followed by their exposure to the programmes, interventions and ready-made social networks and communities and their acquiring of new, eclectic forms of capital enabled them to begin to retreat back from the subfield they had inhabited and enter a new social subfield. In the process, there was a gradual softening—or even feminizing—of the habitus projected by the men as they were slowly 'un-becoming' gang members (or, in a minority of cases, retreating from non-gang-related offending) (Brenneman 2012, p. 88). A new sense of status was being gained from narratives of recovery, generativity and 'countercultural frames of masculinity' as identity markers (Johnson 2017, p. 112).

By beginning to re-shape their identities in this way and experiencing influential types of interaction, encouragement and support from mentors, pastors and peers, they were earning what I characterise as *masculine spiritual distinction*. Within this subfield they were still very much marginalised and still in a state of flux and transition, but they also managed to avoid becoming emasculated (Flores 2014; Deuchar et al. 2016). They were beginning to draw upon their new forms of capital and habitus to transition from dark, difficult pasts into lighter, optimistic presents and possible futures, to 'make good' and 'give back' through

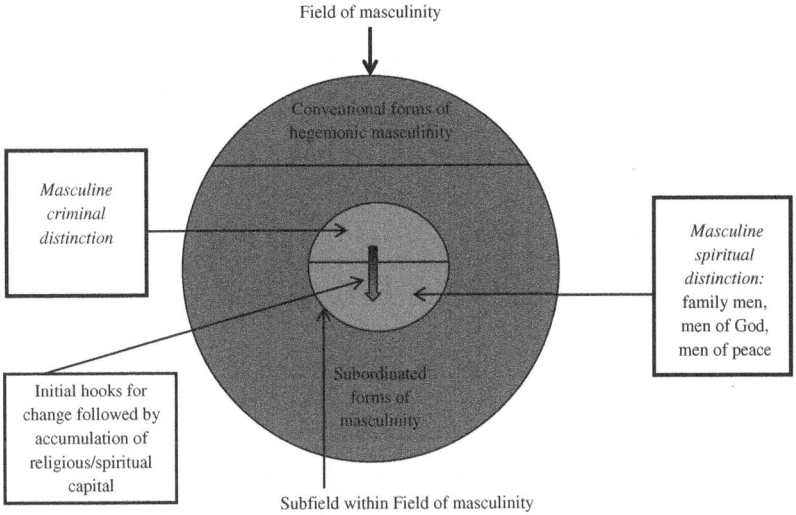

Fig. 11.2 Subfields in the *field of masculinity* and the transition from *'masculine criminal distinction'* to *'masculine spiritual distinction'* (Adapted from Coles 2009, p. 40)

becoming family men, men of peace and/or men of God (Maruna 2001; Healy 2012; Flores 2014). The natural proclivity towards moral and ethical values and principles that the majority of the men held was becoming nurtured and re-applied in non-criminal contexts within the subfield. As such, they were gaining a growing determination to continue to engage with the desistance process.

Final Reflections and Implications

Religious and spiritual interventions are rarely featured within criminal justice policy in many parts of the world, and so it is important that we draw upon applied research to shed light on the potential impact they may have. The research contained within this book has illustrated that religion and spirituality can provide some male gang members and offenders who have entered a liminal phase with the opportunity to enter a new social sub-field, often characterised by the presence of substitute forms of brotherhood and trust and alternative forms of masculine status gained from *masculine spiritual distinction*.

This type of distinction provides these men with an emerging ability to gain access to supportive communities, to new ideologies, rituals and practices, continued opportunities to disseminate explanatory narratives about previous wrongdoings and a sense of hope for the future. Most of all, I have found that it enables them to find and project a legitimate reason for leaving gang lifestyles behind and to draw upon their emerging religious and social capital to problematize caustic and toxic conceptualisations of manhood (Connell and Messerschmidt 2005; Deuchar and Weide 2018). In the process, the concept of criminal desistance literally begins to become masculinized (Deuchar et al. 2016). While it was beyond the scope of my research to explore the longevity of this change process, several of the initiatives I studied that had post-rehabilitation employability elements embedded within them or opportunities for post-prison support services attached to them offered some hope that initial primary desistance could become sustained and evolve into secondary desistance (Maruna and Farrall 2004).

Given the deeply entrenched gender identities that male gang members and offenders create for themselves across the world, it is important that policy-makers and practitioners understand the extent to which religious and spiritual practices may enable them to discover (or re-discover) *alternative* masculine identities and begin to view desistance as a realistic goal that they can achieve (Dufour and Brassard 2014). Religion and wider forms of holistic spiritual interventions need to be given cognisance in criminal rehabilitation policy and seen as feasible and credible alternatives to psychological and psychosocial interventions across the globe. Adequate State funding also needs to be made available for them in order to avoid the type of budget shortfalls that limit their reach and influence and the sustainability of their impact.

Clearly, the research outlined in this book had its limitations. For instance, although I have defined it as 'global', it was in reality limited to a four-country focus and was restricted to emerging insights captured by small samples of men in particular geographical locations during transitional phases when they were still emerging from offending lifestyles. I believe that further research in this field is needed, which moves beyond the locations where I have worked to capture, for instance, the experiences of male offenders in Latin America due to both the religiosity and sheer volume of gangs to be found there. Further, although my inclusion of a small group of other types of offenders allowed some illuminating contrasts and analysis of how religious/spiritual interventions may impact beyond gang-related contexts, the numbers were small and access in some cases was limited, and additional studies that focus on the experiences of wider groups of offenders who engage in spiritual interventions would be valuable in the future. In addition, a longitudinal element to future research would be beneficial to allow us to begin to consider the longer-term impact of religious and spiritual interventions on gender identity reconstruction and desistance among gang members and wider samples of offenders.

I was driven to write this book because my experience has told me that, underneath the tough exterior of many male gang members, there is an ethical, moral and softer side that simply needs to be nurtured in the right way in order to allow it to flourish in contexts outside of crime. One of my Danish participants (referred to in Chapter 8) summed this up best when he mused:

> You are not born a tough guy … I was born like a creature who was open and full of love and creativity. (Hans)

It is my hope that this book will stimulate researchers, policy-makers and practitioners across the world to work together and ensure that wider religious and spiritual interventions can be drawn upon to enable more 'tough guys' to become 'creatures full of love and creativity'.

References

Baird, A. (2012). The violent gang and the construction of masculinity amongst socially excluded young men. *Safer Communities, 11*(4), 179–190.

Bourdieu, P. (1969). Intellectual field and creative project. *Social Science Information, 8,* 189–219.

Bourdieu, P. (1984). *Distinction: A social critique of the judgement of taste* (R. Nice, Trans.). Cambridge, MA: Harvard University Press.
Bourdieu, P. (1990). *The logic of practice.* Cambridge: Polity Press.
Bourdieu, P. (1991). *Language and symbolic power.* Cambridge: Polity Press.
Brenneman, R. (2012). *Homies and hermanos: God and gangs in central America.* Oxford: Oxford University Press.
Cohen, A. K. (1955). *Delinquent boys: The culture of the gang.* New York: The Free Press.
Coles, T. (2009). Negotiating the field of masculinity: The production and reproduction of multiple dominant masculinities. *Men and Masculinities, 12*(1), 30–44.
Connell, R. W. (2005). *Masculinities.* Cambridge: Polity Press.
Connell, R. W., & Messerschmidt, J. W. (2005). Hegemonic masculinity: Rethinking the concept. *Gender and Society, 19*(6), 829–859.
Decker, S. H., Pyrooz, D., & Moule, R. K., Jr. (2014). Disengagement from gangs as role transitions. *Journal of Research on Adolescence, 24*(2), 268–283.
Densley, J. (2013). *How gangs work: An ethnography of youth violence.* London: Palgrave Macmillan.
Deuchar, R. (2009). *Gangs, marginalised youth and social capital.* Stoke on Trent: Trentham.
Deuchar, R., & Weide, R. (2018). Journeys in gang masculinity: Insights from international case studies of interventions. *Deviant Behavior,* 1–15. http://doi.org/10.1080/01639625.2018.1443761.
Deuchar, R., Søgaard, T. F., Kolind, T., Thylstrup, B., & Wells, L. (2016). 'When you're boxing you don't think so much': Pugilism, transitional masculinities and criminal desistance among young Danish gang members. *Journal of Youth Studies, 19*(6), 625–742.
Dillon, M. (2001). Pierre Bourdieu, religion and cultural production. *Critical Methodologies, 1*(4), 411–429.
Dufour, I. F., & Brassard, R. (2014). The convert, the remorseful and the rescued: Three different processes of desistance from crime. *Australian and New Zealand Journal of Criminology, 47*(3), 313–335.
Flores, E. O. (2014). *God's gangs: Barrio ministry, masculinity and gang recovery.* New York: New York University Press.
Fraser, A. (2013). Street habitus: Gangs, territorialism and social change in Glasgow. *Journal of Youth Studies, 16*(8), 970–985.
Fraser, A. (2015). *Urban legends: Gang identity in the post-industrial city.* Oxford: Oxford University Press.

Giordano, P. C., Cernkovich, S. A., & Rudolph, J. L. (2002). Gender, crime and desistance: Toward a theory of cognitive transformation. *American Journal of Sociology, 107,* 990–1064.
Guest, M. (2007). In search of spiritual capital: The spiritual as a cultural resource. In K. Flannagan & P. Jupp (Eds.), *A sociology of spirituality* (pp. 181–200). Aldershot: Ashgate.
Hall, R. E., Livingston, J. N., Brown, C. J., & Mohabir, J. A. (2011). Islam and Asia Pacific Muslims: The implications of spirituality for social work practice. *Journal of Social Work Practice, 25*(2), 205–215.
Harding, S. (2014). *The street casino: Survival in violent street gangs.* Bristol: Policy Press.
Healy, D. (2012). *The dynamics of desistance: Charting pathways through change.* New York: Routledge.
Johnson, S. A. (2007). *Physical abusers and sexual offenders: Forensic and clinical strategies.* London: Taylor and Francis.
Johnson, A. (2017). *If I give my soul: Faith behind bars in Rio de Janeiro.* Oxford: Oxford University Press.
Klein, M. (1971). *Street gangs and street workers.* Englewood Cliffs, NJ: Prentice Hall.
Lindsay, R. (2002). *Recognizing spirituality: The interface between faith and social work.* Crawley: University of Western Australia Press.
Maruna, S. (2001). *Making good: How ex-convicts reform and rebuild their lives.* Washington, DC: American Psychological Association.
Maruna, S., & Farrall, S. (2004). Desistance from crime: A theoretical reformulation. *Kolner Zeitschrift fur Soziologie und Sozialpsychologie, 43,* 171–194.
McLean, R., Densley, J., & Deuchar, R. (2017). Situating gangs within Scotland's illegal drug market(s). *Trends in Organized Crime.* https://doi.org/10.1007/s12117-017-9328-1.
Messerschmidt, J. (2005). Men, masculinities and crime. In M. S. Kimmel, J. Hearn, & R. W. Connell (Eds.), *Handbook of studies on men and masculinities* (pp. 196–212). London: Sage.
Patrick, J. (1973). *A Glasgow gang observed.* London: Eyre Methuen.
Pitts, J. (2008). *Reluctant gangsters: The changing face of youth crime.* Devon: Willan.
Schroeder, R. D., & Frana, J. F. (2009). Spirituality and religion, emotional coping, and criminal desistance: A qualitative study of men undergoing change. *Sociological Spectrum, 29,* 718–741.

Swartz, D. (1997). *Culture and power: The sociology of Pierre Bourdieu*. Chicago: University of Chicago Press.
Thrasher, F. (1927). *The gang: A study of 1313 gangs in Chicago*. Chicago: University of Chicago Press.
Verter, B. (2003). Spiritual capital: Theorizing religion with Bourdieu against Bourdieu. *Sociological Theory, 21*(2), 150–174.
White, R. (2013). *Youth gangs, violence and social respect: Exploring the nature of provocations and punch-ups*. Basingstoke, UK: Palgrave Macmillan.
Whitehead, P. L. (2013). Touching the void: Community chaplaincy as an ethical-cultural agency in criminal justice re-formation in England and Wales. *Social and Public Policy Review, 7*(1), 40–54.
Williams, R. (1977). *Marxism and literature*. Oxford: Oxford University Press.
Yablonsky, L. (1967). *The violent gang*. Middlesex: Pelican.
Yablonsky, L. (2000). *Juvenile delinquency into the 21st Century*. Belmont, CA: Wadsworth and Thomson Learning.

Index

A

Agnew, Robert 130, 133, 204
Alcoholics Anonymous 100
alcoholism 23
Anderson, Elijah 24, 51, 83
anger management 90, 93, 99, 175
anti-depressants 185, 186
anxiety 45, 50, 150, 151, 171, 179, 185, 188, 230
Art of Living Foundation 170, 172
Asia 3, 4, 12, 28, 190, 195, 207. *See also* Hong Kong
Australia 27, 152

B

Bandidos 120
baptism 155, 156
bereavement 125, 153, 154, 156, 163

Bible, the 155, 159, 164, 220, 230–233, 236–239
Black Power movement 64
Bloods 64. *See also* gangs
bodybuilding 132–134, 138, 150, 176, 181, 185
Boston 24, 43. *See also* United States of America
Bourdieu, Pierre 6, 26, 246, 247, 252
Boyle, Father Gregory 90, 174
Breathe Smart 125, 172–175, 177, 182, 183, 189
breathing practices 124
brotherhood 13, 28, 51, 127, 134, 135, 138, 196, 207, 209, 213, 219, 236, 237, 239, 240, 250, 256
Buddhism 50
bullying 197, 203, 204

C
cannabis 129, 185, 207. *See also* drug addiction/dealing; marijuana
capitalism 196, 204
Catholicism 155. *See also* Christianity; faith; religion
Chicago 24, 64, 65. *See also* United States of America
Chicago School of Sociology 24
China 28, 49, 196, 221
Christianity 43, 48, 147, 150, 154, 155, 158, 164, 220, 223, 238. *See also* religion; faith; Catholicism
 conversion to 44, 226
 evangelistic 220
 fundamentalist 238
 holistic forms of 227
 and music 231
 Pentecostal-influenced 231
 and proselytism 226
 and worship 159, 220–223, 227, 228, 231
Cincinnati Initiative to Reduce Violence 43
Civil Rights Movement 83
Cloward, Richard A. 24
cocaine 70, 129, 150, 185, 186, 207, 212, 235. *See also* drug dealing
codes 4, 11, 22, 27, 44, 52, 75, 118, 135, 220, 239
Cohen, Albert 20, 24, 246
community-building 96, 105, 110, 227
Connell, Raewyn W. 20, 22, 23, 122, 163, 181, 246, 248, 250, 256

counselling 90, 144, 150
Crips 64. *See also* gangs
cultural capital 247, 253

D
Decker, Scott H. 5, 9, 28–32, 65, 71, 76, 79, 81, 84, 97, 146, 160, 178, 187, 197, 205, 208, 209, 213, 251
Denmark 3, 8, 11, 111, 117, 118, 120–127, 131, 135–139, 147, 148, 150, 156–159, 161–164, 172, 173, 176, 184, 187, 200, 214, 248, 249, 253. *See also* Europe
Densley, James 4, 26, 30, 32, 47, 51, 78, 82, 84, 92, 129, 138, 188, 215, 246, 251
depression 45, 101, 150–153, 163, 171, 186, 188. *See also* mental health
desistance
 and identity theories 32
 life course perspectives on 5, 29
 primary and secondary 29, 81
 progression towards 7, 39, 40, 51, 52, 82, 170, 179, 234
 and push/pull factors 29
differential association theory 42, 164
discrimination 10, 53, 63
drive-by shootings 4, 73, 74
drug addiction 64, 83, 131, 199, 207, 208, 212, 213, 220–222, 226, 232, 233, 250

drug dealing 8, 21, 23, 26, 28, 74, 77, 83, 120, 122, 123, 129, 131–135, 138, 147, 152, 174, 188, 197, 206, 207, 209, 212, 214, 233, 247, 249
Durkheim, Emile 41

E

El Salvador 47
emotionality 75, 130, 163, 221, 253
employability 224, 256
ethnography 3, 6, 8, 10, 24, 26, 43, 78, 89, 119, 199
Europe 11, 25, 111, 117–120, 189, 240. *See also* Denmark; Germany; Netherlands; Norway; Scotland

F

faith 6, 7, 39, 45–47, 52, 53, 90, 102, 144, 145, 148, 154, 155, 157, 159, 161–165, 223, 224, 229, 231, 234–237, 239. *See also* Catholicism; Christianity; religion
Flores, Edward O. 24, 25, 30, 31, 40, 47, 51, 65, 75, 82–84, 90, 92, 98, 100, 103, 105, 107–110, 164, 179, 188, 215, 220, 226, 231, 238, 248, 251, 254, 255
football hooliganism 25
forgiveness 154–156, 158, 164, 187, 220
Fraser, Alistair 4, 27, 119, 196–198, 213, 215, 246, 249

G

gambling 197, 207, 209
gangs
  Crips and Bloods 64
  and disengagement 3, 5, 6, 9, 30, 31, 40, 52, 161, 162, 164
  and embodiment issues 82, 108, 109, 179, 238, 251
  and exploitation 208, 209
  female members 91
  and initiation 71, 198
  and loyalty 22, 134, 135
  Latino members 10, 63, 64, 75, 80
  motorcycle 4, 120, 121, 176, 214, 249
  and physicality 28, 31, 46
  and prisons 78, 117. *See also* prisons
  and respect 22, 214, 249
  and 'stigmata' 30, 32, 82, 84, 92, 179, 215, 251
  and tattoos 74, 82, 96, 108
  triad 12, 195–198, 208, 211–214, 222, 240
  and violence 3, 4, 6–8, 12, 13, 19, 20, 23, 31, 52, 82, 92, 108, 110, 129, 131, 132, 138, 169, 188, 203. *See also* violence
generativity 137, 145, 156, 165, 234, 254
Germany 25. *See also* Europe
Giordano, Peggy C. 5, 29, 32, 41, 42, 45, 49, 79, 80, 84, 92, 106, 136, 137, 161, 164, 175, 178, 221, 229, 251
Glasgow 3, 4, 25, 27, 119, 120, 129, 196. *See also* Scotland; Europe

group therapy 10, 84, 89, 91, 103, 105, 109, 254
guanxi 196, 209, 214, 239, 240, 250, 253
guns 72–74, 107

H

Hallsworth, Simon 22, 26
Harding, Simon 23, 26, 129, 130, 178, 196, 197, 246, 247, 249
healing circles 105
Healy, Deirdre 5, 6, 8, 9, 11, 29–31, 45, 47, 66, 82, 89, 92, 97, 107–109, 135–137, 143, 156, 160, 165, 175, 187, 200, 209, 210, 212, 214, 215, 236, 237, 251
Hell's Angels 120
heroin 69, 70. *See also* drug addiction/dealing
Homeboy Industries 10, 11, 53, 66, 67, 75, 82–84, 89–94, 96, 97, 99, 100, 102, 105–111, 227, 238, 239, 254
homelessness 70, 226
homicides 65, 118, 196
Hong Kong 4, 8, 12, 13, 28, 190, 195–200, 202–205, 208, 210, 213–215, 219, 221–226, 237, 238, 240, 249, 253. *See also* Asia
hooks for change 79, 81, 84, 92, 106, 136, 178, 199, 251, 254

I

identity reconstruction 6, 7, 14, 30–32, 39, 44, 45, 146, 190, 251, 257

immigration 24, 25, 65, 122, 127, 128, 137, 138, 158, 173
impression management 73, 78
India 49, 171
Islam 148, 150, 158, 159, 162. *See also* religion
Islamic-Christian Study Centre 162

J

Japan 49

K

ketamine 205–208, 212, 235
Klein, Malcolm W. 24, 25, 152, 246
knife carrying 207

L

liminal theory 5
London 22, 26, 27, 249
Los Angeles 4, 10, 25, 53, 63–70, 75, 76, 82–84, 89, 108, 128, 135, 137, 139, 160, 171, 174, 184, 196, 214, 227, 238, 249, 254. *See also* United States of America
Lo. T. Wing 28, 51, 196–199, 205, 208, 209, 211, 213, 214, 224

M

machismo 78, 83, 106, 144, 249
Mafia 78, 133, 197, 210, 214
  Mexican 78
  Sicilian 197
marginalisation 7, 10, 19, 21, 22, 24, 27, 28, 63, 68, 75, 119, 128, 135, 138, 162, 213

marijuana 70, 74, 150, 185. *See also* cannabis; drug addiction/dealing
Maruna, Shadd 5, 7, 29, 32, 39, 43, 48, 80, 81, 98, 105, 109, 145, 156, 159, 165, 184, 188, 220, 233, 255, 256
masculinity
  and criminal distinction 248–252, 255
  fields and subfields 247, 248, 255
  hegemonic 6, 13, 20, 21, 23, 25, 27, 28, 31, 53, 75, 83, 138, 148, 181, 240, 245–248, 251, 252
  hyper- 23, 46, 52, 134, 156, 160, 172, 176, 181
  marginalised 23, 25, 30, 31, 46, 138, 163, 188, 248–250
  and spiritual distinction 254–256
  toxic forms of 72, 73
McKay, Henry D. 24
meditation 12, 49–52, 100–102, 124, 139, 151, 165, 169–172, 177, 179–182, 184, 185, 187, 189. *See also* mindfulness
mental health 27, 46, 49–51, 93, 125, 129, 131, 144, 148, 151, 153, 156, 171, 185, 189, 211, 213. *See also* depression; suicidal thoughts
mentoring 10, 89, 109, 162, 222, 239
Merton, Robert K. 204
Messerschmidt, James W. 122, 250, 251, 256
methamphetamine 70. *See also* drug addiction/dealing

mientze 202, 214, 250
Miller, Walter B. 24
mindfulness 49–51, 100–102, 254. *See also* meditation
money laundering 197
morality 81, 128, 135, 139, 181, 183, 184, 236

N

narratives 46–48, 52, 98, 104, 105, 107, 110, 136, 145, 156, 161, 188, 220, 232, 254, 256
neoliberalism 83
Netherlands 25. *See also* Europe
Norway 25. *See also* Europe

O

Ohlin, Lloyd E. 24
organised crime 120, 196–198, 205, 210, 211, 213, 235, 250
outreach work 223–225, 227

P

parenthood 29, 80, 137
pastoral care 224
Patrick, James 25, 119, 246
physical capital 133, 176, 247, 249–251, 253
Pitts, John 23, 46, 71, 73, 246
poetry writing 103
police 43, 68, 82, 111, 118, 120, 127, 134, 138, 198, 206–209, 211, 215
  corruption 198, 215
  harassment 82

suppression tactics 68, 120
poverty 23, 24, 68, 83, 118, 126, 131, 135, 138, 226
prayer 45, 104, 105, 153–158, 160, 164, 180, 181, 227–232, 234, 238, 239
prisons
　chaplaincy services 144, 148, 165
　and codes 11, 118
　conversion in 145
　gangs in 10–12, 76–78, 84, 108. See also gangs
　segregation in 138
　solitary confinement in 76, 163
Prison Smart 172–175, 177, 178, 183, 186, 189
prostitution 197
psychological problems. See mental health
Pyrooz, David 28–30, 47, 65, 71, 79, 81, 105, 197, 205, 208, 213

Q
Qur'an, the 157, 159, 164

R
racism 24, 26, 27
redemption scripts 7, 39, 48, 52, 109, 145
religion 7, 13, 19, 31, 32, 40, 41, 44, 45, 47, 52, 150, 152, 154, 156–160, 162, 164, 180, 198, 215, 220, 221, 229, 231, 234, 236, 239, 245, 252, 253, 255. See also Catholicism; Christianity; faith; Islam

residential care 125, 126
Rio de Janeiro 43, 149

S
Sadarshan Kriya Yoga 125
Scotland 3, 8, 11, 27, 104, 111, 117–126, 129–131, 135, 136, 138, 139, 147–150, 153, 154, 156–164, 187, 214, 248, 249, 253. See also Europe; Glasgow
sectarianism 120
secular support 164, 183
secure accommodation 144
sex offenders 11, 117, 123, 139, 149, 150, 163–165, 253
shame 47, 48, 96, 97, 105
Shaw, Clifford R. 24
signalling theory 78
social capital 32, 42, 43, 52, 247, 256
social control theory 164
social field analysis 6, 13, 26, 240, 245, 246, 252
social justice 94, 110
spirituality 3, 5–7, 13, 19, 31, 32, 40, 41, 48, 51, 52, 66, 84, 91, 100, 102, 104, 109, 110, 123, 170, 180, 188, 227, 245, 252, 253, 255
　definitions 41, 253
　eclectic forms of 100
　Hindu 170
　Journeys 109, 180, 184
　and masculine distinction 254, 256. See also masculinity
steroids 133, 134, 150–152, 178, 185
story-telling 98

street capital 26, 28, 129, 209, 212, 247, 249, 251, 252
study groups 11, 124, 143, 146–150, 155, 158, 159, 161, 164, 199, 222
suicidal thoughts 150, 151, 212, 233. *See also* mental health
Sutherland, Edwin 20
symbolic capital 247

T

tattoo removal 90, 108. *See also* gangs
territoriality 120, 121, 138
Thrasher, Frederic M. 24, 246
transitions 6, 7, 9, 31, 32, 40, 81, 82, 84, 160, 211, 215, 250
trauma 27, 45, 46, 65, 70, 75, 81, 83, 106, 109, 128, 138, 148, 153, 175, 185, 186
triads 198, 206, 207, 209–211, 233. *See also* gangs

U

unconditional love 94, 95, 99, 105, 109, 228, 238, 254
United States of America 8, 10, 11, 24, 25, 30, 53, 63, 65, 110, 111, 117, 187, 204. *See also* Boston; Chicago; Los Angeles

V

values 6, 7, 11, 22, 28, 39, 41, 51, 52, 77, 107, 135, 143, 153, 160, 164, 184, 187, 188, 196, 197, 201, 203, 205, 209, 214, 226, 232, 235, 240, 250, 255
Victory Outreach 238
Vigil, James Diego 21, 24, 53, 64, 66, 69–71, 75, 78, 83
violence
  and anger 22, 50, 70, 138
  capital 84, 133, 176, 179
  domestic 64, 71, 83
  in gangs 8, 19, 22, 26, 31, 52, 84, 203, 205. *See also* gangs
  inter-cultural 7, 19, 65
  sexual 8, 26, 70, 138

W

Wacquant, Loic 64, 83
Weide, Robert D. 65, 67, 68, 73, 92, 174
White, Rob 4, 22, 27, 32, 40, 51, 183, 252
Whyte, William F. 24
working class 22, 24, 28

Y

Yablonski, Lewis 24, 246
yoga 12, 49, 50, 52, 124, 139, 165, 169–172, 175, 179, 181, 182, 187–189, 253

The manufacturer's authorised representative in the EU is Springer Nature Customer Service Centre GmbH, Europaplatz 3, 69115 Heidelberg, Germany. If you have any concerns regarding our products, please contact ProductSafety@springernature.com

Printed and bound by CPI Group (UK) Ltd, Croydon, CR0 4YY

23/03/2026

02076735-0010